Entrepreneurialism in Universities and the Knowledge Economy

Diversification and Organizational Change in European Higher Education

Edited by

Michael Shattock

UNESCO
United Nations
Educational, Scientific and
Cultural Organization

in association
with **UNESCO**

International Institute
for Educational Planning

Society for Research into Higher Education
& Open University Press

Open University Press
McGraw-Hill Education
McGraw-Hill House
Shoppenhangers Road
Maidenhead
Berkshire
England
SL6 2QL

email: enquiries@openup.co.uk
world wide web: www.openup.co.uk

and Two Penn Plaza, New York, NY 10121–2289, USA

Published in association with UNESCO

First published 2009

A catalogue record of this book is available from the British Library

ISBN-10 0 335 23571 9 (pb)   0 335 23570 0 (hb)
ISBN-13: 978 0 335 23571 1 (pb)   978 0 335 23570 4 (hb)

Library of Congress Cataloging-in-Publication Data
CIP data has been applied for

Typeset by RefineCatch Limited, Bungay, Suffolk
Printed in the UK by Bell and Bain Ltd., Glasgow

The *McGraw·Hill* Companies

Entrepreneurialism in Universities and the Knowledge Economy

SRHE and Open University Press Imprint

Current titles include:

Catherine Bargh *et al.*: *University Leadership*
Ronald Barnett: *Beyond all Reason*
Ronald Barnett: *Higher Education: A Critical Business*
Ronald Barnett: *Realizing the University in an age of supercomplexity*
Ronald Barnett and Kelly Coate: *Engaging the Curriculum in Higher Education*
Tony Becher and Paul R. Trowler: *Academic Tribes and Territories (2nd edn)*
John Biggs: *Teaching for Quality Learning at University (2nd edn)*
Richard Blackwell and Paul Blackmore (eds): *Towards Strategic Staff Development in Higher Education*
David Boud and Nicky Solomon (eds): *Work-based Learning*
David Boud *et al.* (eds): *Using Experience for Learning*
Tom Bourner *et al.* (eds): *New Directions in Professional Higher Education*
Anne Brockbank and Ian McGill: *Facilitating Reflective Learning in Higher Education*
Stephen D. Brookfield and Stephen Preskill: *Discussion as a Way of Teaching*
Ann Brooks and Alison Mackinnon (eds): *Gender and the Restructured University*
Sally Brown and Angela Glasner (eds): *Assessment Matters in Higher Education*
Burton R. Clark: *Sustaining Change in Universities*
James Cornford and Neil Pollock: *Putting the University Online*
John Cowan: *On Becoming an Innovative University Teacher*
Sara Delamont and Paul Atkinson: *Successful Research Careers*
Sara Delamont, Paul Atkinson and Odette Parry: *Supervising the Doctorate (2nd edn)*
Gerard Delanty: *Challenging Knowledge*
Chris Duke: *Managing the Learning University*
Heather Eggins (ed.): *Globalization and Reform in Higher Education*
Heather Eggins and Ranald Macdonald (eds): *The Scholarship of Academic Development*
Gillian Evans: *Academics and the Real World*
Merle Jacob and Tomas Hellström (eds): *The Future of Knowledge Production in the Academy*
Peter Knight: *Being a Teacher in Higher Education*
Peter Knight and Paul Trowler: *Departmental Leadership in Higher Education*
Peter Knight and Mantz Yorke: *Assessment, Learning and Employability*
Ray Land: *Educational Development*
John Lea *et al.*: *Working in Post-Compulsory Education*
Mary Lea and Barry Stierer (eds): *Student Writing in Higher Education*
Dina Lewis and Barbara Allan: *Virtual Learning Communities*
Ian McNay (ed.): *Beyond Mass Higher Education*
Elaine Martin: *Changing Academic Work*
Louise Morley: *Quality and Power in Higher Education*
Lynne Pearce: *How to Examine a Thesis*
Moira Peelo and Terry Wareham (eds): *Failing Students in Higher Education*
Craig Prichard: *Making Managers in Universities and Colleges*
Stephen Rowland: *The Enquiring University Teacher*
Maggi Savin-Baden: *Facilitating Problem-based Learning*
Maggi Savin-Baden: *Problem-based Learning in Higher Education*
Maggi Savin-Baden and Kay Wilkie: *Challenging Research in Problem-based Learning*
David Scott *et al.*: *Professional Doctorates*
Peter Scott: *The Meanings of Mass Higher Education*
Michael L. Shattock: *Managing Successful Universities*
Maria Slowey and David Watson: *Higher Education and the Lifecourse*
Colin Symes and John McIntyre (eds): *Working Knowledge*
Richard Taylor, Jean Barr and Tom Steele: *For a Radical Higher Education*
Malcolm Tight: *Researching Higher Education*
Penny Tinkler and Carolyn Jackson: *The Doctoral Examination Process*
Susan Toohey: *Designing Courses for Higher Education*
Melanie Walker (ed.): *Reconstructing Professionalism in University Teaching*
Melanie Walker and Jon Nixon (eds): *Reclaiming Universities from a Runaway World*
Diana Woodward and Karen Ross: *Managing Equal Opportunities in Higher Education*
Mantz Yorke and Bernard Longden: *Retention and Student Success in Higher Education*

Contents

Contributors

Igor Kitaev is a member of the International Institute for Educational Planning, UNESCO, Paris, who teaches and writes extensively on educational costs and finance, in particular on higher education in the transitional economies of the former Soviet Union. He was a member of the Steering and Drafting Committees of the World Conference on Education for All (Jomtien, Thailand, 1990) and research consultant for networks and projects of UNESCO and other international organizations. His latest contribution appears in *Private Schooling in Less Economically Developed Countries* edited by P. Srivastava and G. Walford (Didcot, UK: Symposium Books, 2007).

Jenni Koivula is a researcher in the Center for Research and Lifelong Learning and Education at the University of Turku, Finland. She is also a PhD student in the FiGSEL (Finnish Graduate School in Education and Learning); she is writing her doctoral thesis on the new governance, market drift, and cultural changes in higher education politics. Jenni has been working in the EUEREK Project and has written Finnish national reports. She is also co-author of an article entitled 'The changing place of the university and a clash of values' (R. Rinne and J. Koivula, 2005, *Higher Education Management and Policy*, 17(3): 91–123).

Marek Kwiek is Professor in the Department of Philosophy and the founder and director of the Center for Public Policy, an autonomous research unit of Poznan University, Poland. Currently, he is a Fulbright 'New Century Scholar' 2007–2008 ('Higher Education in the 21st Century'). His research interests include globalization and higher education, European educational policy, welfare state reforms, transformations of the academic profession, as well as philosophy of education and intellectual history. Marek has published eighty papers and eight books, most recently *The University and the State: A Study into Global Transformation* (New York: Peter Lang, 2006), a monograph about the impact of global reformulations of the role of the state on the future of public universities.

Bruce Henry Lambert is a Professor of Entrepreneurship with extensive international experience in university entrepreneurship, strategy, and destination marketing. He holds a doctorate in management from the University of Oxford, a masters degree in economics from Tsukuba University, and a recent masters degree in educational leadership and management from Stockholm University. Bruce is currently a Professor of Sookmyung University and Le Cordon Bleu Hospitality Business School in Seoul; managing partner of Helpnet, a destination marketing consultancy; and also holds adjunct posts with the Nordic Institute of Asian Studies, Denmark, and the Helsinki School of Economics. Key past posts have been with KTH (Royal Institute of Technology, Stockholm) and the Stockholm School of Economics. Bruce's research interests include developing a systematized quantitative analysis of university economic footprints. He is also studying the human resource element of cultivating entrepreneurship, with a special focus on legal, logistic, and quality-of-life dimensions that promote the retention and inward mobility of highly skilled people. He has wide-ranging publications and consulting output, and has been visiting professor at many institutions worldwide.

Raphaelle Martinez is a freelance educational consultant. After postgraduate studies in political science at the Sorbonne, she specialized in educational policy, planning, and management, including higher education. She coordinated a network of reference documents in these areas at UNESCO headquarters in Paris. More recently, she worked as a research coordinator for the Committee for International Cooperation in Research in Demography (Paris). At present, Raphaelle is in charge of scientific editing and review of World Bank studies on public expenditure and UNESCO studies on management of education systems worldwide.

José-Ginés Mora is Director of the Centre for the Study of Higher Education Management (CEGES) at the Valencia University of Technology and Visiting Professor in the Institute of Education, University of London. He is Deputy-Chair of the governing board of the Institutional Higher Education Programme (IMHE) of the OECD, former President of the European Higher Education Society (EAIR), and ex-member of the Steering Committee of ENQA. He is associate editor of *Tertiary Education and Management* and member of the editorial boards of *Higher Education Policy, Higher Education in Europe*, and *Higher Education Management and Policy*, and former joint editor of the *European Journal of Education*. His research is focused on higher education. He is author of more than two hundred publications. Two recent contributions are 'Public–private partnerships in Latin America: a review based on four case studies' (in H. Patrinos and S. Sosale, eds., *Mobilizing the Private Sector for Public Education: A View from the Trenches*. Washington, DC: World Bank, 2007) and 'Job satisfaction among recent European graduates: does field of study matter?' (2007, *Journal of Higher Education*, 78(1): 98–118).

Risto Rinne is Professor of Education and head of the Department of Education and the Center for Research on Lifelong Learning and Education (CELE) in the University of Turku, Finland. He is also the director of the Finnish National Graduate School on Educational Research. He is a member of the Finnish Academy of Science and Letters and has published over three hundred scientific publications. His main interests and publications include sociology of education, international comparative education, educational policy, history of education, higher education, and adult education. His recent publications include: 'Too eager to comply? OECD education policies and the Finnish response' (R. Rinne, J. Kallo, and S. Hokka, 2004, *European Educational Research Journal*, 3(2), 454–85) and *Adult education – liberty, fraternity, equality?* (R. Rinne, A. Heikkinen, and P. Salo, eds. Turku: Finnish Educational Research Association, 2007).

Michael Shattock is a Visiting Professor at the Institute of Education, University of London; he was formerly Registrar of the University of Warwick. He was leader of the EUEREK Project. Michael has published over eighty articles and book chapters on higher education policy, history, management, and governance. His three latest books are *Managing Successful Universities* (Maidenhead: Open University Press, 2003), *Entrepreneurialism and the Transformation of Russian Universities* (ed.) (Paris: International Institute for Educational Planning, UNESCO, 2004), and *Managing Good Governance in Higher Education* (Maidenhead: Open University Press, 2006). He is the editor of the OECD journal *Higher Education Management and Policy*).

Paul Temple is senior lecturer in higher education management at the Institute of Education, University of London, where he is co-director of the MBA programme in higher education management. He has worked extensively on higher education projects in Eastern Europe and Asia. He was previously head of the federal University of London's planning division, after working on polytechnic and college planning and finance for the Inner London Education Authority. Paul has written on various aspects of university strategy and management, and is currently researching the role of space and place in the university. His book on this subject will be appearing later this year.

María-José Vieira is a full-time teaching and research assistant at the University of León, Spain, and collaborates in several international projects with the Centre for the Study of Higher Education Management (CEGES) at the Technological University of Valencia. She has a degree in education and a doctorate in psychology and educational sciences. Her research is focused on higher education (student support and guidance, labour market, governance, and quality assurance). María is author of several publications on these subjects. She has worked as adviser for higher education matters for the European Commission and collaborates with the Director-General of Higher Education in the Spanish Central Government.

Gareth Williams is Emeritus Professor of Education Administration at the Institute of Education, University of London, where he was founding head of the Centre for Higher Education Studies. He worked previously as an educational economist at Lancaster University, the London School of Economics, and OECD. Since 1992 he has concentrated on higher education policy and finance. Books include *Changing Patterns of Finance in Higher Education* (Maidenhead: Open University Press, 1992) and *The Enterprising University* (Maidenhead: Open University Press, 2003). Recent articles include 'The higher education market in the United Kingdom' (in P. Teixeira, B. Jongbloed, D.D. Dill, and A. Amaral, eds., *Markets in Higher Education: Rhetoric or Reality.* Dordrecht: Kluwer Academic, 2004) and 'English university responses to globalisation, internationalisation and Europeanisation' (with J. Evans, in J. Huisman and M. van der Wende, eds., *On Cooperation and Competition II: Institutional Responses to Internationalisation, Europeanisation and Globalisation.* Bonn: Lemmens, 2005).

Abbreviations

AESM	Academy of Economic Studies of Moldova
AMU	Adam Mickiewicz University
AUST	Ajman University of Science and Technology
BIBIM	Baikal Institute of Business and International Management of Irkutsk University
BSU	Balti State University
CEO	Chief Executive Officer
EC	European Commission
ECTS	European Credit Transfer and Accumulation System
EEA	European Economic Area
ENS	External Relations Office
EU	European Union
FINHEEC	Finnish Higher Education Evaluation Council
FTE	Full-Time Equivalent
GDP	Gross Domestic Product
GIFO	Government Individual Financial Obligations
GIPE	Employment Initiatives Office (Spain)
HEFCE	Higher Education Funding Council for England
HEIs	Higher Education Institutions
HSE, Finland	Helsinki School of Economics, Finland
HSE, Russia	Higher School of Economics, Russia
ICTs	Information and Communication Technologies
IT	Information Technologies
JBRs	Research and Development Units (Poland)
KTH	Royal Institute of Technology, Stockholm
LEAs	Local Education Authorities
LOU	University Organization Law (Spain)
LRU	University Reform Act (Spain)
LSHTM	London School of Hygiene and Tropical Medicine
MISTRA	Foundation for Strategic Environmental Research
MSU	Moldova State University

MUST	Mediterranean University of Science and Technology
OECD	Organization for Economic Cooperation and Development
ORI	International Relations Office (Spain)
OTRI	Office for the Transfer of Research Results (Spain)
PAN	Polish Academy of Sciences
PESCA	Quality Strategic Plan (Poland)
PKA	State Commission for Accreditation (Poland)
PPP	Purchasing Power Parity
PR	Public Relations
PROPHE	Programme on Research of Private Higher Education
PSI RAS	Institute of Programming Systems of the Russian Academy of Sciences, University of Pereslavl
PUE	Poznan University of Economics
R&D	Research and Development
RAE	Research Assessment Exercise
RAMs	Resource Allocation Models
SAC	State Attestation Committee (Russia)
SAS	State Attestation Service (Russia)
SMEs	Small and Medium Enterprises
SMT	Senior Management Team
STINT	Swedish Foundation for International Cooperation in Research and Higher Education
SUHF	Association of Swedish Universities and University Colleges
TCUM	Trade Commercial University of Moldova
TEKES	Finnish Funding Agency for Technology and Innovation Group
UAL	University of Alicante
UCH	Cardenal Herrera University
ULA	University of Lapland
UMG	University Management
UMH	Miguel Hernandez University
UNESCO	United Nations Economic, Scientific, and Cultural Organization
UNT	Unified National Test (Russia)
UPV	Technical University of Valencia
USD	United States Dollars
UTA	University of Tampere
UV	University of Valencia
VC	Vice-Chancellor
WSHIG	Academy of Hotel Management and Catering Industry
WTO	World Trade Organization

Tables and figures

Tables

Figures

Preface

This book has originated from an EU Sixth Framework Programme Priority 7 grant to study the relationship between university entrepreneurialism and the Europe of Knowledge (the EUEREK Project). Together with the International Institute of Educational Planning, UNESCO, the following universities were partners in the enterprise: the Institute of Education, University of London, UK (coordinator); the University of Turku, Finland; the Moldova State University, Moldova; the Adam Mickiewicz University, Poland; the Higher School of Economics, Russia; the Technical University of Valencia, Spain; and the Royal Institute of Technology (KTH), Sweden. The project coordinators wish to acknowledge the role of Aljona Sandgren in initiating the bid for the grant and the contacts with the research partners.

The grant commissioned the establishment of a theoretical framework for a study of entrepreneurialism in higher education together with case study research. The initial findings on the theoretical framework were published in a special issue of the journal *Higher Education Management and Policy* (2005, Vol. 17(3)). The case study research covered 27 universities/higher education institutions (HEIs) drawn from seven countries: Finland (3), Moldova (4), Poland (3), Russia (3), Spain (6), Sweden (4), and the United Kingdom (4). The names of the institutions are listed in Appendix 2; the full case studies can be consulted on the EUEREK website (www.EUEREK.info). Quotations from the case studies are referenced as follows: (Alicante case study). Some quotations are also drawn from the national case studies that were prepared as part of the project and are also available on the website; these are referred to by the author and are listed in the bibliography. The universities/HEIs were not selected because they were necessarily to be regarded as entrepreneurial, except in the case of Russia, where the size of the higher education system made an approximate representation of the system as a whole impossible, and comprised a cross-section of institutions ranging from comprehensive universities sited in urban locations to regional universities, specialist institutions, and private universities. This selection was made because we explicitly did not want to choose institutions that would replicate those described in Clark's (1998) *Creating Entrepreneurial Universities* but would illustrate how entrepreneurialism flourishes or is inhibited in a broad spread of institutions that operate under different national systems. The inclusion in the study of private universities that might under one definition be described as entrepreneurial in character *sine qua non*, represents a distinctive feature.

Although most case studies were drawn from within the European Union, it was instructive to include Moldova and Russia in the project both because they highlighted the problems of re-establishing viable higher education systems in the transition countries and because they offered comparators to Poland, a transition country, for the purpose of this study, but now within the European Union. In Moldova, we found institutions severely handicapped by the national economic situation yet struggling to follow what might be described as a 'European' agenda. In Russia, however, the volatility of institutional development (well illustrated in our three case studies), created by a period of financial entrepreneurialism that was itself driven by an acute economic downturn that seriously disrupted the university system (Shattock, 2004a), makes the system difficult to characterize, even though a programme of targeted government reinvestment is now underway. Our case studies serve to highlight the fact that this huge higher education system has yet to reach a point of stability from which general conclusions can be drawn, except that in economically turbulent times entrepreneurial approaches offer more promising routes to survival than reliance on state support.

These case studies, the most extensive we believe undertaken in any trans-European higher education research, provide a unique resource to draw from in studying key themes relating to the state of play in the development of entrepreneurialism in European HEIs. As they are publicly available on the web, we hope they will be of use to other scholars in this and related fields. For us what emerges is a highly variegated picture reflecting national systems, institutional histories, locations, and widely differentiated missions but also clear evidence of movement across all twenty-seven HEIs (though often at a different pace) towards new models that are different from the traditional European university. Our conclusions, set out in Chapter 11, are rooted, like the various theme chapters, in this case study evidence.

The study involved a comparison of financial and other data over the period 1994 to 2004. This was undertaken both to identify longer-term trends than would have necessarily been apparent from the case study interviews and because universities, like tankers, have very large turning circles, so that any analysis of changes of direction demands quite long timescales. The findings are described in Appendix 1. The comparison highlighted some important divergences between national systems where differences in semantics disguised real differences of substance. Thus the concept of 'core funding', and therefore of 'non-core funding', was found to be the subject of varying interpretations depending, for example, on the extent to which funding for research was part of the main government grant to the institution or a matter of separate allocation. The availability or lack of institutional financial accounts recording annual surpluses and deficits for institutional spending also illustrated different national traditions of university managerial autonomy and financial accountability. Such differences of practice illustrate the extent to which system management can vary across Europe. In spite of this we believe that these institutionally based data sets offer a unique alternative picture of institutional change to that which might be derived from nationally based comparative statistics that inevitably smooth out institutional diversity. Institutions – that is, universities and other HEIs – are where higher education takes place, where research is carried out, where students are taught, and where interactions, in both directions, between institutions and their regions occur. It is their leadership, organizational cultures, and, ultimately, performance that together make up the systems of higher education described in national profiles. Unless we understand how they respond to funding pressures, expansion of student numbers, regional constraints and incentives, and changes in the economic environment, we cannot interpret national data accurately.

The final chapter sets out the policy conclusions that we have drawn from the project. We believe that by drilling down into institutional case studies, it has been possible to provide an alternative and more nuanced picture of organizational change than in some other accounts and offer a corrective to some of the conclusions reached in policy documents issued by the Commission of the European Communities (CEC, 2003a, 2005, 2006a).

The editor wishes to express his thanks to all the colleagues who participated in the EUEREK Project, in particular Paul Temple and Gareth Williams who formed with him the Institute of Education, University of London's project coordinating team. He would also like to pay thanks to Rania Ofilippakou, also of the Institute, for her scholarly assistance in the editing of the text for publication.

Michael Shattock

1

Entrepreneurialism and organizational change in higher education

Michael Shattock

The European policy context

The European Union has adopted the goal of becoming the most competitive and dynamic knowledge-based society in the world because it sees knowledge production and diffusion as the engine of economic and social progress. Universities are regarded as having a profound influence on the realization of this goal. The European Commission argues that: 'Given that they are situated at the crossroads of research, education and innovation universities in many respects hold the key to the knowledge economy and society' (CEC, 2003a). They are, it says, responsible for 80% of the fundamental research conducted in Europe, they employ 34% of the active researchers, and in 2001 the unemployment rate of their graduate output stood at only 3.9%, one-third of that of people with lower-level qualifications. In addition, universities train increasing numbers of students to higher qualifications, many of whom enter the highly knowledge-intensive sector of the economy; this sector accounted for half of the new jobs created between 1997 and 2000. Universities are also key contributors to lifelong learning (CEC, 2003a).

Constraints on universities

These expectations impose on universities unlooked for, and perhaps unrealizable, roles and responsibilities. Universities – endowed as they are with a long history and as important as they have been in the production of scholarship and new ideas, and for the training of elites – have not until recently been seen as such positive vehicles of economic progress. Like many other institutions they are facing pressures for change and, unlike most other institutions that have historically depended on the state for resources, their history suggests that they operate most effectively if they have a high degree of academic and managerial autonomy. The overall management of university systems remains, however, vested in individual national governments and variations in modes of state governance, funding regimes, levels of investment, and human resource policies can have critical impacts on their outputs, and in particular on their capacity to innovate, introduce organizational change, and act entrepreneurially.

Over the last two decades, all European higher education systems have expanded rapidly to respond to a rising demand for places, driven in part by demography but more particularly by rising expectations of educational advancement. This trend has been strongly encouraged by national governments but funding has failed to keep pace with student numbers. One effect has been some differentiation of roles among universities between the more research intensive, the less research intensive, and the more local or regional institutions. This process has proceeded at different rates and at different intensities in different countries. A second effect has been the encouragement offered by governments to universities to generate a growing percentage of their funding from non-state sources. A third effect, often linked to the second, is for universities to seek to connect more to society through third mission activities that have an industrial or commercial association or are associated with the regeneration of local or regional economies. These developments have led to extensive organizational and cultural changes within institutions that have varied according to national contexts.

Entrepreneurialism in higher education

The concept of the 'entrepreneurial university' was first highlighted by Clark in his 1998 book *Creating Entrepreneurial Universities* and has been the theme since of many publications across the world. The UNESCO-CEPES Institute devoted a special issue of its journal *Higher Education in Europe* to this theme (2004) and the OECD journal *Higher Education Management and Policy* published a special issue on entrepreneurship from papers given within this project in 2005. By implication, it is a major theme in the European Commission's paper 'Mobilising the brain power of Europe: enabling universities to make their full contribution to the Lisbon Strategy' (CEC, 2005). But there is very little hard definition of entrepreneurialism as a characteristic form of institutional behaviour. In a comprehensive literature survey for the Commission, Audretsch (2002) concludes that as an economic phenomenon, 'there is little consensus about what actually constitutes entrepreneurial activity', while an EU Green Paper sees entrepreneurship as the capacity to turn a business idea into success through 'the ability to blend creativity or innovation with sound management' and argues that implicit in the concept is 'a readiness to take risks and taste for independence and self realisation' (CEC, 2003b). It quotes as an illustration of the 'entrepreneurial dynamism' of the United States that it took twenty years to replace one-third of the Fortune 500 companies listed in 1960 against four years for those listed in 1998. This reflects the Schumpeteran thesis that entrepreneurialism is a disequilibrating force, a force for 'creative destruction' where new entrepreneurial firms displace older less innovative ones, thus producing economic growth (Audretsch, 2002).

It should be remembered that entrepreneurialism in the economic sense only began to become fashionable in the modern period after Birch's (1979) finding, published in 1981 in a period of recession, that small firms in the United States were expanding employment more rapidly than larger ones that had hitherto been seen as the prime engines of growth (Birch, 1979). This evoked a strong response from business theorists who argued that entrepreneurialism had a close connection with the size of the company and usually its commitment to new technologies, together with its capacity to take decisions quickly, take risks, and reposition itself in changing markets for success. These were characteristics that were rarely found in traditional companies, mostly built on manufacturing for mass markets.

But while the economic view of entrepreneurialism is certainly reflected in the debates about entrepreneurialism in universities, there are significant divergences. Clark, in the case studies associated with his 1998 book, describes universities breaking out of the constraints imposed by restrictive funding systems or the bureaucratic conventions of state-run higher educa-tion systems by encouraging innovative academic behaviour, engaging in wide-ranging partnerships with external bodies, and generating non-state funding that can cross-subsidize activities and be used to incentivize further entrepreneurial academic activity. Entrepreneurialism stimulates external collaboration, most notably with industry and commerce, but not exclusively so, and reinforces academic performance by attracting additional resources and widening the research agenda. Clark emphasizes the importance of institutional self-reliance and less dependence on the state. In his second book on this theme, *Sustaining Change in Universities,* Clark (2004a) enlarges the concept by referring to 'the adaptive university', the 'proactive uni-versity', and the 'innovative university'. Shattock (2003, 2005) defines entre-preneurialism similarly as *inter alia* 'a drive to identify and sustain a distinctive institutional agenda which is institutionally determined not one [which is] effectively a product of a state funding formula'. A less positive picture emerges from Slaughter and Leslie's (1997) *Academic Capitalism* and from Marginson and Considine's (2000) *The Enterprise University,* which emphasize much more the academic and organizational downsides of universities being forced to diversify their resource base by engaging in the search for non-state income. The latter define the Australian 'enterprise university' as having the first three of Clark's characteristics of the entrepreneurial university – the strengthened steering core, the expanded developmental periphery, and the diversified funding base – but significantly not the enhanced academic heartland or the integrated entrepreneurial culture. There is also concern, particularly voiced in some European university systems, that by increasing university dependence on non-state resources and deepening their engage-ment with industry and commerce, universities will lose their freedom to act in their traditional role as critics of society. In *The Enterprising University,*

Williams (2004) confirms the view 'that the emergence of enterprise as a powerful and possibly dominant force in universities inevitably raises fundamental questions about their nature and purpose'.

This study does not accept that entrepreneurialism in higher education should be defined wholly in economic terms. Entrepreneurialism in a university setting is not simply about generating resources – although it is an important element – it is also about generating activities, which may have to be funded in innovative ways either in response to anticipated and/or particular market needs or driven by the energy and imagination of individuals, which cumulatively establish a distinctive institutional profile. Entrepreneurialism is a reflection both of institutional adaptiveness to a changing environment and of the capacity of universities to produce innovation through research and new ideas.

One of the principal reasons why entrepreneurial universities acquire a reputation for entrepreneurialism is the extent to which they offer encouragement to 'intrapreneurs'. There is a substantial literature quoted in Kirby (2003) devoted to intrapreneurs in the world of business (Kantor, 1983; Drucker, 1985; Pinchot, 1985; Sinetar 1985; Ross and Unwalla, 1986) but very little within higher education. A university can be viewed as a collection of departments (which behave a little like small and medium enterprises, SMEs) or even as the organizational framework that encloses an accumulation of individual lone scholars (though this applies much less in the sciences than in other disciplines). It is nevertheless the case that departments and even universities are heavily dependent for their reputations on the capacity of a more restricted number of scholars, 'academic intrapreneurs' (Perlman *et al.*, 1988; Shattock 2003), who build substantial research or teaching enterprises outside traditional structures funded largely from external sources. Individual programmes and research teams may be built up by combining grants from research councils, contracts from industrial or other sponsors, and fees from postgraduate students to create new academic enterprises initially on the back of 'soft money' but perhaps eventually, as the research findings are translated into teaching programmes and the teaching programmes become mainstreamed, as part of the new permanent shape of the university. Academically, entrepreneurial universities are distinguished by the apparently untidy array of research centres, research institutes, and special units, which, through their individual drive to attract new resources, are enabled to invest in new facilities, recruit additional staff, and repeat the process again and again by winning new research grants and contracts and engaging in further income-generating activities. Entrepreneurial universities will be flexible in regulating such enterprises, will incentivize and reward them, and be sympathetic to giving them substantial autonomy and freedom to develop and grow. One way to characterize an entrepreneurial university is by identifying its number of successful 'intrapreneurs'.

But we should not see entrepreneurialism simply or even necessarily in relation to research, or in the exploitation of research findings. As we shall see from our case study evidence, entrepreneurialism involving innovation and academic and financial risk can be found in regional outreach programmes, in economic regeneration activities, and in distance learning ventures, as well as in investment in spin out companies, the establishment of overseas campuses, and the creation of holding companies to house different sets of income-generating activities. For many universities, entrepreneurialism can be found in various innovative forms of teaching either to new clientele at home or embodied in programmes for internationalization (themselves often involving both financial and reputational academic risks).

Financial trends 1994–2004

In economic terms, this data set of universities presents a very interesting picture. Statistical material was collected for a 10-year period (see Appendix 1). This was a decade when in almost all the universities there was a significant rise in student numbers not compensated for by pro-rata increases in core income. These increases were spread fairly evenly across the different categories of comprehensive, regional, specialist, and private higher education institutions (HEIs), with Nottingham seeing a rise of nearly 200%, Moldova State one of over 150%, and Tampere one of 24%, though Lund saw a rise of only 13%. In the regional and specialist categories, not counting institutions that were newly founded or had very small numbers (like the London School of Hygiene and Tropical Medicine, LSHTM), both Balti and Lapland doubled in size while Jaume I Castellon, Plymouth, Umeå, the Stockholm Royal Institute of Technology (KTH), and the Poznan University of Economics all saw rises of between 35% and 60%.

If we exclude the public universities in the transition countries that received a very high proportion of their income from fee-paying students (Moldova State University 83%, the Academy of Economic Studies, Moldova 90%, the Poznan University of Economics 51%), the institutions with the highest non-core income in 2004 were from the UK (Nottingham 65% and LSHTM 73%) with KTH (Sweden), a highly research active institution, at 45%, against Plymouth (also from the UK), an essentially regional university, at 43%. But if we look at the change between 1994 and 2004 we find a very different picture, with the UK universities, although seeing very substantial growth in their student numbers and in their external funding, nevertheless showing zero growth in the proportion of non-core to total income and with Plymouth even showing a fall from 62% to 43%. In contrast, the other national systems showed a considerable increase in the proportion of non-core income, with Tampere (Finland) moving from 24% to 34%, the Helsinki School of Economics (HSE, Finland) from 29% to 34%, Jaume I Castellon from 35% in 1999 to 40% in 2004, and the Swedish universities all showing a considerable reliance on non-core income (KTH 45%, Lund 38%, Umeå 32%, and Jönköping 28%). What this suggests is that the UK public universities were already operating in a marketized system and generating substantial non-core income by the early 1990s, and although they have grown their non-core income considerably in volume terms since 1994, the growth has done no more than keep pace with the growth of core income. The other countries, starting later, have begun to move rapidly in the direction the UK followed before 1994; in all these universities, there is a much greater dependence on non-core income than there was a decade ago.

In part, these figures are skewed by fee income, in particular by fees charged to international students. Thus in the UK[1], at Nottingham and Plymouth, fees make up 28% and 27% respectively of the total university income (LSHTM is postgraduate only and therefore much lower at 13%) and in Spain, the Technical University of Valencia and the University of Valencia fees comprise 16% of total income; Finnish and Swedish universities, on the other hand, show no dependence on fee income. However, leaving LSHTM (63%) to one side, universities from Sweden (Lund 31%), Finland (Tampere 22%), and Spain (Jaume I Castellon 27%, the Technical University of Valencia 21%, the University of Valencia 18%) have much higher proportions of income derived from research than Nottingham at 15% (the university's considerable growth in research income is balanced by a student growth of 200%) and Plymouth at 5%. Such figures emphasize that judged simply on the basis of dependence on non-core income and particularly in relation to research income, the UK is much less different from the rest of Europe than might be supposed. While Nottingham generates 22% of its income from 'other services' – that is, from income-generating activities outside teaching and research – the Helsinki School of Economics generates 34%, the Adam Mickiewicz University (AMU) 28%, and the University of Lapland 22%. If fees for overseas students were introduced in Scandinavian countries, something that is under discussion in Sweden, the balance of core to non-core income would be even further diminished. These figures somewhat contradict the accepted EU view, as described in 'Mobilising the brain power of Europe' (CEC, 2005), that European universities are overdependent on the state, at least in financial terms, and they suggest that if our data set of institutions is typical, the market-led reforms that once seemed to set the UK apart are proceeding throughout the European higher education sector.

However, what the figures also demonstrate is the widely different contributions that universities make to a European research and development (R&D) target. In effect, a line can be drawn between a group of comprehensive and specialist institutions (Lund, Nottingham, Tampere, LSHTM, KTH, and the Technical University of Valencia), all located in major urban areas, and the comprehensive universities in Moldova and Poland and the regional and other specialist universities. Thus if the sole purpose of policy was to meet the Lisbon target, a concentration of additional resources in these institutions and their comparators around Europe would add the most value, because they are already research intensive and would be most likely to be effective in exploring research outcomes in the knowledge economy. However, this would tend to undervalue the contribution of the regional universities in particular, where fundamental research is much less evident and conventional technology transfer is therefore likely to be much more patchy, and where a wider range of entrepreneurial activities is often deployed to the benefit of rural populations.

Organizational change

These financial changes and the take-up of new activities are mirrored in wide-ranging organizational change. It is not simply that these institutions have created research offices or technology transfer units, outreach arms and new decision-making structures to manage international activities, but they have found that the more they engage with external markets the more decision-making systems have to be made more flexible. Internal governance arrangements have needed to change to match the new demands made upon them. It is here that often the greater difficulty lies, and where the greatest impediments to change can be found. Chapter 6 describes the situation revealed by the case studies in more detail. It suggests that the UK model of the university as an independent legal entity with full autonomy can be seen to be better placed to adapt to changing circumstances than universities that are closely integrated with state ministries or government departments. The non-traditional constitution of Jönköping University represents an attempt by the Swedish Government to provide a new model for Swedish higher education that will be of interest to many countries. If we accept that in companies 'organizational design is the key to unlocking the opportunities of the 21st century' (Bryan and Joyce, 2007: 16), the same may be true of universities. If, as these authors argue, internal organizational design changes could add between 30% and 60% to the profit per employee of companies with high proportions of 'thinking-intensive jobs', how much could universities add to their innovative capacity by further organizational change? Our case studies suggest that while considerable organizational change is taking place, many national systems of higher education still have considerable impediments to innovation in place.

Entrepreneurialism and the knowledge society

Fully state-funded national higher education systems do not provide the challenges that diversified funding systems offer institutions to break out of a common, state-constructed, model. Entrepreneurialism, through the generation of new and innovative activities, therefore, makes a distinctive contribution to the knowledge society; a diversified income base and institutional competitiveness are forcing houses for new ideas and new programmes. From this one might anticipate that private universities, funded entirely independently of the state, might be in the forefront of entrepreneurial activity, but in Europe at least, judging by our case study evidence

(Chapter 8), this is not the case because they are themselves dependent on a single source of income – student fees. This seems to have the effect of concentrating their energies on maximizing this single stream to the exclusion of others, and they are generally not entrepreneurial in the sense in which we understand it. By contrast, many universities in our study, substantially core funded by the state, have diversified their activities into externally funded research and technology transfer, regional outreach, and into internationalization ventures of astonishing breadth and ambition. Publicly funded universities, provided the funding is adequate (which is not the case in, for example, the transition countries), appear much more likely, on the basis of our case studies, to provide the innovation and intellectual dynamism to fuel the knowledge society than the private sector. The picture, therefore, that emerges is that state investment in university institutions in Europe provides a necessary platform from which diversification and entre-preneurialism can take place. How this platform is constructed, what incentives it contains, and what organizational forms and missions are adopted by or provided to institutions determines to a significant extent the degree to which they develop a culture that encourages entrepreneurialism.

Note

1. In quoting practice with respect to fee charging in the UK, it is important to remember that fees are not charged to Scottish (and other EU member) students in Scotland.

2

Finance and entrepreneurial activity in higher education in a knowledge society

Gareth Williams

Introduction

Entrepreneurialism is fundamentally about innovation and risk taking in the anticipation of subsequent benefits. Neither the innovations and risks nor the expected benefits need necessarily be financial, but it is rare for them to have no economic dimension. Finance is a key indicator and an important driver of entrepreneurial activity.

The main link between entrepreneurial activity in universities and the knowledge economy is Adam Smith's 'invisible hand'. Universities are institutions that advance their reputations and their wealth by creating and disseminating knowledge. If the innovations that they make and the risks that they take accelerate useful knowledge creation and its transfer into social and economic practice, their entrepreneurialism contributes to a knowledge-based society.

Any organization with an assured income at a level that is adequate in relation to its needs and aspirations has little motivation to undertake risky innovations. In addition, if a university is not able to retain the external income it generates, there is little economic incentive to seek to supplement its core allocations from government by selling academic services. This was the situation in many European countries until the 1980s. While some individual members of academic staff may have had a predisposition towards innovation – the urge to discover and interpret natural and social phenomena, for example – there were few economic reasons to make any findings widely available outside the academic world or seek practical applications for them. In contrast, when the assured income is inadequate to meet the goals of an organization and the university is able to retain any supplementary income it generates, incentives are created to seek new sources of revenue and this often means developing new ideas, and taking risks to transfer knowledge into productive activity. Financial stringency and financial opportunities have been the main drivers of entrepreneurial activity in the case study institutions.

However, some case study reports also suggest that severe financial stringency can inhibit creative entrepreneurialism because many innovations require some initial investment and usually some financial risks that institutions that are severely short of money cannot afford to take.

Governments can stimulate entrepreneurial behaviour through the mechanisms they use to allocate resources to universities. If subsidies are based on formulae for staffing establishments and physical facilities, there is little incentive for universities to do more than accept the cash and spend it in accordance with the legal regulations. If, however, government allocations take the form of payment for services rendered, either for research achievements and aspirations or for recruiting and graduating students, the institutions are encouraged to be achievement orientated and entrepreneurial behaviour is encouraged. The 'new public management' and 'steering from a distance' put into practice by many governments in the 1990s stimulated such responses.

There are similar incentives in the allocation of resources within institutions. A traditional way of managing the finance of a university or college was for all resources to be allocated and administered from the top of the institutional hierarchy. The task of departmental and faculty staff was to undertake teaching and research according to the rules of the institution and to follow prescribed procedures if they needed to purchase equipment or employ assistants. Any supplementary income resulting from the research or teaching was paid to the central management of the university. Such arrangements do not encourage entrepreneurial behaviour by individuals and working groups within the university.

In the more entrepreneurial universities covered in the case studies, departments and faculties are treated as more or less independent franchised businesses. A university or college has certain legal obligations, which must be enforced on everyone employed within it, and it has its own rules and conventions to ensure the distinctiveness and quality of its own 'brand'. But beyond this, deans and heads of departments often have very considerable autonomy in managing their own budgets, allocated according to the amount of teaching and research they undertake, and have the authority to generate additional income in ways that are consistent with the institution's, usually broadly defined, mission. In these circumstances, departmental and faculty leaders and individual members of staff have many opportunities for innovative entrepreneurial initiatives.

Income profiles in the case study institutions

In broad terms, most European higher education institutions now receive their income via three main routes:

- regular core income from government for teaching and (in most countries) basic research;

- additional research funds mainly from government that are earned, at least in part, competitively;
- 'third stream' or 'third mission' income earned on a quasi-commercial basis for contract research and teaching and use of university facilities by outsiders.

The key financial indicators of the potential for entrepreneurial activity by higher education institutions are:

(a) sources of income;
(b) mechanisms through which income is received by universities and colleges;
(c) resource allocation procedures within the institution.

As a general rule, institutions that receive all – or most – of their income in the form of line item budgets that must be strictly adhered to are unlikely to have the incentive or the opportunity to generate additional income through entrepreneurial initiatives. At the other extreme, universities that receive generous public funding with little accountability over how it is used have little incentive to attempt to make the services they can provide widely available outside academia. In contrast, if their core funding is not generous and they are able to retain any supplementary income they can generate, they have an incentive to show many more aspects of entrepreneurialism and to sell their services in the wider society.

The institutional case studies that are part of the EUEREK Project have very different income profiles. Table 1 shows that in 2004 the percentage of income recorded as core income from government ranged from over 70% in some universities in Finland, Poland, and Spain to zero in private universities in Moldova, Poland, Spain, and the UK. Fee income is usually the complement of these extreme cases, and ranged from over 90% in the private universities in Poland and Spain to zero in Finland and Sweden. The percentage of non-government income from research ranged from over 60% in one of the UK institutions to zero in some Moldovan and Polish universities. It was not possible to separate third mission activities from research and teaching budgets in all cases but where this can be done the figures range from nearly 30% in one Swedish university to less than 5% in some Moldovan and Polish institutions.

Many of these differences are a result of the legal and political context of universities in different countries. For example, in Finland and Sweden the educational activities of universities are still regarded as a public service and they are not allowed to charge fees for any of their regular teaching, although recent changes in their legal status now permit universities to charge some fees for courses that are not part of their mainstream academic work. At the other extreme, the private universities in the UK, Poland, and Spain, and all the case study universities in Moldova, are almost entirely dependent on student fees. In Spain, the public universities obtain between 10% and 20% of their total income from fees, and in the Russian case study institutions fee income ranged from over 60% of total income to nearly zero in the case of Pereslavl University, which is concerned mainly with teaching higher-level computer technology and applications. In the UK, the corresponding figure is between 10% and 30% and in Poland between 20% and 40%. It is a moot point whether dependence on fees encourages entrepreneurial attitudes. On the one hand, there is an incentive to develop new courses and adapt existing programmes to make them more attractive to students; on the other, the recruitment of students can be such a time- and resource-consuming activity that little surplus is left for innovation. There are examples of both in the case studies.

Research profiles are equally varied. In the UK, one institution obtains nearly two-thirds of its income from research while in another the figure is less than 10%. In Sweden, the variation is almost as wide, from over 50% to less than 20%. In Finland, where it is not possible to distinguish between research and education/teaching income in the case of government grants, external research income ranges from 10% to over 30% of total income. In Spain, the situation and the variance is broadly similar to Finland, while in Poland and Moldova research generates relatively little income from either government or external sources.

Third mission income, which is likely to encompass the greater part of what is usually understood by entrepreneurial activity, varies similarly: ranging from 4% to 16% of total income in the Swedish case study institutions, 6% to 23% in the UK, 12% to 22% in Finland, 0% to 13% in Moldova, and 3% to 10% in Poland. In Spain, none of the income of higher education institutions is treated as third mission. This highlights one problem of making international comparisons of these new university activities: the definitions of third mission vary considerably. Spanish universities have several 'satellite campuses' that undertake many of the kinds of work that the UK and Sweden treat as third mission. It is also the case that the boundaries between many kinds of applied research and income-generating consultancy are very blurred and may be defined differently in different institutions in one country as well as between countries. The figures given in Table 1 must, therefore, be considered as indications rather than definitive measurements. They do, however, provide a starting point for more general discussion of the economics and finance of university entrepreneurialism in the EUEREK countries.

Between 1994 and 2004, the proportion of income from non-core government sources increased in slightly more than half the case study institutions for which the information is available, but the reasons for the increase differ considerably. In Moldova and Poland it is almost entirely due to the growth in fee income, while in Finland it is mainly a result of increased third mission activity. In the UK universities, there was a slight decline in the proportion of income from non-government sources over the decade but this can be attributed to the fact that the figures were already high by 1994 and the greatly increased first-degree fee income had not come into operation in 2004.

Table 1 Income profiles of case study institutions, 2004

	Core government		Other			Index of increase as % of income from non-state sources 1994–2004
	Education/teaching	*Research*	*Research*	*Fees*	*3rd mission, etc.*	
Finland	64		23	0	13	
HSE	66	12	0	22	19	
Lapland	78		8	0	14	22
Tampere	66	22	0	12	61	
Moldova†						
MSU	13	4	0	83	0	>100
AES	10	0	0	77	13	>100
BSU	26	3	0.1	70.7	0.2	>100
TCUM	0	0	0	100	0	
Poland	52	9	2	31	6	
(Public)	62	11	3	19	6	
(Private)	0.3	0.4	0.3	96	3	
AMU	62	9	1	18	10	45
PUE	44	5	1	41	9	28
WHSIG	0	0	0	94	6	0
Russia						
BIBIM Irkutsk	14		1	62	33	−8*
Pereslavl	72	17			11	0
HSE	22	12	21	17	28	28
Spain†						
Alicante	70		14	16	0	
Hernandez	85		3	12	0	
Herrera	0		1	99	0	
Jaume I of Castellon	74		13	13	0	
UP Valencia	70		9	21		
U Valencia	73		9	18		
Sweden	65		16	0	19	
Jönköping	65	7	10	2	16	
KTH	55		32	9	4	
Lund	32	30	26	5	7	
Umeå	68		18	0	14	
UK	30	8	16	25	21	
Buckingham	0	0	11	70	19	0
LSHTM	18	26	37	13	6	−1
Plymouth	54	3	5	27	11	−31
Nottingham	21	13	15	28	23	−1

* 1999–2004.
† Not available.

Dimensions of university entrepreneurialism

Finance can enable and stimulate entrepreneurial activity or it can discourage and obstruct entrepreneurial initiatives depending on where it originates and how it is made available to a university.

Five different categories of entrepreneurial behaviour can be observed in the case studies:

(a)   new private higher education institutions;
(b)   new developments in public universities stimulated by government;
(c)   major institution-wide initiatives by public universities;
(d)   smaller-scale departmental, faculty, and centre ventures;
(e)   freelance teaching, research, and consultancy.

Private universities

In some countries, of which the United States is the best-known example, private universities have a long history and predate the public systems of higher education. In these countries, the public system of higher education was established to make the benefits of higher education available to a much wider cross-section of the population. Among the EUEREK countries, the UK comes close to this model. The legal status of UK universities has always been very similar to that of the traditional private universities in the United States. They are autonomous organizations with the legal status of charitable foundations, which means that any income they receive must be used to support the charitable purposes for which they were founded, but with this restriction they are legally able to undertake any activity their governing bodies consider appropriate. Where the UK differed from the United States was that for four decades after 1945 the British Government made available to the universities massive institutional subsidies with very little requirement on them to account for how the money was spent other than in accordance with their charitable status. During the same period, the UK authorities developed a public sector of higher education, analogous to the pubic universities of the United States, with the aim of making some provision for students who could not afford the costs of university education, and to provide high-level vocational and professional qualifications that the universities did not provide. Nevertheless, the autonomous university with full responsibility for its own financial arrangements remained the dominant model of higher education provision, so that when, at the end of the 1980s, the Government decided to create a unitary system of higher education, it was based on the autonomous university model and all higher education institutions became self-governing institutions. Much of the literature on university governance during the past two decades has drawn parallels between university governing bodies and the boards of directors of private companies.

In the other EUEREK countries, publicly provided state systems of higher education were established in the nineteenth century and remained the dominant sector throughout the twentieth century. The state assumed full responsibility for financing higher education and for much of its management and academic content. This was, of course, particularly evident, from the 1920s onwards, in countries controlled by Communist parties in Eastern Europe, but was also the case in Spain among the EUEREK countries.

These two traditions led to different responses when public finance for higher education became very much less generous in the last two decades of the twentieth century. In higher education systems with a strong tradition of dependence on government funding and control, public universities found it difficult, and were often unwilling, to adapt to new circumstances. Legal and cultural restrictions inhibited the development of new curricula or charging student tuition fees to help cover the costs of doing so. After 1990 in Moldova, Poland, and Russia individual entrepreneurs and groups of entrepreneurs established private universities to take advantage of gaps in public sector provision, especially in information technology, social and business sciences, and in language education. It will be interesting to see whether the greater autonomy and flexibility granted to the public universities, and their growing realization that survival depends on finding non-government sources of finance, since the middle of the 1990s will result in some of the recently established private universities becoming less financially viable.

In Poland, for example, the competition of public and private institutions for students, and especially fee-paying students, is increasing. The case study private university, the Academy of Management and Catering Industry (WSHIG), established in 1993 as a private entrepreneurial venture, has found a useful niche in the tourism industry, in close collaboration with the tourist and hotel authorities. However, the WSHIG case study shows that in recent years student recruitment has become more difficult. In 2000, a major public university in the same city, Adam Mickiewicz University (AMU), established a course in tourism and recreation studies. Similar courses have been established in the other major higher education institution in the city, the Poznan University of Economics (PUE). It remains to be seen whether the private university will be able to survive if the public universities start to compete seriously. In Moldova, too, in recent years the public universities have begun to behave more like private institutions, adapting their curricula to twenty-first century needs and charging significant fees to their students.

In the UK, the universities were able to use their autonomy to generate income in most of the ways private universities can: they developed new courses; they charged fees for all students other than European Union (EU) students on first-degree courses[1]; they sold consultancy services; they rented out their facilities for conferences. An interesting exception to this general rule was the private University of Buckingham, one of the case study institutions, which was established in 1976 by a group of academic and political entrepreneurs who were concerned that the growing dependence of universities on public funding threatened to give the government too much control over higher learning. As is evident from the UK case studies, the continued autonomy of the traditional universities to generate financial surpluses from everything except their first degree teaching of EU students made Buckingham relatively unattractive to UK students and research sponsors with the result that it has remained a very small contributor to the total provision of higher education in the country. To date it has remained financially viable largely because of the students from other countries it attracts. It remains to be seen whether the much higher fees to be paid by all UK students from 2006 onwards will encourage more UK and other EU students to consider Buckingham.

In general, it is apparent from the case studies that, apart from the initial entrepreneurial act of establishing them, the management of the private universities has shown little evidence of entrepreneurialism in the period covered by the case studies. This appears to be largely due to the lack of any financial surplus that would enable them to take the financial risks of uncertain new ventures. All available energy is used in recruiting and satisfying the students who are paying fees that are higher than those in public sector institutions. The need to concentrate on providing value for money for the students has also meant that there is very little funded research in the private universities. This raises a more general issue about successful entrepreneurialism and entrepreneurial higher education institutions in particular. In a competitive environment, any university or college must be prepared to innovate, but it must also be able to sustain and develop those innovations that are successful and to discontinue those that are unsuccessful. Both are easier if there is a financial cushion. New private universities may be justified in seeking to establish a firm financial footing before undertaking costly new ventures.

During the period covered by the study, the Scandinavian countries, represented by Finland and Sweden, have been in an interesting intermediate position. Traditionally, the national governments have exercised quite close control over universities but it has also funded them quite generously. During the 1990s, government began to loosen its grip, especially in Sweden, but reductions in funding were not severe. The no-fees policy has made it impossible for any commercial private universities to be established, but the established public universities have been able to adapt gradually to the new circumstances and increase their applied research and consultancy, and also to undertake some contract teaching for public and private organizations. In Sweden, some new universities have been established, Jönköping University among the case studies, with a legal status similar to universities in the UK. These universities receive funding from government in lieu of student fees, which they are not allowed to charge for regular academic courses, but otherwise they are encouraged to raise income in any ways they consider to be appropriate.

Government initiatives

One of the main ways in which national governments play a part in promoting entrepreneurialism in universities and their contributions to the knowledge society is by establishing an appropriate legal framework for them to operate within. Despite the collapse of centrally planned economies and the global spread of market ideas in higher education, national governments still exercise considerable power and influence over their universities and colleges. Indeed, in countries with a long tradition of university independence, such as the UK, it is usually claimed that central governments have, over the past twenty years, increased rather than reduced their regulatory powers over higher education. This is largely due to their control of substantial financial resources but governments also have political powers of persuasion. A remarkable development of the past two decades has been the extent to which European governments have begun to see higher education institutions as potential spearheads of technological advance and hence of economic and social well-being (see, for example, Kitagawa, 2005; Williams and Kitaev, 2005). This was extended to a European level concern with university contributions to European economic success through the Lisbon agenda and the debates surrounding it. In May 2006, for example, the European Commission took a position on how best to modernize Europe's universities:

> This is fundamentally important for them to make their contribution to the EU's objective to become a leading global and knowledge-based economy. European universities have enormous potential, much of which unfortunately goes untapped because of various rigidities and hindrances. Freeing up the substantial reservoir of knowledge, talent and energy requires immediate, in-depth and coordinated change: from the way in which systems are regulated and managed, to the ways in which universities are governed. (CEC, 2006a)

Governmental financial incentives have influenced entrepreneurial initiatives in the case study universities both positively and negatively. Positive references are largely about funds that are made available for research and sometimes to promote university–industry partnerships. In the Finnish University of Lapland (ULA), for example, 'the connection between funding and steering is emphasized. It is seen that the financiers have lots of influence on the functioning of the university. The structural fund system of EU has probably been the most significant resource base which has made many activities possible at the ULA' (Lapland case study).

Research in Polish higher education is funded mostly 'through different slots in state subsidies for research. Additionally, the University makes use of EU research funds, currently mainly through the 5th and 6th Framework Programs' (Kwiek, 2005b). The state 'also provides financial support in the form of generous tax incentives for academics (and other so-called in Poland "creative" professions such as journalists, artists, lawyers etc)'. In Spain too, 'the production of new knowledge is initially financed with both national and regional public funds. After that, if successful, they look for other public and private sources' (Kwiek, 2005b).

In the extremely research-intensive UK case study, one respondent remarked that:

> the role of the UK Government should not be overlooked. Although the HEFCE commitment to the School is relatively small, the UK Government remains an important source of research funding and the G8's initiatives towards the Third World and the Government's commitment to 'the South' has been beneficial to the School's progress. Every grant from the Department for International Development now carries a requirement that researchers should commit themselves to publishing their findings outside the usual academic journals, thus forcing the School to be more active in contributing to the public understanding of science. (LSHTM case study)

Government influence need not, however, always be directly financial – or legal. In Nottingham University, leading members of the University expressed the view that they need to talk constantly to government, as well as research collaborators and a wide variety of people, if the University is to play its part in providing the innovation the UK needs as the country moves into the twenty-first century. In the same university, according to one senior member of staff:

> Over time the third stream area is being seen more and more as what a University would naturally be doing. And sometimes it is politically appropriate: the government is expecting us to do something and will look at us more favourably if we do it. (Nottingham case study)

In Finland, universities have been allowed, since 2005, to establish and retain the income from companies they set up to exploit their research. This practice has been common in UK universities since the 1970s and in Sweden since the early 1990s. In Poland, new laws on public–private partnerships and on intellectual property are too recent to identify their impact but potentially they open new possibilities for spin-off companies run by academics. Such ventures have also begun to appear in Moldova where one of the case studies reported the creation of a business incubator with funds from the EU and other foreign sources.

There were some comments, however, about the inhibiting nature of governmental involvement in some of the initiatives. In Finland, the new university company model was heavily criticized by the Director of Administration at one university, who claimed that the model does not provide opportunities to establish holding companies that would carry their own losses and profits: the returns of the companies must be written into the balance sheet of the university.

I don't think that they've really fully realized all the aspects yet. They want power and are concerned with the commercialization of some innovation and the entrepreneurial possibilities and with the fact that hopefully we don't make too much money and become too rich with all of this. But I don't know of any university anywhere in the world that would've become too rich with this type of thing. What they should be concerned with is making sure that we have operational conditions that are capable of covering the risks. – I think it's quite natural that this model has not cut a dash in the universities. It's still based on that mistrust. As I see it, people don't have confidence in the universities' abilities of doing it successfully. (HSE, Finland case study)

In Poland, history was held to be responsible for the underdevelopment of university–industry cooperation for two reasons:

first, the industry, and especially heavy industry, has been in a very difficult financial position in the recent 15 years due to the passage from command-driven to market economy and heavy competition with foreign products; second, the university in previous decades under communism was focused much more on state-supported basic research, rather than on industry-supported applied research. (Kwiek, 2005b)

In Poland, one – probably unintended – outcome of the 1991 Law on Higher Education that was in operation until July 2005 was that it did not prevent staff from holding multiple positions in several institutions: 'Consequently, faculty members have been much more interested in teaching in several places than in thinking in an entrepreneurial manner in the institutional context of PUE' (PUE case study). Under the 2005 Law, university staff members were restricted to holding only two full-time academic posts.

In Spain, the fact that academic staff are employed and paid as permanent civil servants was felt by some respondents to be a factor inhibiting entrepreneurial activity within the university. The head of a research institute at the Technical University of Valencia (UPV) remarked that:

If you guarantee someone that, whatever he/she does, nothing is going to happen to him or her, you are reducing his/her motivation to work. Therefore, in our system, the stimulus is personal; whoever wants to work does so. I have tried to motivate some civil servant academic staff but sometimes it is impossible. A civil servant does not have any obligation to research because there is no formal control of these activities. (UPV case study)

The head of one UK institution expressed a similar point from a diametrically opposed starting position.

The University is, then, reacting to market pressures, much in the way that (presumably) government intended – behaving as a commercial corporation would, competing for market share by offering new products and improved services, while seeking to expand the market. Staff are aware that, while they arguably work in the public sector, their jobs depend on the University's success in this way. (Plymouth case study)

Major institutional initiatives

In some cases, a university is entrepreneurial in the sense that its senior management undertakes large-scale and possibly risky investments on behalf of the institution as a whole. Whether it is able to undertake such ventures depends on the legal and administrative setting, the nature of the senior management team, the academic culture of the university, and its financial situation. A university is unlikely to be entrepreneurial if it is legally prevented from being so, if the senior management team is more concerned with stability than with testing the boundaries, if the academic culture values traditional mainstream teaching and research above all else, or if there is insufficient financial security for major new investments that inevitably carry an element of risk. Given these parameters, it is not surprising that there are relatively few examples of such ventures among the case study institutions and a high proportion of these are in two UK universities (Nottingham and LSHTM) that have long experience of financial autonomy.

There are some other examples. The business incubator of the Academy of Economic Studies of Moldova (AESM) has already been referred to. Here the financial uncertainty was met with grants from the EU and from other external sources. In Poland, the legal and financial situation is such that there are very few examples of institutional initiatives of this type, though the recent change in the law that makes it possible for a university to establish an income-generating company may change the situation.

One interesting development in the Poznan University of Economics (PUE) in 1993 was the establishment of the PUE Foundation to support the academic work of the University. In 2000, the Foundation established a consultancy office with the legal form of a company, 80% of whose shares belonged to the Foundation. The establishment of this company was undoubtedly an entrepreneurial venture but its links to the University are tenuous. The University bears no financial risks, exercises no control over the company, and no financial surpluses are returned to the University. One lesson of such examples is that university managers should understand that a prestigious name can have considerable commercial value and the university needs to control the use made of its name in commercial as well as academic ventures.

A somewhat similar situation of entrepreneurial initiatives taking advantage of the name and facilities of the university but with only tenuous links in practice is reported from Spain.

It could be said that the UPV is not an entrepreneurial institution (this is, in fact, true of any Spanish university). However, it is full of entrepreneurs who are relatively free to work as they wish within the UPV.

They have been helped by the creation of independent satellite centres which have become the driving force behind entrepreneurial activity at the UPV, yet the institution's core, and to a great extent, the university's formal teaching methods, are still highly conventional and insist on using outdated practices. This is a clear case of 'institutional schizophrenia', i.e. the two live together in harmony as long as there are no clashes between the two cultures. This balance has been maintained up until now thanks to the previous rector's leadership. The situation's Achilles heel is that the whole house of cards could come tumbling down if the governing bodies advocate radical change in the university. (Technical University of Valencia case study)

The 'tumbling down' presumably refers to what might happen to the satellite centres if the governing body of the University decided to try to harness all this entrepreneurial effort to the interests of the University as an institution.

In Finland, recent changes in the law now make it possible for universities to undertake large-scale entrepreneurial ventures and some of the tensions and teething problems have already been referred to above. Belief in the importance of university autonomy is very strongly held in Finland and many income-generating activities are undertaken with this in mind, to protect academic values rather than undermine them. In the Helsinki School of Economics (HSE, Finland), for example, The rector stated that they have consciously and actively raised the proportion of external funding to increase the autonomy of the university. Establishing companies has naturally assisted reaching this goal'. The view that this aim of enhancing autonomy is being achieved was underlined by one professor of economics whose experience was as follows:

But we have been in a good situation in a sense that we haven't had to do research for money. We've gotten funding for projects we've felt are feasible and sensible. We've got so much of surplus that we haven't had any financial problems at all while I've been here. In fact, quite a lot of savings have been transferred from us to other subjects. (HSE, Finland case study)

It is in the UK, and in Nottingham University in particular among the case study institutions, that large-scale entrepreneurialism reaches its zenith. During the period covered by the EUEREK case study, Nottingham University has established new campuses in Nottingham, Malaysia, and China, created a new Veterinary School, and played a leading role in the establishment of 'Bio-City', a collaboration between the two universities in Nottingham and the local authority, to develop a major research and development centre in commercially exploitable biosciences. The case study report attributes these ventures primarily to the leadership of its vice-chancellor over the past twenty years: 'There is widespread agreement within the University that the immediate driver of change is the vice-chancellor'. One senior and long-serving academic commented that:

If 20 years ago I was told that one person could make such a big difference to an institution . . . I would have refused to believe it. I think he is
an exceptionally talented individual and particularly suited to the kind
of institution we are because we are akin perhaps to a firm of solicitors
with 1,400 partners. The individuals are important and the management
makes a difference. (Nottingham case study)

This case study report also points out, however, that 'the vice-chancellor,
like all chief executives works within a context bounded by external constraints and internal pressures'. External constraints are political and legal as
well as financial and the internal pressures are created by the culture and
vested interests of the people working in it. The task for managers is to find
ways of manipulating and evading the external pressures and to create an
internal culture, such as that already referred to in the context of the HSE
(Finland), in which new ventures are seen as bolstering the mainstream
academic work rather than detracting from it.

The importance of adequate finance is also mentioned in the Nottingham
report:

[The University] has been able to maintain a healthy overall financial
situation since 1990 despite the stringency in public funding and several
new ventures, which the University has undertaken. This is due in part
to the healthy overall financial reserves held by the University . . .
Against such a background a university can afford to take some well-
considered financial risks. (Nottingham case study)

This contrasts sharply with the situation in Polish universities where:

It is difficult to talk about more entrepreneurial missions and strategies
in a severely under funded public system which has marginal chances
for either international funding or funding from the industry and which
a few years ago was not able to pay salaries at some point. (AMU case
study)

Another large-scale form of institutional-level entrepreneurial activity is
the establishment of partnerships with higher education institutions in
other countries, which enable students to benefit from teaching and qualifications of the European university but to spend much less time and money
outside their own country. This is common in UK universities, but was
not reported in any of the case study institutions (except in Russia). A
somewhat similar kind of partnership, reported in the Plymouth University
and the Lapland case studies, is participation with other institutions in
regional partnerships to enable students in relatively remote areas of a country to participate in higher education. The Plymouth case study poses the
question:

Can these partnerships be classified as entrepreneurial in the sense of
the diversification of income and the extent to which they draw the
University into non-traditional activities? Or are they simply another way

for the University to gain access to public funds, in response to current funding priorities? (Plymouth case study).

However, although the motivation for such activities is rarely exclusively financial, they are a risky venture to some extent, but if they are successful it is in a university's financial interest to be able to attract new categories of student.

Small-scale entrepreneurialism

In nearly all the case study institutions, there is a wide range of relatively small-scale entrepreneurial activities by faculties, departments, research centres, and individual members of staff. There are examples from all the participating countries in teaching, research, and knowledge transfer.

In teaching, many examples are reported of new ways of recruiting fee-paying students, within the law, often by the creation of innovative short non-award-bearing courses and, in some countries, through the creation of one-year master's degree courses that do not form part of the national qualification framework. MBA programmes are often quoted as falling into this category. To do this on a large scale, as happens in two of the UK case study institutions, involves considerable investment and some financial risks in that the market can never be certain. According to some understandings of the word 'entrepreneurial', any new award-bearing courses where income is dependent on recruitment of students, for example the new courses in tourism and hotel management in Polish public institutions, can be considered to come into this category of small-scale entrepreneurialism. Another example from Poland at the very small-scale and low-risk end of the spectrum is the common practice of individual teachers holding teaching posts at more than one university, though this can also be classified as an individual initiative (as we will see in a later section of this chapter).

It is in research that small-scale entrepreneurialism is most widespread. It is innovative research that also makes the most obvious contribution to European and global knowledge economies. Nearly all new externally funded research can legitimately be considered as entrepreneurial since, by definition, it is innovative to some extent, it involves some financial investment, in the form of staff time if nothing else to prepare a proposal, and the outcomes are uncertain both in the sense that the project proposal may be unsuccessful and, if the money is obtained, the research itself may finally prove to be of little value. Nearly all the case study institutions obtain external research funds, as Table 1 shows. The extent varies very considerably, however, from a few hundred euros in some instances (which may, however, reflect considerable entrepreneurial effort by one individual) to well over 30% of the total income of the institution (or several million euros) in two of the case study institutions (see Table 1).

Third mission

Almost as widespread as research in terms of income generation is the 'third mission' work, which covers a wide range of activities, including consultancy, which is usually distinguished from research in being more routine and commercial in nature, short periods of non-award-bearing professional retraining, and letting out university facilities to other users, for example conferences. The very wide range of activities that can be included under this heading and its relative newness means that there are serious problems of definition in making comparisons of income from them between countries or even between institutions. Table 1 gives some indicative figures, which show that in all the participating countries except Spain, there is some income that is not from teaching or research and again this varies from a few hundred euros to around 20% of the income of some Finnish, Swedish, and UK universities. The Spanish case highlights the definitional problems, since the case study reports do make clear that there is work that in other countries would be considered as third mission but it does not appear in the university financial returns as such.

There is a more general issue in connection with the financing of third mission activities. Are they undertaken as an end in themselves on a par with teaching and research? In other words, have they become part of mainstream higher education? Or do universities seek third stream income to generate a surplus for the university that enables regular teaching and research to be done better? Williams and Kitaev (2005) have found that:

> Government policies on such matters are often opaque. Are universities encouraged to generate income from private sources in order to relieve government from some of the costs of teaching and research – in which case the work is worth doing by a university only if it generates a surplus over and above the full costs of doing it. Or are third mission tasks genuine new roles for the university arising from the pervasiveness of 'knowledge' as an economic and social good? In this case these activities can claim as much right to be financed from public funds as conventional teaching and research and universities should not be expected to make a profit from them. (Williams and Kitaev, 2005: 128)

The case studies suggest that the universities themselves are ambivalent about this issue. There is considerable evidence that lack of conventional funding is a spur to innovation. One example is the University of Tampere, where:

> The interviewees at the University of Tampere think that the reasons for increased share of external funding are both that the state funding has decreased and that the university is more active and willing to seek funding. When the budget funding decreased and the demands for universities increased, it was the only way to make extra resources. (Tampere case study)

In the University of Lapland, it was reported that 'the decrease of the state funding was an important reason also at the ULA to start to seek external funding'. However, this contrasts with the other opinions in Finnish universities, which claim that shortage of money does not seem to have been a prime motivating factor. This is discussed in a later section.

In Sweden, a senior member of the Law Faculty at Lund University remarked that 'Without external resources we cannot survive. Every senior lecturer needs to find 50% of the salary and every professor needs to finance one doctoral student' (Lund case study). In the Social Sciences Faculty of the same university, a respondent remarked that 'lack of money forces new ideas to come forward' (Lund case study).

In Spain, the head of a research institute at the University of Alicante stated: 'We need support for projects when we are trying to get them started not at the end when we have done all the leg work' (Alicante case study). In the Technical University of Valencia:

The general opinion was that yes, the benefits of entrepreneurial activities do end up paying for academic activities:

- A maximum of 30% of the funding goes to the researcher, the remaining 70% goes to the university.
- The money that the university obtains from R&D activities (€46 million) benefits students as well because money from R&D activities pays for many other infrastructures. (UPV case study)

At the University Jaume I of Castellon, 'most of the people interviewed agreed that economic factors are decisive, because without the necessary funds it is impossible to develop university activities'.

In the UK, the case study on the LSHTM reports that 'The School receives only 21% of its income from HEFCE sources and is therefore, under a financial definition, highly entrepreneurial'. The University of Plymouth is:

behaving as a commercial corporation would, competing for market share by offering new products and improved services, while seeking to expand the market. Staff are aware that, while they arguably work in the public sector, their jobs depend on the University's success in this way. (Plymouth case study)

However, remarks about shortage of money driving entrepreneurial third mission ventures were outweighed in the case studies by two types of contradictory comment. One is a quite widespread view that lack of money, by reducing the ability to take risks, inhibits entrepreneurial activity; the other is that some kinds of commercial activity, and any entrepreneurialism associated with it, have become (and may indeed always have been) part of the mainstream ethos of universities, to increase their autonomy and to bolster their more conventional academic work. It is generally agreed, however, that such activities have expanded very considerably during the past decade.

The clearest exponents of the view that shortage of money *inhibits* entrepreneurialism are in the private universities. One frequently expressed view in private universities is that public universities can afford financial and other risk because they have the cushion of public funding. For example the main concern of the rector of the Polish private case study institution (WSHIG case study) is whether 'the income from student fees [will] cover the expenditure (including debt instalments to the banks) from its own resources, with no state subsidies'.

In the private Spanish Cardenal Herrera University, respondents were 'unanimous in the fact that it is fairly difficult to obtain public resources to finance entrepreneurial activities in private universities'. In the University of Buckingham in the UK, 'reliance on fee income alone had meant that the University had not until recently shown any entrepreneurial capability'. According to one senior member of staff at the University when asked about inhibitors of entrepreneurialism: 'If I had to say one word it would be "money", getting the required investment is really linked very much on maybe this traditional over-reliance on student fee income' (Buckingham case study).

The inhibitions of lack of money are felt beyond the private universities, however, particularly in Moldova and Poland. The Polish report remarks that 'It is difficult to talk about more entrepreneurial missions and strategies in a severely underfunded public system. . .' (Kwiek, 2005b) Academic staff in Polish universities have spent most of their spare time in part-time appointments teaching in other universities to boost their inadequate incomes. This leaves very little time for research, let alone entrepreneurial ventures.

> What most academics are selling today are not research results but teaching services: both for their home university (teaching part-time fee-paying students for additional money) and for other educational institutions. Just as university has been becoming increasingly a teaching institution, staff have been becoming increasingly teaching staff. This issue . . . borders directly with staff's entrepreneurialism. (AMU case study)

In the UK, at the University of Plymouth, one interviewee remarked that a major inhibition to entrepreneurial activity is:

> lack of money, and that links to what we charge in terms of doing our research in the region because sometimes we don't necessarily charge enough. That's because the fact that businesses are small or there is not a culture of it or they don't know what price to charge, so we often subsidize what we do when perhaps we should be making a profit. (Plymouth case study)

In Spain, several respondents said that 'the time factor is the main inhibitor for entrepreneurial activity'. Though this may not be entirely due to lack of finance, it is often a shortage of money that requires staff to spend large amounts of time on routine teaching and academic research to further their own careers.

Is finance the dominant driver of university entrepreneurialism?

There were also indications, however, that an entrepreneurial ethos and a desire to sell academic services in new and innovative ways can permeate the mainstream life of a university. The concept of Mode 2 knowledge (see Gibbons *et al.*, 1994) is linked in part to the idea that real-world problems generate progress in research. This chapter is concerned with the financial dimensions of entrepreneurialism but there is ample evidence that entrepreneurial third mission activities are seen in several of the case study universities as interesting activities to undertake. Indeed, one of the concerns of some senior managers is that academic staff are liable to become engrossed in particular projects but they do not cover their costs properly.

It has already been shown that in Finland external income, and hence incentives to be entrepreneurial, are seen by at least some respondents as enhancing a university's autonomy and reinforcing conventional research and teaching in ways other than the purely financial. One professor in the HSE responded by saying that:

> In this sense our autonomy has grown. Now we can do projects we couldn't do before. And also train new doctors. We wouldn't have to. We could just decide that fine, we won't take any external funding, we'll just operate on our own budget. We have the right to choose. But we've adopted this policy because now it's possible and I think has worked quite well up to this day. (HSE, Finland case study)

The report on the University of Lapland refers in this context to the interests of the teachers and researchers to seek external projects and also 'the university's responsibility for its environment'. Again in Finland, at the University of Tampere, the Head of the Planning Office remarked that 'With external funding we can employ people. These new people of course provide the department with some latitude, so I think there's something like this going on' (Tampere case study).

In Spain in the University of Alicante, 'the majority thought that . . . in practice entrepreneurial behaviour mainly depends on individual behaviour', and in the University Cardenal Herrera, 'The general opinion was that the entrepreneurial attitude is influenced by education-related factors'. Similarly in the Technical University of Valencia, 'most people interviewed felt that entrepreneurial activities are not motivated exclusively by economic factors; at least, not as much as some people believe'.

The head of a research unit at the University Jaume I of Castellon expressed what is probably the most widespread view, that it was a combination of the need for money and academic interest that stimulated entrepreneurial initiatives:

> On the one hand, entrepreneurial attitudes are motivated by economic constraints but on the other hand we have to approach companies. Activities are carried out because companies ask for them, but also because the Institute is enriched by doing these activities. These activities finance themselves and improve knowledge. (Jaume I case study)

The conclusion of the University of Lund case study expresses a similar, widely held view:

> Few of our informants claim that Lund University as a whole is characterized by an entrepreneurial culture. Equally few say, with conviction, that the university by no means could be considered as entrepreneurial. Instead, most of our interview persons say that there has been a marked shift toward encouraging and supporting entrepreneurial activities at the university, and point out some units and also some individuals that could be labelled as particularly entrepreneurial. The many mechanisms created by the university, supporting entrepreneurship and innovation, are an indication of an ongoing transformation process. However, a culture resting on old traditions with a focus on academic excellence has its own incentives and rewards, not always with the same goals as those that characterize enterprises. It is a question of mind-set, according to several interviewees. (Lund case study)

At the LSHTM, whose income depends very largely on external competitive sources, a senior member of staff summed up the institution's entrepreneurialism thus:

> The School does not have the money-making entrepreneurialism, but the School is very academically entrepreneurial in constantly looking for new sources of funding and keeping that going. Many people in this School are very altruistic; they are interested in the School's mission, improvement of health worldwide. They really believe in it, that's what motivates them. You have to be creative and inventive to be able to do that, you have to keep your research and funding going. If that is entrepreneurialism, then we are good at that. (LSHTM case study)

Incentives and impediments

It is clear from the examples given in this chapter that the lessons for the finance of universities are not straightforward. Money is important but, while the need for resources often stimulates entrepreneurial knowledge transfer, extreme financial stringency is often seen as an inhibiting factor in that it makes it difficult to take risks and staff have to devote so much of their time to mainstream teaching that they have little energy for new initiatives. Much depends on individuals. In at least three of the case study universities (Nottingham, UPV, and HSE (Finland)) it is clear that the attitudes and character of institutional leaders have contributed to a very large extent to their entrepreneurial character. In many of the case studies, it is apparent that smaller-scale entrepreneurial ventures, the establishment of a research centre, or of an income-generating MBA course for example, it is individuals who have had ideas and carried them forward while colleagues have been content to confine themselves to conventional teaching and research.

It is also clear, however, that financial incentives do have an important part to play in both enabling and encouraging innovative income-generating activities. Before the 1990s, many higher education institutions were not permitted to retain any income they generated outside the core income from their governments or officially recognized research projects. The transformation, which occurred suddenly and dramatically in the nations of the former Communist Bloc and in a more measured way in Spain and in the Nordic countries, changed very considerably university opportunities with respect to external income. However, the cultural attitudes created by generations of reliance on public funds do not adjust so quickly and much of the ambivalence in the views expressed about entrepreneurial activities may be due in large part to beliefs, so firmly established it may be legitimate to call them ideologies, that scholarly teaching and research depend on public funds being made available without detailed specification of the outcomes expected. At the level of whole universities, some senior managers have eagerly grasped the opportunities the new funding policies offer for the aggrandisement of their universities, others are cautiously following suit after seeing how successful the early adopters have been, while others remain to be convinced.

Within the universities there are similar disparities. When all financial decisions are taken by the central administration and all income earned is retained by the centre, there is very little incentive for departments or individual members of staff to proactively seek external income. Where it does happen it takes the form of individual members of staff freelancing on their own behalf, as is the case with academic staff in Polish universities who take part-time appointments in several universities.

This illustrates an important issue that arises in recognizing an entrepreneurial university – the management of third stream income. The nature of academic work and the very high-level knowledge and skills required to perform it mean that academic staff have been able to operate as independent professionals and supplement their salaries by selling their expertise to outside individuals and organizations. This ranges from a small amount of part-time teaching to the income from intellectual property that has commercial value. The universities' only interest was to ensure that teaching and research responsibilities were not neglected. In recent years, shortage of core funds is encouraging universities to take a much stronger commercial interest in the ability of their full-time staff to generate independent income. Many require their staff to contribute at least part of such freelance income to general university funds, sometimes by contributing to their own university salaries. Many have set up university consultancy companies to promote the services the universities' can provide and to ensure that some of the cash generated is returned to the universities. There are several examples earlier in this chapter of such practices being fairly widespread:

> Staff are aware that, while they arguably work in the public sector, their jobs depend on the University's success in this way.

> Every senior lecturer needs to find 50% of the salary and every professor needs to finance one doctoral student.

> A maximum of 30% of the funding goes to the researcher, the remaining 70% goes to the university.

An illustration of the issues is provided by Nottingham University, which:

> has a traditional approach to consultancy work by individual members of staff. Academic staff are allowed to spend up to 50 days a year in private paid consultancy. They have to pay full cost for any university facilities used in providing the consultancies and they are advised to insure themselves against civil or other liabilities since the University will not accept responsibility. The University also requires staff to disclose whom they are working for and when they are doing it but they do not need to disclose how much they are paid. This enables the University to monitor the amount of such work that is being done but 'we don't need to know the private arrangement'. The University takes the view that some external consultancy work, as well as helping members of staff to supplement their academic salaries, helps to broaden their experience of the real world in their areas of expertise. (Nottingham case study)

The formalization of freelance work is thus one important way in which a university can 'become entrepreneurial' in the sense of what has been described in this chapter as small-scale entrepreneurialism. Traditional methods of financing universities gave no incentive for the management of the university to take any interest in such activities provided the staff members met their contractual obligations with regard to teaching students. New public management types of funding arrangements, whereby universities become autonomous financial enterprises, give them a much larger financial interest in the income-generating capacities of their employees and very many of the case studies describe schemes, mainly through the application of funding formulae, whereby staff are encouraged to earn additional income on behalf of the university, and to retain much of it, either themselves or on behalf of their department or research centre, if they do.

It is clear from the case studies that many of the Spanish universities are in this transitional phase, while the LSHTM and Jönköping University have reached a stage where earning external income on behalf of the institution is part of the normal expectation of its academic employees.

In general, the critical financial management issues that determine the extent and nature of entrepreneurialism in a university are concerned with who earns the money, how it is distributed internally, who controls its use, and how spending decisions are taken. Unless control of the uses of resources and spending decisions are closely linked to the authority and ability to earn income for the institution, there will be little incentive to make efforts to innovate or to take risks on behalf of the institution.

An example of the perception that regulations discourage this kind of initiative is a remark made by one of the Finnish interviewees: 'we have more prohibitions to make revenues than instruments to make revenues' (HSE, Finland case study). The Polish study considers that the job security of academic posts discourages risk-taking effort, referring to 'the academic post as an almost fully safe, non-competitive working environment' (AMU case study). In Spain, also, there is a widespread feeling that the status of academic staff as permanent civil servants often does not encourage them to be entrepreneurial. A remark made in one of the Swedish case studies illustrates a transitional stage of thinking about the issues: 'in the area of incentives, it is clear that it would help a lot if successfully landing large projects or patents obtained could count as merits in the academic career race' (Lund case study). One of the UK case studies also illustrates such 'transitional' thinking from another angle: 'some in the University are said to believe that consultancy activities are only filling the pockets of individuals rather than bringing any added value to the University more broadly' (Plymouth case study).

In the UK, two of the case study universities do illustrate that they have come to terms with the financial implications of twenty-first century policies regarding the economic position of universities. In one, 'funding allocations to academic Schools are related directly to the earnings they bring to the University, thus increasing the incentive of generating additional revenue' (Nottingham case study). In the other, the School 'allocates the whole overhead to the department, thus encouraging the department to negotiate hard with the awarding authority for high overheads' (LSHTM case study).

Concluding comments

The case studies suggest that institutional entrepreneurial activities are encouraged when:

- core income from government is tight but not inadequate for some new initiatives;
- when governments promote and support third mission activities;
- when a significant part of any income earned from new initiatives goes directly or indirectly to the groups and individuals that have the ideas, take the risks, and do the work;
- when a commercial culture is acceptable to a significant number of the academic staff;

- when unofficial individual private entrepreneurial or freelance ventures are regulated;
- and when the university is active in subject areas where continued professional development and research findings are commercially or socially valuable.

Conversely, entrepreneurial activity may be discouraged if:

- core income from government is too generous;
- core income is inadequate for investment and risk taking;
- financial regulations are too burdensome;
- the traditional academic culture that became dominant in much of the twentieth century remains in place.

However, it was also pointed out that sometimes the regulatory demands of other financing bodies are more demanding than those of national governments and there is considerable uncertainty about too great a dependence on external income. However, the UK institution with the greatest dependence on external income of all the EUEREK case study institutions countered this by claming that 'it continues to be important to diversify the sources of the School's income to provide greater stability and to protect it from policy changes of its current significant funders' (LSHTM case study).

As a final remark, an examination of the finance of entrepreneurial activities in universities highlights the issues of definition. If risk is the determining criterion, nearly all externally funded research should be included, since all research carries an element of risk with respect to its outcomes. If innovation in the sense of doing something that universities have not done before is the criterion, and once it has been done successfully it is treated as routine, then there are very few examples of ongoing entrepreneurialism. It is when trying to determine which parts of the income and expenditure of an institution it is legitimate to consider as entrepreneurial that such questions become acute. This chapter has adopted a broad definition that includes all the activities of a university apart from its mainstream, core-funded, teaching and research. It finds that all the case study institutions have some entrepreneurial features but it is much more developed in a few universities than in most of the others.

Note

1. It is widely believed that UK first-degree students were not charged fees because it was illegal to do so. In fact, there was no legal restriction on the fees universities could charge until 1998, but if a university did charge undergraduate student fees it risked losing the very large sums of money it received from government in lieu of tuition fees. This changed in 1998 when Parliament passed a law fixing a maximum fee a university was allowed to charge its first-degree students.

3

Research, technology, and knowledge transfer

Michael Shattock

The EU communication 'Mobilising the brain power of Europe: enabling universities to make their full contribution to the Lisbon Strategy' (CEC, 2005) emphasizes the 'innovation gap' between European and some other economies and identifies a number of bottlenecks. The first is uniformity of programme and conformity to a standard model, a consequence of which is that Europe 'has too few centres of world class excellence'. Insularity is a second – European universities remain largely 'insulated from industry, with limited knowledge sharing and mobility . . . most universities are strongly dependent on the state and ill prepared for world wide competition over talent, prestige and resources'. A third is over-regulation so that 'Minute *ex ante* control hinders universities' capacity to react swiftly to changes in their environment'. Finally, under-funding is the fourth: EU countries spend 1.9% of gross domestic product (GDP) on research instead of the 3% adopted as the target for 2010 (CEC, 2005). Our study confirms that all these bottlenecks inhibit the development of research and of technology transfer and knowledge transfer (the two being distinguished in this discussion between the transfer of specific and mostly scientific/technological findings, and the transfer of knowledge that may contribute to broader social as well as economic good). But it also suggests that generalizations on this scale about what generates research and encourages technology/knowledge transfer are dangerous in over-simplifying a complex picture. In particular, innovation, exploitation, and entrepreneurialism need a 'pull' factor from society and from local, regional, and national economic forces as well as a 'push' factor from governments. Innovation and entrepreneurialism are not spread evenly across all institutions and national systems of higher education, but we show in this chapter and in others that different kinds of universities can generate different kinds of innovation and entrepreneurial activity, and that the uniformity and insularity criticized in the EU paper is not as persistent as might be supposed. This leaves the inadequate investment in research in many countries as perhaps the major obstacle to change in the direction which the Commission is looking for.

Defining diversity among institutions

In our data set of universities drawn from seven countries, three of which are transition countries, we can identify four major categories of universities:

1. Comprehensive, some of which are research-intensive
2. Regional
3. Specialist, some of which are research-intensive
4. Private

In the first category, we find Lund (Sweden), Nottingham (UK), Tampere (Finland), Valencia (Spain), Adam Mickiewicz (Poland), and Moldova State (Moldova) Universities. Of these, Lund and Nottingham are large (around 30,000 students), research-intensive universities where external research funding constitutes about half their total income. Both are strongly engaged in technology transfer, Lund holding some 500–600 patents and Nottingham generating €3 million each year through its intellectual property. Tampere, located in a heavy manufacturing area, was originally orientated towards vocational programmes and teacher education but adopted a new strategy in 2001 that placed research as its main strategic aim, and has grown its external research funding from only 11% of its total income in 1990 to 22% in 2004, in spite of the fact that it still has a bias towards the humanities and social sciences, which do not traditionally generate large external research incomes. On the other hand, we have Adam Mickiewicz University (AMU), an old university like Lund, and located like Nottingham and Lund in a provincial capital, where, as in other old universities, we might expect to find a heavy research orientation (Gueno, 1998), but which has seen funding for research fall from 15% to 9.5% of its total income between 1994 and 2004. In the same category we find Moldova State University; only 8% of the national research and development (R&D) budget in Moldova is approved for financing research in universities, 37% going to the Academy of Sciences and 55% to research institutes attached to various ministries. Although some internally funded research continues to be carried out at AMU, both Universities have become largely teaching-only essentially because of acute funding restrictions. Finally, we have the University of Valencia, like Lund a very old and large (over 50,000 students) university and the 'mother university' of the Valencia system. This university might be described as 'research active' rather than 'research intensive', generating some €25 million (10% of total income) from research, and could be seen as falling into the traditional mould described above by the Commission.

A second category, the regional university, embraces Lapland (Finland), Alicante, Miguel Hernandez, Jaume I Castellon, the Technical University of Valencia (Spain), Umeå (Sweden), Plymouth (UK), and the Alecu Russo State University of Balti (Moldova). None of these universities are research intensive, although all have research interests that are geared primarily towards research of economic relevance to their regions. The Technical

University of Valencia comes closest to the description of research intensive with a research income of some €34 million (14% of total income), and could certainly be described as entrepreneurial, largely as a result of the vision promoted by its former Rector, Justo Nieto, who adopted a policy of strong collaboration with the socio-economic environment, supporting the establishment of autonomous teams generating external funding and an emphasis on technology transfer. This is an example of a university that has been strongly led away from the traditional model to the kind of innovative and entrepreneurial university the Commission's paper seems to envisage. Umeå, too, incentivized by its isolated northern location, has developed significant research interests in specialist areas.

The third category, the specialist institutions, also offers considerable diversity. The London School of Hygiene and Tropical Medicine (LSHTM) in the UK and the Helsinki School of Economics (Finland) are both ambitious research-intensive institutions with strong international presences in their specialist areas. LSHTM could legitimately claim to be 'world class' in its research and intensely entrepreneurial in a research sense (that is, in the mode of research, and the diversity of external funding support) but not at all in the commercial (that is, in exploitation through spin-off companies and the development of intellectual property rights) use of the word. The Poznan University of Economics, the Academy of Economic Studies of Moldova, and the Baikal Institute, on the other hand, are primarily specialist teaching institutions. Jönköping University fits uncomfortably into this group: on the one hand, it must be classed as specialist in that it is restricted to four schools – engineering, business, education and communication, and health sciences – but on the other, its special Foundation status (one of three such institutions in Sweden) gives it a greater degree of autonomy than other Swedish universities and its establishment in 1994 was geared very strongly to the economic interests of the region, which has a long tradition of starting and running small and medium enterprises (SMEs) and emphasizes entrepreneurialism as the driving force for development. The University derives nearly 30% of its income from non-core funding, a very high proportion from third mission activities. Similarly, the Higher School of Economics, Moscow, founded on the model of the London School of Economics (LSE), represents a reforming model for Russian state universities and has developed three branch campuses and a range of international partnerships.

The fourth and last category is made up of private universities, Buckingham (UK) and Cardenal Herrera (Spain) Universities, the Academy of Hotel Management in Poland (WSHIG), the Trade Cooperative University of Moldova, and Pereslavl University in Russia. These institutions have relatively little or no research capacity because their energies are primarily concentrated on attracting fee-paying students. Buckingham would argue that it is 'research active' because it has two self-financing research groups and has an expectation that its staff will undertake research, but its very small size means that it is not competitive in research output with larger publicly financed universities in the UK. Pereslavl, which was founded on the basis of an Academy of Science research institute, retains a research/consultancy capacity but derives the majority of its income from tuition fees. It could be argued that the financial stringencies affecting higher education in Poland and Moldova, which have led public universities to adopt survival strategies of recruiting high numbers of fee-paying students in addition to state-funded quotas, have created private/public institutions that share with the private universities the need to give a higher priority to student recruitment than to research.

Research intensity and technology transfer

Entrepreneurialism is often identified in official (and certainly EU) documents as being most closely identified with technology transfer, with commercial exploitation of research outcomes, and partnerships with industry. Our interpretation of entrepreneurialism is wider than this, but if it was restricted to this more narrow definition, then the most entrepreneurial universities in our study would very clearly be those that are the most research intensive. Thus, the greatest amount of 'entrepreneurial science' to use Etzkowitz's (2002) phrase is with the exception of LSHTM concentrated in those institutions that excel in fundamental research. The 'triple helix' of government–industry–university support (Etzkowitz and Leydesdorff, 1998) (or in the case of LSHTM, government–international agency–university support) is most evident in large research-intensive institutions (whether 'comprehensive' or specialist).

Lund and Nottingham provide excellent examples. In Lund, where it is accepted that fundamental research has the highest status, innovative/ entrepreneurial structures abound: 'The leaders of the most renowned research groups are key personalities with charisma, knowledge and dedication as well as the entrepreneurial spirit' (Lund case study). In the Institute of Technology, one of Lund's faculties, professors are expected to raise 40% of their salaries from grants and contracts and all PhD students undertake part of their study working in industry. The University founded LUAB as a holding company in 2001 with nearly €2 million capital to invest in commercializing knowledge; its managing director is also chief executive of CONNECT, a platform for linking scientific innovators to the market; and it has a subsidiary, UNIVA, which has been founded to create partnerships with companies that are looking for ways to improve their products, technology, staff, and organization using the University's resources. The company's success can be judged by its turnover in 2004 of over €29 million; one of its projects, TANGO, funded by a three-year EU grant, involved 117 commercial partners in the mechanical and food production areas. Venture Lab, an incubator for start-up companies, which is a joint project between three faculties – Technology, Medicine, and Economic Research – and IDEON, the University's Science Park, which has housed over 500 companies since its foundation, represent exemplars of entrepreneurial breakouts from a university committed to fundamental research. Nottingham tells a similar story. Here the pro-vice-chancellor for research and knowledge transfer reported that 'the majority of our money comes from fundamental research' but 'knowledge transfer and commercialization is a major plank of the University's strategy'. The University's Research and Innovation Services Office employs 45 staff and owns or is a partner in 27 spin-out companies. As reported above, it generates a substantial income from its intellectual property portfolio.

The two research-intensive specialist institutions tell a similar story, although their disciplinary focus imposes different research outcome profiles. The Helsinki School of Economics, where research staff numbers have grown from 13 in 1994 to 102 in 2004, has established HSE (Finland) Research as a network to establish a brand for research at the School and has given it a separate advisory board. It has founded two companies: LTTR Ltd., which markets the School's research services, and HSE (Finland) Executive Education Ltd., which manages the profitable Executive MBA programme. The School's case study draws the distinction that: 'LTT strives to produce solutions for its clients while the university is advancing science. The outputs of LTT are the property of the clients whereas academic research should be available for all' (HSE case study). The LSHTM has a very different approach. It generates 63% of its income from research, but while it is not entrepreneurial at all in terms of the commercial exploitation of its research, it is highly entrepreneurial in its modes of research, in the way it focuses its research on changes in global health issues, and addresses long-run problems like poverty, nutrition, and HIV through research that can be both fundamental and very applied, and also in the way it approaches the generation of funding support for such projects from a wide range of international sources. LSHTM's attitude to exploitation in the commercial sense can be summed up by its decision to withdraw from consultancy work to concentrate more on fundamental research because it felt that it was from this source that it would expect to contribute to major advances in the reduction of disease.

Two other institutions offer contrasting outcomes. At Jönköping, two of the schools are strongly attuned to local and regional interests: the School of Engineering, which specializes in technological improvements in SMEs, and the School of Business, which specializes in entrepreneurship and business renewal. The School of Health Sciences is primarily national and international in its approach, with a major programme in psycho-geriatrics and strong links with universities in Africa. The impact of Jönköping, which is still a very new university, can be seen in the fact that such a high proportion of its income comes from specifically third mission activities, and the success of its Science Park, with its incubator building, has been driven by the activities of its graduates. The Technical University of Valencia, on the other hand, a much larger and older institution, while it has increased its R&D contracts from 98 in 2000 to 154 in 2004 and its technological support and consultancy projects from around 1000 in 2000 to over 1700 in 2004, has nevertheless been inhibited in its transfer of technology through the creation of spin-off companies, licensing agreements, and patents by the economic structure of its region and the lack of the 'pull' factor that is apparent around Jönköping.

The evidence, however, seems to point clearly to the fact that the more research intensive an institution, whether a fully comprehensive university or a specialist school or institute, the more likely it is to be a leader in technology transfer. The old divisions of pure/fundamental research and applied research no longer seem to apply: the institutions most supportive of fundamental research are leaders in its application and exploitation. Such evidence would also support arguments for concentrating research funding in universities that have demonstrated their research effectiveness rather than spread it thinly around all universities, because this will achieve a higher level of technology transfer. This is not at all to minimize the contribution of regional universities (see next section) but merely to emphasize that research-intensive higher education institutions based in centres of high economic activity, as all these are, have a potential for Mode 2 research (Gibbons *et al.*, 1994) that rural locations, locations with low population densities or a weak industrial base simply cannot provide.

Regional universities and the development of 'third mission'

'Third mission' represents a concept that defies clear definition. Originally first used in the UK to describe a funding stream (third stream) to universities intended to support the processes of technology/knowledge transfer, it has become more generally used in the UK and the rest of Europe to denote activities primarily designed to support regional engagement and regional economic growth more generally. This widening of the concept, therefore, embraces various forms of continuing education, and widening participation in higher education by economically disadvantaged groups, as well as offering support to SMEs, the creation of investment funds to found spin-off companies, and developing partnerships with companies. In this second stage of the concept, it is recognized that many such activities, while generating income, will not be self-financing and that state or regional funding support may be required to incentivize local and regional impact. Third mission activities tend to be funded programmatically so that each country is inclined to adopt its own definitions as to what these are designed to achieve. Third mission activities may not, therefore, be entrepreneurial in the strictly financial sense, but most universities regard them as such and they may certainly involve many of the characteristics of individual leadership, innovation, and risk that are normally associated with entrepreneurial behaviour.

Of course, all universities might be expected to undertake third mission activities, whether a large, research-intensive, city-based or even private university (as at Buckingham), but their regional aspect is of particular relevance to universities that have adopted or been given a regional role and may demonstrate other forms of research-based entrepreneurialism than can readily be identified in the specifically research-intensive institutions. Here location and local economic factors can determine both the character of the university and the kind of third stream activities it engages in. Thus, in Poland and Moldova the industrial collapse characteristic of many transition countries, and the conditions of financial stringency mitigated by the recruitment on a large scale of fee-paying students, has inhibited the development of third stream work. On the other hand, some universities benefit from particular local environmental features where close collaborations are producing economic advantage. Jaume I Castellon University is sited in a great centre for the ceramics industry with which it works closely and its Ceramics Technology Institute is the result of a cooperation agreement with the Ceramics Industry Research Association. The success of this partnership accounts for the University's high rating among Spanish universities for R&D expenditure per member of staff. Plymouth University, located in an economically disadvantaged part of the UK, has used its physical location to develop the Plymouth Marine Sciences Partnership with the City of Plymouth and other organizations, including the government-supported Plymouth Marine Laboratory. It plans to create a major Marine Biology/Maritime Centre that will also involve commercial maritime interests in boats, tourism, and so on.

In Sweden, the 1997 Higher Education Act required Swedish universities 'to cooperate with the surrounding community and inform it about its operations', thus making it mandatory for them to engage in this 'third task'. Umeå represents a particularly good example of this. Situated in the north of Sweden, some 300 km from the Arctic Circle, it was founded in 1965 with a regional mission, essentially to cooperate with its community. In doing so, it draws no distinction between collaborating with industry and engaging in other educational and research outreach activities. The case study suggests that its geographical position has encouraged it to become entrepreneurial to overcome what would otherwise be its isolation. Its success can be seen in the economic and population growth in Umeå itself, in contrast to the depopulation in general in the north, and the extent to which a municipality like Ormskoldsvik (population 56,000) has seen the University as an integral part of its development. Although it is not research intensive, its Medical Faculty is research active with particular interests in malaria, and its demographic database in medical history, for which the government provides nearly €2,200,000 per year, is unique. With its special mission in internationalism, it attracts considerable numbers of international students and runs 22 master's programmes in English.

In the Valencia region, the state government gives universities special research funding to encourage research with regional companies and agencies. Alicante University, for example, which is located on the coast away from major industrial centres, has 88 grants from the national government but 145 from the Valencian Government and 379 from private contracts, mostly local, and has a business incubator unit that has links with about 40 companies. The Technical University, although it has many of the characteristics of a research-intensive university, 'aims to be entrepreneurial with a technical innovation and regional background' (UPV case study). Miguel Hernandez University, established only in 1977, which has adopted a strongly vocational or 'practical' approach to its courses, sees itself 'born into an entrepreneurial culture' and one research centre head reports that his centre receives 80% of its funding from external sources (Miguel Hernandez case study).

Perhaps the most extreme example of a university with a regional mission is the University of Lapland, which is essentially the regional university for the north of Finland. Low on external funding, an inevitable reflection of the economic circumstances of the area, it is yet described as 'breathing with the region' (Lapland case study). It argues that it is not possible to be entrepreneurial in a commercial sense in Lapland, but that it is entrepreneurial 'in a soft sense' in building local networks and conducting long-term research and basing its education programmes on it. But even in this university there is an exception, the Faculty of Art and Design, which is seen as having a much more marketized and commercial approach because it can generate interest from outside the region.

What the case studies of the regionally orientated universities demonstrate is that the 'pull' factors that can be exercised by major industrial centres such as in southern Sweden (Lund), in Tampere, in industrialized areas around Nottingham, or in the depth of SME activity around Jönköping, do not exist for them except in individual and particular cases, such as at Jaume I (ceramics) and Plymouth (maritime activities), so that the universities have to take a much more proactive role. Here Umeå and Lapland are especially interesting examples because of their intrinsic regional missions. The decision by Umeå to create ENS, a centralized office to act as an inward and outward gateway for collaboration with business and public organizations, although quite controversial within the University, represents a response to this need. The consequence of locations in low-population areas is that research is more difficult to initiate and to sustain, and research expertise *per se* is only one of the elements in a third stream programme, and not necessarily the major one. The entrepreneurial researchers and designers in Lapland's Faculty of Art and Design will have to work infinitely harder than if they were based in Helsinki or London to generate an external income, and require a much higher proportion of state investment to make their mark. The literature about 'the learning region' (Lundvall and Johnson, 1994) emphasizes the importance of the contribution of a university to a regional economy but by the same token a regional economy can make an important contribution to a university's ability to be entrepreneurial.

Developing research-led entrepreneurialism in non-research-intensive universities

In research-intensive universities, research is driven by organizational culture and by internal competition and is facilitated by external reputation. Research-intensive universities have a research infrastructure that speeds up research outcomes and attracts large numbers of doctoral students and research manpower that can be deployed to create research teams. At the LSHTM, for example, although a significant proportion of staff members are employed on non-permanent contracts co-terminus with the duration of research grants, the capacity of the institution to generate major research grants and contracts means that it is possible to move seamlessly from one contract to another and the School provides bridging finance between contracts to established researchers to give them time to generate new funding, a facility only possible in an institution confident in its ability to attract external research funding and an important adjunct to the retention of key research staff.

These advantages are not so likely to be available at non-research-intensive universities, thereby making it more difficult for individual academics to get research off the ground and to sustain it. Another inhibition may be the constraints, financial and otherwise, imposed in non-research-active academic departments on individuals who want to be 'intrapreneurs' but who need support outside the usual conventions or regulations to progress their projects. Such individuals may want to engage in a mix of activities – research, consultancy, and short courses – which do not fit into standard financial arrangements and which appear to conflict with bureaucratic procedures. Many universities that are traditionally not research active have for this reason chosen to concentrate their research in specialist research institutes or have facilitated 'academic intrapreneurs' to set up quasi-autonomous research centres outside the conventional departmental structures.

The best example of this is to be found in the Technical University of Valencia, where a traditional university structure exists side by side with an entrepreneurial periphery of self-financing centres, units, and special institutes. Perhaps as a consequence of the University's innovative Rector moving on to become the responsible Minister in the Valencia Government, the creation of special institutes is a feature of the Valencian university system. Thus, the University of Valencia was not considered by its staff to be entrepreneurial but entrepreneurial attitudes were to be found in the research institutes, which 'are conceived as multi-disciplinary research structures beyond the framework of the departments [which] are useful in so far as they are better prepared to meet the economic and social demands of society' (Valencia case study). Interviewees, quoted in the case study, give mixed interpretations as to the extent to which the apparent independence from departmental controls gave real autonomy to the researchers to self-manage their own efforts to generate external income to fund research. A similar picture emerges at Alicante, where the research institutes 'are the best examples of the [university's] activities aimed at maintaining links with the business world' (Alicante case study). The Ceramics Technology Institute at Jaume I, described above, represents another example of the entrepreneurial benefits of breaking out of the traditional departmental structures.

In Tampere, the creation of quasi-autonomous research centres and institutes has had two important organizational effects. Traditionally a teaching-based university, the creation of non-departmental structures took the University into a much more strongly demarcated research mode, and the need for greater financial autonomy to enable staff to function effectively led to their being so critical of the central bureaucracy that financial devolution was introduced for all departments. This, however, has had the effect of hardening the boundaries between departments and placing more emphasis on the interdisciplinary character of the research centres and institutes. Two of these in particular have been important. The Institute of Medical Technology was formed as a result of the downsizing of the Faculty of Medicine and quotations from the Rector and the Director of Administration emphasize that the freedom to recruit appropriate people and the 'impulse to a new applied research area, practical applications of medical science and industrial applications [and] . . . some spin offs' represent 'a new way of action' (Tampere case study). The second is the Hypermedia Laboratory, which has been so financially successful that it has been able to use the surpluses generated by its activities to cross-subsidize undergraduate study in the subject. The director of the latter, in the case study, sums up the difference between these new structures and the traditional departments:

> There are over 50 units within the University of Tampere . . . You could say that we have a lot of units, like the hyper lab, for example, that live under constant change and uncertainty, but are proactive and establish national cooperation and networks. Then we also have these traditional departments that have strong established teaching and research traditions and quite clear paradigms. They haven't really had to think about these up to now. They've settled with the traditional idea of the university as an institution of civilization and with the Humboldtian identity and they've functioned under these principles. Now this is being questioned. (Tampere case study)

But, as at the Technical University of Valencia, these entrepreneurial entities tend to concentrate on the periphery and are not located in 'the academic heartland' (Clark, 1998). They are, thus, changing the outward face of the university but not yet having much of an influence on the core structures. Nevertheless, the acceptance that one approach to changing traditional structures is to facilitate breakouts into special research centres and institutes or to create new academic organizations outside traditional departmental structures, represents a major step forward for universities that are constrained by government bureaucracy and conservatism in academic decision making. In research-intensive universities where funding and other structures are responsive to the flexibility required by 'a diversified funding base' (Clark, 1998), creating new quasi-autonomous research centres and institutes is a recognized process in generating space for particular research and development programmes to develop, but in universities that are less research active, it can represent a major concession to the persistence of an entrepreneurial individual or a major initiative to free up individuals to collaborate across departmental boundaries, and can be the first step, as at Tampere, in loosening up structures across the whole university.

The growth of organizational support for knowledge transfer

It is now widely recognized that technology/knowledge transfer involves more than just the existence of research or teaching capacity, but also technical skills in exploitation, whether in the commercialization of research or the launching of community engagement programmes. Within our data set of institutions, size, research intensity, and mission seemed to be the critical determinants to what infrastructure had been put in place, but perhaps what was surprising was the extent to which nearly every university had recognized the need to broaden its mission in this way. The structures set up at Lund, the size of the Research and Innovation Services Office at Nottingham, and the commercial organization of the Helsinki School of Economics have already been described. But in every Valencian university there is a Vice-Rector appointed for Innovation and Technology Transfer, while in the Technical University there are Research Incentive and Innovation Incentive Funds and a Researchers Activity Index to stimulate performance. In spite of the state of the national economy and industrial infrastructure, the State University of Moldova has a technology transfer office (although it is funded on a three-year Tempus grant and when that runs out it must become self-supporting), while at the Alecu Russo State University consultancy is offered through an SME centre. At the LSHTM, in spite of its disinclination to commercialize its research, there is a highly qualified Business Development Officer whose task is to protect and exploit intellectual property as it becomes available. At Umeå, where the ENS organization has already been mentioned, and at Lapland, there are extensive networking devices to stimulate regional cooperation, while at Plymouth there is a Research and Innovation Office, a consultancy company earning some €2 million, and two distinctive centres established within academic departments, the South West Regional Food Technology Centre and the South West Economy Centre, which are directly focused on regional issues. What this tells us is that in a formal sense nearly every institution in our data set has recognized the importance of generating entrepreneurial/innovative/third stream activity and has invested resources in terms of offices and other support to encourage it, albeit their effectiveness is limited by institutional capacity to respond to external needs and the strength or otherwise of local and regional 'pull' factors. This represents a transformation from the position a decade earlier.

Bottom up and top down

The interface of research and technology/knowledge transfer raises interesting organizational tensions. Although in the UK the regular Research Assessment Exercise (RAE) that rewards universities, and therefore indirectly their staff, for research quality and in Spain the national research bonus that rewards staff for publication (but, therefore, discourages entrepreneurial research) are direct research incentives, where questions are asked about where the drive for fundamental research comes from, it is clear that the pressure is bottom up not top down. Although this might seem an obvious conclusion to reach in research-intensive universities like Lund and Nottingham, it is also true in the Universities of Valencia and Alicante. In other words, although universities may claim in a mission statement to make research a priority, the research drive actually comes from the individual, and the research centre/institute/department. This conclusion is as true for universities as different as AMU and Lapland, as it is for LSHTM. Institutions through their human resource policies and by offering financial and other support can maximize their research output, but there is little sign from this data set of universities that they can direct, in any top-down fashion, that research shall take place or that any one topic is to be researched more than another. Research represents a prime area of interest for the academic intrapreneur. The LSHTM case study illustrates clearly that personal motivation, the intrinsic interest in the research outcome, and the competitive spirit are the key drivers, and that the role of the School, and its academic departments, is not to direct research but to provide focus and coordination and infrastructural support in terms of finance, facilities, and legal and other support. The case study makes clear that an important component to this is a research-orientated organizational culture that fosters internal, as well as external, competition and that can sustain a researcher, such as is described in the LSHTM case study, who is willing to take the risk of stepping away from active research and publication for two years to redesign equipment for future work.

By contrast, although research motivation was bottom up, the technology/knowledge transfer process seemed to be more top down with pro rectors or their equivalent and technology/knowledge transfer officers being appointed with a remit to be proactive in translating fundamental research into commercial exploitation. Although the Technical University of Valencia states that entrepreneurialism is embedded among its researchers, the case studies suggest that in most universities the staff of the technology/knowledge transfer offices act as a 'pull' and sometimes a 'push' factor in encouraging exploitation. This is not to say that in some universities there are not individual academics who see themselves as entrepreneurs (cf. Nottingham's 27 spin out companies), but in general it is the central university authorities that have seized the exploitation agenda rather than the individual researchers. This would be less true in respect of knowledge transfer, which comprises community teaching services, though the creation of ENS at Umeå seems to be an exception where centralized top-down decision making might seem to have been substituted. This bottom up/top down thesis has important policy implications for funding strategies. Fundamental research, which provides the seed corn for innovation, exploitation, and the creation of intellectual property, requires secure funding over a significant period before it can transform itself into an operation capable of attracting a self-sustaining portfolio of research grants and contracts. It is incredibly hard, for example, in Poland to develop a research trajectory if for personal finance reasons staff have to take on teaching assignments in several universities. Technology/knowledge transfer offices, on the other hand, are unlikely to be funded from research income streams and have to be top sliced from university budgets with little expectation in most universities that they will ever become self-financing. Relatively small earmarked support from the state is probably the most effective way of protecting this function or of stimulating further activity in these financially stretched times.

Competition and research intensity

In the research-intensive universities competition among their external peers represents a critical element. The Helsinki School of Economics describes itself as aiming to be 'the leading research based School of Economics in Europe' (HSE, Finland case study); the Lund University Faculty of Economics and Management says it is 'hungry for fame' (Lund case study) and the University as a whole has been invited to join a highly selective consortium of European research universities. The LSHTM sees itself competing on equal terms (and also collaborating) with the Harvard School of Public Health and with Johns Hopkins Medical School as one of the leading centres of expertise in its field in the world. The Royal Institute of Technology (KTH) in Stockholm has undertaken an 'Entrepreneurial Faculty project' in which it has benchmarked itself against an international group of universities of high reputation and sees itself driven by international competition. Even in universities that overall are not research intensive, like Tampere, Jaume I, or Plymouth, there are research fields like the Institute of Technology, the Ceramics Technology Institute or the proposed Marine Biology/Maritime Centre that compete for national and international standing in their specialism. Research by its nature is competitive, with individual researchers wanting to be first in the field and institutions to be regarded as sites where cutting-edge research occurs. Most national and international league tables make research the most influential indicator of institutional standing. Competition drives individual entrepreneurialism in looking for research funding from external sources and establishes the case for internal investment in promising research groups. Competition represents, therefore, a considerable 'pull' factor for fundamental research and will operate almost irrespective of recurrent funding levels, but governments can augment it as a tool for generating research outcomes by tailoring funding mechanisms towards research excellence. The UK Research Assessment Exercise is the most notable example of this. The downside of such mechanisms, of course, if applied indiscriminately, is the way they can distort the mission of universities created to have a primarily regional role.

The role of the state as a stimulus and an inhibitor of technology/knowledge transfer

We cannot ignore the important role of the state in acting sometimes simultaneously as a stimulus and an impediment to knowledge transfer. A good example of this can be found in Spain where the region allocates 10% of its institutional allocations competitively for research but the civil servant status of the individual academic and the national research incentive scheme based on publication alone represents discouragement to devoting time and effort to technology transfer. The UK Research Assessment Exercise, which gives additional resources to universities based on the research performance of their staff, represents the most extreme form of state incentivization of research. However, broadening the RAE to take account of knowledge transfer activities has been more problematic. But a separate 'third stream' funding line has been introduced in the UK earmarked to help universities establish research, innovation, and knowledge transfer offices so as to provide support for the exploitation of the extra research that the RAE concentration effect is intended to produce.

Whether such direct state steering is the most appropriate approach may be arguable but the role of the state in creating a framework to encourage research is not in question. Examples of this include the Swedish legislation imposing on universities a duty to collaborate with their regions and the Polish legislation in 2005 designed to reduce the multiple teaching contracts that Polish academics have to engage in to provide an adequate reward structure. This latter represents a first step only, however, in providing a framework to reverse the trend for Polish universities to concentrate on teaching at the expense of research. Further actions, as in the UK, might be the liberalization of intellectual property rights to transfer the rewards from the state to the individual researcher and the institution, and to invest in venture capital funds exclusively devoted to university spin-out companies. Nevertheless, in some countries the state remains the 'bottleneck'. In Spain, as has already been mentioned, the civil service status of academic staff represents a protection that can act as an inhibitor of performance. In Moldova, the reforms undertaken in some other transition countries with respect to the academies of science have not yet taken place so that universities are unable to claim a substantial slice of what is a very small research cake. But perhaps the most significant statement was from Finland, where at Tampere:

> the interviewees were unanimous. The view is that the steering of the Ministry of Education has not loosened although the administrative autonomy may have increased. The lump sum budgeting has increased autonomy only in theory. (Tampere case study)

Here the Rector said that although universities now had their own employment structure and could make their academic appointments with complete freedom, 'steering through funding has tightened all along' and 'the Ministry of Education strongly influences the universities' actions through its policies'. A professor said that 'the universities aren't powerful enough yet' (Tampere case study). In the UK, which in many ways might seem to have the greatest degree of informal as well as formal autonomy, because of universities' long tradition of legal independence, lump sum budgeting, and freedom in making appointments, state steering has noticeably increased as steps to open the universities more to market forces have proceeded. This has been engineered through funding strategies and through the weakening of the independence of the intermediary body, the Higher Education Funding Council. UK universities like Nottingham that have strong financial reserves are able to continue autonomous developments, such as the creation of its two overseas campuses and the establishment of a new department of veterinary science, but universities like Plymouth, lacking substantial non-state funding, and not benefiting from the RAE, are much more constrained by state policies.

Indeed, what our data set of universities has shown is that while state steering has been beneficial in pushing higher education systems towards a closer integration with society and towards market conditions, and in devolving budgets to universities to create a greater sense of autonomy, this devolution of budgets has often been more symbolic than real, with universities in fact being steered through variations in line budgets; state steering as a whole has been reinforced by conditions of financial stringency, which has given universities little freedom to exercise their new-found independence. Creating market conditions for universities will not make them autonomous in their decision-making unless some of the mechanisms of steering them are relaxed. There is a danger that 'derived autonomy' – that is, the power to spend but only to spend according to the state's priorities – will supplant 'self-directed autonomy' where the university decides its own spending priorities (Shattock, 2003). Moreover, while it is healthy to maintain diversity within higher education systems so that some universities have primarily regional and some national roles, some should concentrate more on teaching and some more on fundamental research, all universities must be the subject of adequate investment if they are to fulfil their roles. It is a truism that states are competing internationally in an academic 'arms race' for talent, and if EU countries are to fulfil the Lisbon aspirations, fundamental research that, as we have seen, provides the seedbed for subsequent exploitation must be funded adequately and the inhibitors to the conduct of successful research must be removed. Entrepreneurialism in the area of research is dependent on a secure funding base and the creation of a supportive infrastructure; as the private universities in this study demonstrate, a reliance on market forces alone does not generate a research culture. For technology/knowledge transfer to take place effectively, the academic community must have the time, the freedom, and the motivation to produce the knowledge that can be transferred.

4

Teaching and learning: an entrepreneurial perspective

Paul Temple

Teaching and learning in the entrepreneurial university: an introduction

Teaching and learning is, in financial terms and in the use of academic and other resources, the core business of nearly all institutions of higher education, even in those institutions that consider themselves to be strongly research-led. In our case studies, only at the London School of Hygiene and Tropical Medicine (LSHTM) – a highly specialized research institute, on a small central London site, working in a field in which well-funded projects are available – is income from activity other than teaching the dominant revenue stream. The distinctiveness of LSHTM's finances reflects the institution's distinctive nature in other respects.

Yet despite this near-universal institutional importance, I suggest that in considering the nature of the entrepreneurial university, teaching and learning activities often seem to be overlooked, apparently taken for granted. Surely this is paradoxical: can a university be considered entrepreneurial if this entrepreneurialism does not extend to its dominant activity?

Clark (1998) recognized the significance of teaching and learning in his case studies that led to his definition of the entrepreneurial university. He saw the need for universities to respond flexibly and innovatively in this field as much as in more obviously entrepreneurial fields such as technology transfer. He noted that a significant expansion of student numbers, and the effects of widening participation taking in different types of students, perhaps with different expectations, would place new demands on universities. These demands, he thought, would be 'organizationally penetrating', and could, in the right circumstances, produce what he would consider to be an entrepreneurial response. Clark's entrepreneurial university should respond to changed student needs in teaching and learning just as it would respond to demands for new research outputs. Some later writers have seen university entrepreneurialism in this broad perspective (for example, Barnett, 2005).

Others, however, have tended to overlook the possible interactions between teaching and learning and the other aspects of organizational change wrapped up in the notion of the entrepreneurial university (for example, Etzkowitz et al., 2000a).

Of course, if the term 'entrepreneurial' is given its usual business connotation of financial risk taking, then entrepreneurial approaches to teaching and learning in higher education are nothing new: private colleges, sometimes with a for-profit motivation, have been with us for a long time. The long tradition of private (though usually not-for-profit) higher education from the United States (Bok, 2003) has made some inroads in Europe and Asia, and the uncontrolled growth during the 1990s of private 'universities' in the European former communist states is a well-studied phenomenon (Darvas, 1997; Dahrendorf, 2000). Our case studies present examples of private (or at least, non-state) institutions in Poland, Russia, Moldova, and the UK. But I want to suggest here that approaches to teaching and learning differ between state institutions at least as much as they do across the public–private divide. Here, I propose what the factors might be that cause these differences.

We may see examples of Clark's 'organizationally penetrating' impact in the UK, where the rapid expansion of student numbers since the 1980s has caused universities to undergo major changes in their structures and management methods. One of our case studies, the University of Plymouth, a teaching-orientated institution of about 20,000 full-time equivalent students in south-west England, shows how some of these changes have come about. The public funding model for English universities – the 'manipulation of the small print of the [government's funding] formulae' (Williams, 2004c: 249) – has caused Plymouth to become very effective in widening its student catchment, by encouraging people from its relatively economically deprived hinterland to apply to become students there. This has changed the management priorities in the University's faculties to focus on student recruitment, retention, and progression: the effectiveness of staff members as teachers and as managers is now, to a significant extent, assessed on this basis. Similarly, course design is now centred on the interests and abilities of its target students. These people typically are different from the type of student recruited to UK universities in earlier periods, who possessed good groundings (as shown by highly academic school-leaving examinations) in the proposed subject of university study. Courses now at Plymouth may be designed to fit precise niches in the student marketplace, to attract students who may be rejected elsewhere as not having the prerequisite qualifications.

In this case, the university has developed a new strategic and managerial emphasis, and has effectively staked out a new student market: arguably, an entrepreneurial response to changed circumstances. Another example of this type comes from Umeå University, in northern Sweden. Here, an institution in a remote region has become known nationally for its emphasis on studies to do with 'the great outdoors' (as our case study puts it) – health, sport, and the environment. The University has a well-thought-out internationalization strategy, aimed at ensuring that all its graduates 'can successfully operate in international environments' (Umeå case study). It is also cooperating with other Swedish universities in providing courses taught in English, so increasing its attractiveness to students from outside its region. The University seems, as a result, to have been crucial in reversing the depopulation that has affected other communities in northern Sweden. Although Umeå, like Plymouth, relies almost entirely on public funding, it can be seen as having responded entrepreneurially to challenging circumstances.

What factors might make this type of response more likely?

Entrepreneurialism in teaching in our case study universities

Clark's comment about pressures from changes to teaching and learning being organizationally penetrating suggests that a closer look is needed at what teaching and learning means in terms of practice in the university, and how these activities may be conceptualized. What might be the organizational implications of changed teaching and learning?

Barnett and Coate (2005: 48) approach this issue by theorizing that the university curriculum may be considered in terms of *knowing, acting,* and *being*. 'Knowing' is about the knowledge component of the curriculum, in constant need of updating and challenging, and helping the student to engage with it as part of an academic community. 'Acting' is about the student's engagement with the outside (say, the professional) world, but also about the student's engagement on tasks within the institution. 'Being' relates to the development of the student's abilities to live in a changing world, to act capably, self-confidently, and with self-knowledge. All three domains are present in the balanced curriculum but in differing amounts, depending on the epistemological approach adopted.

How might this theoretical proposition help us in this study? I suggest that a university that is acting entrepreneurially in relation to its teaching and learning functions will (implicitly, at least) be reviewing its curricula in terms of *knowing, acting,* and *being*. This is because the university will want to be sure that it is offering a curriculum that is current in knowledge terms; that seeks to assist in students' engagement with external settings; and that may expand its students' confidence to live in a changing, complex world. I have indicated briefly how the Universities of Plymouth and Umeå try in different ways to do these things: through new course designs, or by ensuring that students receive international exposure, for example. Different learning objectives will lead to different mixes from these three domains. I shall try to show how this may be happening.

But there are other dimensions on which entrepreneurialism may be manifested in teaching and learning in our case studies: the range of our cases allows us a perhaps unique perspective here. I propose that we may see four factors driving changes in teaching and learning, through which we may see entrepreneurial effects operating (see Figure 1):

- regional impact;
- widening participation function;
- commitment to a professional domain;
- the traditional view of teaching linked closely to research.

I propose that the examination of these factors allows us to explain something of the distinctive character of our case study institutions towards the organization of teaching and learning. Naturally, in most institutions, more than one of these factors will be relevant, although I argue below that one or two are normally dominant.

It is possible that there may be tensions in some instances between these externally actuated factors (the first three, at least) and the more internal knowing/acting/being conception of the curriculum. Could a university's focus on a particular professional domain, say, lead to a greater emphasis on acting, rather than knowledge, in the curriculum? I hypothesize that the emphasis might be something along the following lines:

Curriculum focus on:	Teaching and learning emphasis on:			
	region	widening participation	professional	teaching and research
knowing			◆	◆
acting	◆	◆	◆	
being	◆	◆		

Figure 1 Typology of teaching and learning

Underlying all these factors is the relevant national funding model for higher education, which provides the framework within which public universities pursue their various missions. These policy frameworks encourage Plymouth to pursue its widening participation activities, and Umeå its northern focus. Private universities are also affected indirectly by the public funding model, as the quantity, quality, and perhaps fee levels of public higher education will in part determine the extent of local demand for private higher education.

Regional impact

In Finland, the University of Lapland's mission is relatively unusual, in that it ties the University very closely to its region. Its mission is focused, according to the case study, on 'societal and cultural development [in Lapland] as well as [the] well-being of the people living in northern regions'. As the case study also reports, 'all the strategic goals [of the University] are somehow connected to the relationship between the University and its environment and region ... society is not only a passive framework to the university, but the university is an active part of that society' (Lapland case study). This focus is demonstrated in the *thematic*, rather than discipline-based, approach to the University's academic structure and its teaching – themes of research methodology, or tourism, for example. The University also has special units directly related to its regional role: the Arctic Centre, the Regional Services Unit, and the Meri-Lappi Institute, which provides R&D and other services to small and medium enterprises (SMEs) in the area.

The University describes itself as applying 'soft entrepreneurialism', by which it means that it tries to respond to regional needs, in teaching and in other areas, but not in the sense of trying to maximize income. We see here an example of a teaching and learning strategy driven by the regional dimension of the University's existence.

According to one respondent in the case study:

> When the university was founded it started out as this institution focused on service expertise. People were initially quite skeptic about how the University and all its fields, such as social sciences and art and design that became a part of the University later on, had anything to do with Lapland or how they contributed to Lapland, even if the University was the University of Lapland and focused on northern issues. But when you think about our society today, our society in which this kind of service expertise is very important, you can see that many changes have taken place. (Lapland case study)

We may see here an emphasis on the *acting* part of the curriculum, but perhaps even more strongly on the *being* part: the sense that a University serving a region with unique characteristics and needs could not adopt a 'let's do it like before' approach, as the Rector put it, but had to address the way the people of Lapland lived their lives. Of course, knowledge is not absent from the curriculum, but the regional dimension perhaps gives the University its distinctive character.

Lapland's northern neighbour, Umeå University in Sweden, is also strongly connected with its region, but is taking a different approach in terms of the regional dimension by working to develop an international focus, requiring that 'all students should benefit from internationalization regardless of their program of study'. This involves study abroad opportunities, English-medium courses, and the opportunity 'to experience an international environment at home' (Umeå case study). Thus, regional goals are being pursued by different means from those adopted by the University of Lapland.

Widening participation

In the case of the University of Plymouth, a strong regional dimension also exists in its work, seen in its engagement with firms and public sector organizations in its sub-region in the south-west of England. However, the University is strongly driven by the UK Government's current policy on widening participation in higher education. This encourages the University to be innovative in the ways it which it recruits students from its region: these are often people without the traditional qualifications for university entrance, posing particular challenges for academic and administrative staff in managing student retention and progression.

Public funding flows to the University in part as a result of its meeting targets on widening participation, enabling it to earn additional income over and above what it would normally receive through the student number-driven funding formula. It has therefore developed an effective central unit that manages the widening participation strategy, but the whole structure of the University is, in a sense, focused on this goal, as individual faculties and departments are required to meet widening participation-related goals. The University's close relations with vocational colleges throughout south-west England, unusually attempting to make them in effect into a faculty of the University, shows that widening participation is a dominant factor in the organization of the University, and is changing the conception of what a university might be.

Although about 20% of the University's students are postgraduates, its research income is small, at a few percentage points of total income. Despite public pronouncements emphasizing its commitment to research, the University's second mission, after teaching, is in reality 'third stream' service to its regional communities. In so far as the University of Plymouth may be said to have an entrepreneurial character, it is becoming a particular sort of university, driven largely by the teaching and learning needs of its sub-regional student population. Its entrepreneurial character in relation to business-related activity is, while significant, less distinctive, and in reality little different from what any institution in its location would do. The curriculum at Plymouth may be said to be focused on the *acting* and *being* domains: its widening participation work requires it to persuade students, who often lack formal academic qualifications, that they can, in fact, succeed at university-level study and go on to professional careers. They are, in effect, asked to see themselves as different people from the ones they thought they were: they are asked to *be* different.

As with Plymouth's adjoining county of Cornwall, the northern Norrland region of Sweden, where Umeå University is located, is Objective 1 status for EU structural funds. Umeå has been successful in attracting students from its region and from across Sweden who in earlier years would not have participated in higher education. Its emphasis on sports and outdoor pursuits (there are similarities here with Plymouth's emphasis in its publicity materials on its attractive coastal position) suggests that its focus, like Plymouth's, is on the *acting* and *being* domains.

The University of Alicante (UAL) might also be considered as an institution with widening higher education participation for its region and sub-region at the centre of its mission. Founded in 1979 on the basis of a local centre for university studies, it is now a large institution of some 27,000 mainly local students, overwhelmingly at first degree level, with just over 600 students (about 2%) studying for higher degrees or specialist courses. Although it operates doctoral programmes, fewer than 10% of students on these programmes finally graduate with doctoral degrees: while the case study does not explain why the completion rate is so low, it may perhaps be associated with the attainment level of its student intake. UAL has a strong social science focus: some 55% of its students are in this area. It operates a 'Lifelong University' aimed at meeting the educational needs of older people.

Some 8% of UAL's total budget relates to research and development work, about the same order as at the University of Plymouth. In 2004, its research income amounted to €11.3 million from public sources and €3.9 million from private sources, a total of €15.2 million. (As a comparison, the LSHTM, a very much smaller research-led institution with only 1750 students in 2003/04, earned €52 million.) UAL is another institution where teaching and learning has had to develop in distinctive ways to meet the needs of its sub-regional student market. It has responded entrepreneurially to its circumstances.

Professional commitment

The Technical University of Valencia (UPV) provides an example of a university pursuing innovation in teaching and learning as a result of its professional commitment. The independent Higher Schools of Engineering that existed in Spain until the beginning of the 1970s, and which were based on the French *Grandes Écoles* tradition, were the basis of the creation of the UPV. From the start, UPV accepted only students who obtained high marks in their secondary school examinations. The first years of the degree courses are also highly selective, and this causes a large number of students to drop out. However controversial this system is, it does create what is described as an exclusive academic environment, where continuing students are committed and have demonstrated their academic abilities.

As befits a technical university in which the majority of lecturers are engineers, relations with the local business community are much better established than they are with other, more non-technical universities in the Valencia region. This open, forward-looking character is said to define the nature of the UPV. This character was impressed on the University by its previous Rector, Professor Justo Nieto, during his 18-year term of office (an exceptional length of time in a Spanish university – most rectors hold office for 4–8 years). During his term of office, our case study argues, the University changed from being an inward-looking centre of higher education to an entrepreneurial university of regional, national, and to an extent international, prestige and influence, but one still focused around its professional mission.

We may see here that the curriculum emphasis is on *knowing*, based on disciplinary understandings – it is knowing that provides the initial access to the University – but also, as befits an institution dedicated to professional achievement, *acting*.

Poznan University of Economics (PUE) offers another example of the pursuit of innovations in teaching and learning underpinned by professional commitment. PUE ranks third in terms of student numbers among economics universities in Poland (the Polish system has a large proportion of specialist, rather than multi-faculty, universities), and second or third in recent external reviews of quality among comparable Polish institutions. While its research work is well-regarded, and is considered to be important within the University, research income accounts for only 6% of the University's total income. It must therefore be considered, by international standards, a teaching-orientated university. The University recognizes these relativities when it states that teaching activities will be the main criterion for assessing staff appointments and promotions.

PUE has set the following priorities for the years 2003/04–2006/07:

- further internationalization of teaching and research;
- development of student exchange;
- improvement in teaching quality;
- expansion of staff training.

These priorities are, on the whole, clearly focused on teaching rather than research; indeed, research priorities themselves relate to the 'needs of the educational offer determined by the needs of the educational market' (PUE case study). It seems clear that the increased competition for students that has developed among Polish universities over the last decade or so has had the effect of driving curriculum change and making the universities more responsive to student demands.

PUE is aiming to enhance the teaching and learning of its students through international cooperation and mobility involving both staff and students, curriculum updating, foreign language teaching, and other matters. The main thrust is the internationalization of the University in order, it seems clear, to ensure that its graduates are able to operate effectively in the global economy, whether in business or the public service. The University has responded in an innovative manner to changes in its external environment, particularly with regard to the ways in which its own professional field is changing, and it has reorganized its structures and processes accordingly. Its focus, as a professional university, is on the *knowing* and *acting* domains, producing graduates with the professional knowledge and confidence to act in wider national and international arenas.

The University of Buckingham is the UK's only private university, in the sense of having UK degree-awarding powers but not receiving any public funds. Its mission statement clearly identifies it as a teaching institution: 'To provide high quality, personal, small-group teaching for our community of UK and international students, and to deliver an excellent student : staff ratio' (Buckingham case study). It is a very small institution, with fewer than 700 students in 2004 (down from a 1995 peak of just over 1000), of whom 75% are studying for law or business studies degrees. Its academic focus is therefore on a relatively narrow professional or vocational range. The case study argues that the University has taken few initiatives that might be considered as being entrepreneurial; rather, it has simply struggled to achieve financial viability in difficult market circumstances. Its approach to teaching and learning seems to be traditional, rather than innovative – and it presents that as a selling point, along with its small size, on its website. As with any organization in survival mode, new initiatives may appear to be unaffordable luxuries. Buckingham may therefore be classed as a non-entrepreneurial university in teaching and learning terms, with a strong emphasis on the *knowing* domain.

The London School of Hygiene and Tropical Medicine (LSHTM), as already indicated, provides a highly distinctive case for study. It operates as a national school for public health in the UK, while pursuing a strongly inter-national mission in this field, with staff drawn from some 40 countries and students from 120. It is a highly research-intensive institution, with a research income of €52 million (2003/04) and it appears that its teaching role follows from its research mission: teaching is seen as one of the means of disseminat-ing the School's research and scholarship – although its distance-learning MSc programme was set up with a clear income-generation remit as well. I therefore classify LSHTM as an institution where teaching is powerfully influenced by its professional mission and commitment.

In curriculum terms, LSHTM must aim to work strongly in all three domains of *knowing, acting,* and *being.* It clearly aims to ensure that its students are rigorously trained and possess accurate and up-to-date scientific knowledge; but it is also engaged in the formation of public health profes-sionals, who will probably have to take, literally, life-and-death decisions in perhaps physically risky situations. The case study does not pursue this point, but as the LSHTM mission involves 'educating public health researchers, teachers and practitioners' (LSHTM case study) from all parts of the world, then the *acting* and *being* components of the curriculum should be pro-nounced if the institution is being innovative – entrepreneurial – in its approach to teaching and learning.

Teaching in the research-led university

The University of Nottingham may be seen as a classical public research university. It traces its origins back to the late nineteenth century, and is now a large institution by UK standards, with some 30,000 FTE students and nearly 2500 academic staff. Although its annual income from research grants and contracts is comparatively large, at about €95 million, it is still a modest proportion of the University's total annual income of some €400 million. Even so, the University regards its mission, so far as teaching and learning are concerned, as being 'to complement its research commitments with the provision of an excellent learning environment' (Nottingham case study). Nottingham sees itself, then, very much as a research-led institution.

The University undertook a major academic restructuring in 1998, which seems to have been driven both by teaching and learning and by research considerations. The view, reports the case study, was that there should be:

> basic organizational units that are intellectually and academically coherent and that they should ensure that (i) they are large enough to have a devolved budget with flexible decision-making, (ii) they cover wide enough subject areas to minimize interdepartmental competition for students, thereby releasing staff time for research, and (iii) that the units have several professors so that the leadership roles can be shared. (Nottingham case study)

We again see a strong research commitment providing the basis for its teaching and learning work.

Nottingham is distinctive in the UK (and relatively unusual internationally) in having developed overseas campuses, first in Malaysia, in 2000, and more recently in China, where the first students were admitted in 2005. These were (and, perhaps, remain) both relatively risky ventures – certainly in reputational terms: other UK universities have considered offshore campus concepts, but few have decided to pursue them. The approach can be seen in terms of the University wishing to take its existing successful mix of teaching and research and transplant it to another setting. This may certainly be considered to be an entrepreneurial approach, searching for new opportunities where the existing business model can be deployed, while accepting that there are inherent risks, both financial and reputational.

It is clear from the case study that the Vice-Chancellor was the driving force behind these international developments: 'The VC has a particular vision about the international agenda . . . he believes that we need to be a global player to be a fully successful institution' commented a senior manager at Nottingham (Nottingham case study). This, together with other evidence from the case study, suggests that, unlike the cases of say Lapland or Umeå, there is no sense that Nottingham has some kind of social mission to provide higher education in China: its international activities arise from its wish to be 'a global player'. In this sense, Nottingham's offshore strategy is perhaps a more purely entrepreneurial activity, in the usual business sense of the word, than most of the other activities described here.

The University of Nottingham aims to encourage an entrepreneurial attitude among its staff and students, and is a UK leader in producing spin-out companies from its research activity. As the case study concludes, as well as research, the main contribution that the University makes to the knowledge society is the production each year of 7000 graduates who find employment in all parts of the world. We may think that these graduates have taken part in an education that generally emphasized the *knowing* domain, though the other domains will not have been absent.

Lund University in Sweden is an even larger institution than Nottingham, with some 28,000 FTE undergraduates. Strongly research-led, Lund has a complex structure of faculties and research units of many kinds, to such an extent that internal competition arises between different units offering similar programmes – a development 'not considered as positive', our case study reports. (We may note Nottingham's organizational approach to this problem.) Lund has, however, adopted innovative approaches to the organization of teaching and learning, notably though the development of Öresund University, a collaborative venture between Lund and other Swedish and Danish universities in its region. The case study suggests that, while a culture of research-led excellence and competition pervades the University, different approaches to teaching and learning occur in different faculties. The Lund Institute of Technology, for example, is characterized by especially close links with industry, with 70% of its budget coming from external sources, and it is likely that this will give teaching and learning in the faculty a particular flavour.

It is clear that most of Lund's faculties focus a great deal of energy on obtaining external research funding: as the case study concludes, obtaining 'external money [for research] has become a matter of survival'. As state funding for undergraduate education has lagged behind the cost of providing it (the case study reports undergraduate teaching as producing a small loss in 2004), some cross-subsidization must take place within faculties from research to teaching. It will also be the case that resources for teaching are better than they might otherwise be as a result of facilities of all kinds receiving funding through research income streams. Lund therefore seems to be a good example of a high-quality research university, where teaching is often not the highest priority, but which nevertheless attracts able students because of its academic reputation. (It may be worth noting that in the 2006 Shanghai Jiao Tong league table of European universities, Nottingham is placed at 24 and Lund at 29. In this sense, they are comparable institutions.)

Adam Mickiewicz University (AMU) in Poland is also a classical university, whose mission starts with the goal of 'educating students and preparing them to professional lives; and conducting research, especially in basic fields of knowledge' (AMU case study). Financial difficulties in recent years have, however, severely undermined AMU's research capabilities: the data show that less than 10% of its total income in 2004 supported research, though this is said to understate actual research activity because of the way in which the statistics are collected. Funding for teaching, in contrast, has been buoyant, partly as a result of the levying of student tuition fees for so-called part-time students: these fees alone represented a 2004 income figure for the University close to its total income for research. The case study shows that the gap between teaching and research income for the University has steadily increased from the mid-1990s, to the extent where it might be classified, on a European basis, as being a mainly teaching university (though allowance must be made for the under-stating of research spending noted). AMU is therefore in a very different situation from the Universities of Nottingham and Lund in terms of spending patterns, but I class them together because they all represent, in their different ways, a classical European university tradition.

The four most popular areas of studies at AMU in the last decade were law, political sciences, tourism and recreational studies, and educational sciences, reflecting the changed economic situation of post-communist Poland. Tourism, for example, has grown from a zero base to over 1600 students (full- and part-time) in 2004/05. We may see the applied, vocational nature of these areas of study as being likely to take a curriculum approach with an *acting* or *being* emphasis, as distinct from the *knowledge* emphasis that might characterize the scientific and technical faculties of the University.

The relationship between teaching and entrepreneurial activities

The relationship between teaching and research in universities is, generally, a disputed one: to many academics, it is self-evident that involvement with research leads to better teaching (some argue that the relationship runs in both directions), but it has proved very difficult to show the connection empirically. The widely cited meta-analysis by Hattie and Marsh (1996) suggests that there are complex connections between the two activities, but that a statistical correlation has not been demonstrated. The relationship between teaching and the university's position in relation to entrepreneurial activities is less studied (indeed, outside the EUEREK Project, it is not clear that it is studied at all), and it is likely that it will prove even harder to show that there is a correlation either way.

So far as the EUEREK research is concerned, the lack of comparable data on teaching activity and learning outcomes means that a discussion of the relationship between teaching and entrepreneurial activity must be speculative – though the collection, at a cross-national institutional level, of rigorous comparable data would in any event be fraught with difficulty: OECD data on tertiary graduation rates by country, for example, are at far too general a level to allow any assumptions about inputs to teaching and learning activities to be made (OECD, 2004). We can only speculate that, as the argument goes for research, so the involvement of academic staff in various externally orientated activities (working with regional social and economic partners, for example) may broaden and deepen individuals' understandings, which in turn may lead to more effective teaching – and so, it may be hoped, learning. Equally – and again as for the argument around research – the involvement of academic staff in such activities may consume time and energy that would otherwise have been directed towards teaching; and if entrepreneurial activities are seen as a key institutional mission, it may mean that teaching comes to be seen as a lower priority, and perhaps lower status, task.

In our case studies, a distinction might be drawn between institutions such as the University of Lapland and the University of Alicante, where the entrepreneurial function is bound up with the region; and institutions such as Lund University and the Technical University of Valencia, where staff are under pressure to obtain research and consultancy contracts from national and international sources. In the former cases, where the institutions are broadly teaching-led, it is plausible that regionally focused entrepreneurial activity will readily feed through into teaching students who come pre-dominantly from that region. An example from the Lapland case is the way in which the graphic design management master's programme relates to work carried out in design projects for the regional tourism industry. In the latter examples, by contrast, it may be that the requirements of, say, large-scale international projects distract staff from the day-to-day needs of undergraduate students, in particular. An informant at Lund University, for example, was reported as saying that, in the context of ceaseless pressure to generate external funding, 'an incredible amount of time is spent on writing applications [for research grants]' (Lund case study): it seems unlikely that teaching will come at the top of such people's priorities.

More consideration needs to be given to these connections in future work in this area.

Conclusions: teaching and learning and the entrepreneurial university

We can see in our cases, I suggest, how universities in different circumstances are changing their approaches to teaching and learning. I have suggested that four main external drivers – region, widening participation, professional focus, and the research–teaching nexus – may affect the ways in which the curriculum is conceived and delivered, and I have proposed a theoretical framework in which to consider this.

It also seems clear that market-type pressures affecting student recruit-ment have led to substantial changes in the ways in which some of our case study institutions have organized their teaching and learning. A public fund-ing structure that accentuates market pressures, by ensuring that public money to fund teaching follows the student, supports changes of these types. Being situated in a competitive environment, with other institutions recruit-ing from the same student market, also seems to encourage innovation in our cases.

All our cases are working in a changing environment, affecting teaching and learning as much as in other aspects of their work. It is noticeable (even if it is no longer remarkable) that few, if any, respondents in our cases seem to regard themselves as operating in a steady-state environment, reliant on guaranteed public funding: change is part of their existence.

Figure 2 tries to show where some of our sample are located on a teach-ing/research axis and a state/market axis, and to indicate the directions in which the pressures in their environments are causing them to move. Thus, in the top-right quadrant, PUE's (Poland) teaching is driven by

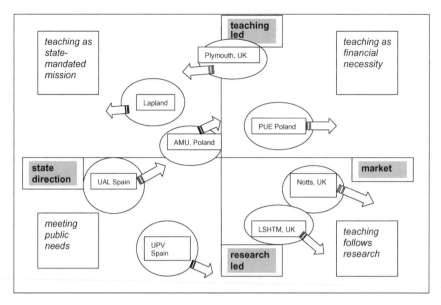

Figure 2   Typology of institutional missions

market pressures. The institutions which I place in the bottom-right quadrant (Nottingham and LSHTM in the UK) are both research-led, and their teaching may be thought of as tending to follow their research agendas, while also being influenced by the demands of the markets in which the institutions variously operate. In the top-left quadrant, two teaching-orientated institutions (Lapland in Finland and Plymouth in the UK) may be thought of as moving, perhaps only slightly, in the direction of state-mandated teaching, as they both respond to different national and regional imperatives for, broadly speaking, social inclusion. We see here the university being used (more or less explicitly) as a state agent for social change. AMU (Poland), by contrast, is responding to market pressures in terms of its teaching patterns, and is moving away from its historical position as a traditional state university. In the bottom-left quadrant, the Spanish examples chosen seem to be moving in different directions, under market pressures, as they seek additional income from teaching or from research, depending on their relative strengths.

The pattern that emerges is one of universities identifying different forces (from the state or from various markets), and acting so as to resolve these forces in ways that might support institutional survival and (it is to be hoped) development. University success in entrepreneurialism might be defined as the extent to which these forces are satisfactorily resolved.

5

Human resource management and the generation of entrepreneurialism

Michael Shattock

Human resource management in an academic context

A conventional, professional view of human resource management might be that it is through contracts, terms of employment, and individual financial incentive-based approaches that academic staff in universities can be motivated to improve their performance or to become more entrepreneurial in their activities. It would be wrong to deny that these traditional modes of human resource management are not important, but the evidence presented in these cross-national studies points to there being much broader influences in play. Our case studies range over comparatively wealthy Sweden and the UK, where academic salaries are low compared with comparable professions in their own countries but relatively high when compared with academic salaries in some other countries, to Moldova, Poland, and Russia, transition countries recovering from the economic crisis of the mid-1990s, where taking on additional paid teaching duties is a necessary requirement to obtain an adequate personal income. But beyond these easy characterizations of national wealth and poverty there lie other distortions based on academic disciplines or on the existence of centralized state controls over salary levels, benchmarks, and nationally based reward systems that may conflict with institutional missions. Finally, any account of human resource management must reflect on the impact of the extent to which a higher education institution (HEI) is autonomous in its ability to manage staff matters, whether a university can act as a legal independent entity to recruit, employ, remunerate, and promote staff according to its own strategic ambitions, or whether it is constrained by national legislation or by the integration of university staff salaries and conditions of service with those of other public services. There are, thus, key economic, social, and cultural constraints that must be taken into account, not to speak of – perhaps the most compelling – academic tradition.

One important test of human resource management in higher education is whether it is adapted to the policy context that the institution finds itself in and whether it is flexible enough to match a changing environment. One case study, that of Plymouth, for example, notes that academic promotion in the University had traditionally been based on research performance even though it was primarily a teaching institution. In 2001, however, it was decided to broaden the criteria to allow professorships, readerships (normally in the UK a post below that of a professor awarded only for research excellence), and principal lecturerships to be appointed on teaching merit alone, and a further signal that the criteria were being broadened was sent out when a lecturer was promoted to a readership without extensive research publications but on the basis of some 70 consultancy reports. This latter action reflected a decisive change in the reward systems that spurred an institution-wide change in academic behaviour to encourage a greater contribution to third mission activity. In Moldova, Poland, and Russia by contrast, the pressure, both with respect to academic status and financial security, for the lecturer to concentrate on preparation for the award of the habilitation, without which a professorship cannot be awarded, has the tendency to exclude activities that do not buttress a publication list. While in Spain the pressure to prepare oneself for the examination to obtain civil servant status (which when achieved provides complete job security and offers no incentive for entrepreneurial behaviour thereafter) again inhibits academics from undertaking activities that might not contribute directly to a high-quality academic profile.

Perhaps the most important element in motivating academic performance is the creation of an organizational culture around an institutional strategic mission. Financial reward systems are necessary but in academic life are perhaps less important in themselves than academic and institutional recognition. At Tampere, for example, financial incentives, though present, are regarded as less important 'because academics fight about glory and merit as well as about money' (Tampere case study). The drive to do fundamental research is motivated by scientific curiosity not financial incentives, but the technology transfer stage and the engagement with third mission activities often can be. There are various ways of handling this dilemma, via direct and explicit rewards to recognize particular performance, such as, for example, allowing an academic to retain a percentage of an external project grant as a personal emolument, or through internal promotion and salary review mechanisms that recognize performance across a broad field of activity. The latter approach is well described and contrasted with the more direct approach in a response quoted in the Helsinki School of Economics case study:

> We don't have a clear system of pay by results. It's been discussed but I guess you could say that if you're active and bring in external funding we've tried to pay attention to it. We've tried to reflect this in people's salaries, we've sort of treated it as extra work which is

compensated – The places where it works, and where it was implemented in a day or two, are in these companies of ours [HSE has established a number of companies to exploit its expertise commercially]. They do have a pay by results system, which also works. If the results are poor, it's reflected in people's salaries, period. (HSE, Finland case study)

It is clear from the case studies that different universities' cultures and economic drivers determine different approaches to how performance is rewarded and that there is no obvious model that could be replicated across national systems. Indeed, while all systems are conscious of the need to motivate improved and diversified performance, it is probably safe to say that there is no aspect of academic behaviour that is more embedded in cultural and social mores and in national academic traditions, and more difficult, therefore, to change. In addition, in many systems, responsibility for the various components of human resource management – salaries, terms of service, incentive systems, and tenure – are divided between the state or other external bodies, the institution, and occasionally the faculty or department. This has the effect of diluting attempts to align human resource management with institutional mission and often builds into the processes inflexibilities and rigidities that contradict local and regional needs. Because these aspects are so important, it is useful to summarize the case study evidence via groupings of countries, rather than on a thematic basis. The groupings are the UK as a group on its own, Finland, Spain, and Sweden as a second group, and the transition countries of Moldova, Poland, and Russia as the third group.

The United Kingdom

UK universities have full, legal independence and employ their own staff and pay them on terms created by themselves. Having said this, salary structures are controlled by national salary negotiations conducted between the universities acting corporately and the academic and other staff trades unions. Within this framework universities have wide discretion over how they pay and grade their staff, a discretion that has been extended since 2004 by the adoption of a nationally agreed salary spine on which it is a matter for individual institutions where to place staff in particular grades. At the professorial level there has never been a prescribed salary scale, leaving universities to award 'spot' salaries that reflect performance and market pressures. Universities are free to adopt their own criteria to appoint at professorial, reader, senior lecturer/principal lecturer, and lecturer level (with equivalent grades for research staff) but the practice of engaging external assessors from other universities to assist in the adjudication of appointments or promotions to professorships and readerships has the effect of not allowing individual institutional autonomy to depart too far from recognized norms. Academic promotions are determined by institutional academic committees and are subject to close peer review. On the other hand, they are not tied to the achievement of particular qualifications or to predetermined numbers, unless this is decided by the institution itself. It is a matter for the institution to decide its own salaries and wages expenditure within its own finances, so that for universities successful in generating a significant proportion of income from non-state sources there is a greater possibility, not always acted upon, to remunerate staff at higher levels, than universities which are less successful. Nottingham, for example, in 2004, paid over 170 of its staff more than €97,000 per annum (that is, more than twice the average academic salary). The most obvious benefit of this legal independence lies in the ability of the universities to adapt their reward structures to match their strategic mission. Thus Nottingham has chosen to offer particular incentives of rank and remuneration as inducements to staff working in its overseas campuses, whereas Plymouth, as described above, has amended its criteria for promotion to senior academic positions so as to greatly reduce their requirements for research and to emphasize teaching performance and third mission activities, steps that have no doubt contributed to its entrepreneurialism in teaching described in Chapter 4.

The London School of Hygiene and Tropical Medicine (LSHTM) has taken this freedom even further. While most full-time academic staff in UK universities, other than research staff appointed on 'soft money', are given permanent appointments (though without the legal definition of 'tenure'), only 40% of LSHTM academic staff hold permanent posts and the remainder are on fixed-term appointments, whether funded from recurrent funds or on 'soft money'. The Director of the School defended this policy on the basis that:

> A lot of it looks tougher than it really is because in fact most people just carry on with their work. One of the problems here is that the institution can become a little top heavy at times: people don't want to leave. (LSHTM case study)

On the other hand, not surprisingly, an LSHTM researcher indicated there were downsides to the policy:

> Most people in the School would say that job security is very important and does create a lot of tensions, particularly perhaps some of the junior staff feel quite badly pulled in different directions (project funding is ending, is something else coming up etc.). That happens in all universities, but here it happens to a much higher proportion of people. (LSHTM case study)

Many of these staff will hold their appointments over a series of research grants and contracts and when there are gaps in external grant income, staff with 10 or more years of service are given 16 months 'underwriting', and with 5–10 years' service 6 months 'underwriting' to prepare new research grant applications. But research performance cannot in all cases be the only criterion for retention. As the Director said:

we have 5–10% of people who don't do research who have important teaching roles. And it is always a question of when someone is valuable enough to institutionally say that it does not matter that they don't do research, we just want them for what other attributes they have got. (LSHTM case study)

Of 234 academic staff, 132 are funded from non-core income; 24 staff are paid over €125,000 and six over €175,000, reflecting the high salaries paid in the UK to staff in clinical medicine. The School is strongly driven by international competition, with the proportion of its income derived directly from external research grants and contracts having risen from 51% to 63% over the 1994–2004 period and has created an organizational culture in which a respondent could say: 'Even though I have a secure contract now, we are still expected to bring in at least part of our salary when we can . . . if none of us could pull in part of our salary the School would go bankrupt' (LSHTM case study). And a head of department could claim: 'An unusual thing about the School is the degree to which a very large number of our staff completely buy into the mission' (LSHTM case study).

It is dangerous to seek to draw too firm conclusions from a specialist institution with a relatively confined academic brief, but the case study does illustrate the extent to which in the right circumstances an institution legally competent to fit its human resource policies with its corporately and collegially determined mission can be innovative and take financial risks to retain its international competitive edge.

Finland, Spain, and Sweden

These three countries offer a more 'European' model of human resource management, though there are important variations between them and within them. However, they share a situation of much heavier state control over staffing issues and policy than would be the case in the UK. A Finnish speaker from the Helsinki School of Economics puts the position forcefully:

The fact that our universities are these sort of accounting offices without their own finances, own money, own accounting and in principle even without, directly, their own employees or without the status of a legal person means that they're totally subdued government agencies that are treated like all other government agencies. This is an obvious structural weakness, which actively undermines our international competitiveness. (HSE, Finland case study).

In fact, the 1997 Universities' Act in Finland gave universities autonomy to allocate their own resources, create professorial chairs, and employ their own staff and the Ministry has tried to steer the universities to a more management-by-results system so that the core funding is based on targets with universities being required to evaluate their own activities. Nevertheless, progress appears to have been slow: a national salary structure remains and personal financial reward systems seem to be limited and based on managerial rather than academic performance. One Tampere respondent suggested that there had been only very modest changes over the last decade but that the limitations were chiefly imposed by internal tradition rather than a lack of autonomy. Another suggested that Ministry financial steering was so strong that unless a university had a 'money maker' it was still heavily controlled. One institution, the HSE, seemed to have been able to create the 'money maker' role by generating resources through a private Foundation and through various companies. Thus the Foundation offers a scholarship of €2000 to academics for a publication in a top journal and some staff can add to their salaries considerably through the companies, but HSE, like LSHTM, is a specialist institution, and such opportunities are not available in the universities generally.

In Spain, 70% of the academic staff are civil servants and central government decides on general personnel policies, including structures, appropriate workloads, and salaries, although regional governments are responsible for payments and can authorize the establishment of new professorships. Universities do have the freedom to decide how many staff should be in each grade and workloads but these decisions are made by the staff through collegial boards. The existence of three sets of authorities – the state, the regional government, and the institutional level of decision making – makes change difficult to achieve and gives rise to considerable discord. There is a national research bonus that rewards publication and in Valencia there is a regional bonus, PAREDITT, which translates university activities, fundable by external bodies, into teaching credits, but this is not seen as having any real impact on entrepreneurial behaviour. Although in the Technical University of Valencia (UPV) there is now a new position of 'contracted doctor', which gives contract staff some job security, it remains the case that non civil servants are prohibited from being project managers, on the grounds that they might resign before the project is completed, so that contract staff are disadvantaged. Teaching workloads are strongly controlled but research is very much left to individual initiative. At UPV, the spectrum of entrepreneurial units surrounding the traditional core of the University offers opportunities for additional earnings and UPV has its own system of incentives including a Supplementary Research Support (ACI) and a project overhead sharing scheme that is very favourable to the project leader, but the overall picture is that of a centralized control of human resources out of line with the mission and objectives of many Spanish universities.

Swedish universities, like Finnish and Spanish universities, do not in general have the corporate legal powers of the UK universities, but in Sweden there are three exceptions: Chalmers University, the Stockholm School of Economics, and Jönköping University. The newest of these is Jönköping, which, unlike Lund, Umeå, and the Royal Institute of Technology (KTH), our other three case studies, has the power to recruit and employ its own staff and reward them for individual merit. Where in traditional Swedish universities an appellant against a university's staffing decision would do so through a central appeal process, at Jönköping it would be via the civil courts. However, this legal freedom has not resulted in a loosening of the human resource framework: there are no developed incentive schemes and although salaries are said to be based on results, it appears that the main incentive is a relief from teaching and more time made available for research. Research leaders can receive up to 4% of a project's funding themselves (1% when the contract is received and 3% when the funding stream is in place) but the University's human resource policies otherwise appear little different from those of other Swedish universities, where staff are recruited and employed on terms comparable to other state agencies except in regard to the exploitation of intellectual property rights (the so-called 'academic exception'). This leads universities to follow the same route as the HSE (Finland) in setting up foundations or companies where incentives and merit awards can be 'privatized'; the existence of such organizations can make the academic department or research group more attractive to potential recruits. (One consequence is a substantial system-wide under-reporting of non-state income into the university.) At Umeå, for example, it was said: 'We are very, very bad at reward systems. Departments get rewards not individuals', while awards and prizes 'have great symbolic value' (Umeå case study). On the other hand, many faculty members generate supplemental income streams via their own private firms. At Lund, however, where the University is organized on a heavily devolved faculty basis, the Lund Technical Institute operates on a much more independent basis with considerable variations in the level of professorial salaries, and with the Dean having a large sum available from which to reward academics bringing in large grants. The Institute is also funded on the expectation (as at LSHTM) that a professor will generate a significant proportion of his/her salary from external sources.

The 'transition' countries: Moldova, Poland, and Russia

The universities in Moldova, Poland, and Russia all inherited a highly centralized higher education system, which nevertheless retained some characteristics from a former Humboldtian past. Thus although the system was directed (rather than steered) to fulfil state requirements and subject to a high degree of central control, institutional integrities such as, for example, respect for the habilitation qualification as a guarantee of academic seniority and research capability were generally maintained. All three countries have seen an extraordinary increase in demand for higher education since the fall of communism, and responding to this while at the same time facing economic crisis has had the effect of reinforcing teaching priorities over research. The absence of state support for a research agenda via research councils or comparable bodies in Russia and Moldova or of a significant 'pull' factor from the economy in any of the countries has also meant that there has been very little project money to stimulate entrepreneurial research undertakings. These factors have conditioned human resource management in all three countries, although the political and historical circumstances of each country (most notably Poland's historical distinctiveness from the Eastern Bloc and its membership now of the EU) and their development profile since the early 1990s, have marked out widening divergences within a Central and East European model.

In Moldova, the expansion of student numbers together with the introduction of tuition fees to substitute for state funding has had a dramatic impact on the financing of higher education. In 1994, the Moldova State University (MSU) received 100% of its income from the state with 8% coming from the state research budget and 92% for teaching; in 2004, 83% of its income derived from tuition fees and 17% from the state, of which only 4% was in respect of research. Since 92% of Moldova's national research expenditure is channelled through the Academy of Science or government research institutes, the low level of the University's research income is not surprising but the transformation of the tuition driven element of the budget in so short a period is extraordinary and dictates human resource management: salary differentials by faculty have been created to reflect student number pressure and monthly premiums have been introduced to recognize high work performance in teaching. At the Academy of Economic Studies, state-controlled salaries can receive an uplift of up to 350% depending on the number of lectures given, the quality of the teaching, the specialism, and the staff member's length of service. The impact on staffing policies can be judged at the MSU by a fall in the number of research staff from 426 in 1994 to 273 in 2004 and a growth in the professoriat of only 40% versus a 400% increase in the number of lecturers. Moldova state-funded universities have in effect become privatized teaching institutions. One consequence of the adverse economic conditions has been an exodus of younger staff and an increasing concentration of staff in older age brackets.

A very similar economic position prevailed in Russia for most of this period and, as in Moldova, the solution adopted was to permit state universities to take fee-paying students in addition to those funded by the state. Our Russian case studies were all of institutions that have sought to break away from this model, which, as in Moldova, concentrated the energy of institutions on teaching by rewarding the recruitment of increased student numbers, but thereby reduced research capacities. The most significant of the case studies from this point of view is the Higher School of Economics in Moscow (HSE, Russia), which has been identified by the government as one of the key university institutions in the reform of Russian higher education. The School operates a very active set of human resource management policies recognizing that the key step must be the recruitment of real talent and positive staff development programmes. Twenty-five per cent of the staff are full professors or hold the habilitation qualification: such staff are attracted both because the School offers 'a unique degree of creative freedom' (HSE,

Russia case study) and because professorial salaries at €14,500 per annum are very high by comparison with the rest of the university system. The School, it is said, 'consistently attracts faculty members dissatisfied with the routinized situation in Soviet academic life and who seek a place to realize their innovative ideas' (HSE, Russia case study) and has embarked on an ambitious partnership programme with leading European institutions. On the other hand, the School's specific human resources development plan illustrates the difficulties implicit in creating an institution of international excellence in the context of a funding environment dominated by teaching numbers. By 2010, the School plans to toughen its recruitment criteria further, ensuring that every academic is research active, that at least 25% of the holders of main chairs will publish internationally (at least 10% regularly), that at least 35% will be engaged in applied research, and that at least 75% will hold PhDs. Staff numbers are planned to rise from 660 to 1100 at a very favourable 1:10 staff:student ratio and base salaries will grow by 300%. The size of the task that confronts the institution, however, is demonstrated by the fact that in the last two years, 25% of staff have not published at all and 46% of staff have never written a journal article; only 19% have ever published in a foreign language, and it is admitted that some staff 'prefer to earn through a greater academic workload in commercial programmes since their courses enjoy effective demand' (HSE, Russia case study).

Poland shares many of the characteristics of the Moldovan and Russian experience in that economic downturn was combined with greatly increased student demand (over 370% growth in the student population between 1990 and 2004) so that universities were permitted by the government to shore up their finances by taking fees-only students, although in Poland the students were part-time and weekend students only. However, Poland also saw an extraordinary explosion of some 315 private HEIs, the teaching for which was provided by staff employed in the state-funded institutions in order to supplement their state university salaries. Indeed, many of the most senior academic managers in Polish universities chose to take leadership positions as well in private universities. In 2005, the government passed legislation to restrict state university staff to hold only one position in another institution, but the basic academic teaching workloads of 180 hours teaching a year for senior staff and 210 hours for junior staff, and the rules for promotion, remain unchanged from the 1970s and 1980s. Salary levels continue to be determined by the state and there are no financial rewards for establishing entrepreneurial units or for special achievements, although staff are permitted to claim a proportion of income from research grants as a personal emolument. The effect of the salary structure is to encourage staff to concentrate on achieving the habilitation milestone, because of the salary reward and lower teaching load associated with becoming a 'senior academic' rather than be distracted by third mission type activities. This coupled with a 'brain drain' of younger staff has pushed up the average age of academic staff, and in the longer term the number of professors is likely to decrease as a result of retirements and an inability to replace them with sufficiently qualified people.

The growth of the private sector of higher education in Poland has protected the state-funded universities from being swamped with fee-paying students, as for example in Moldova, but it is still the case that 82% of the income in state universities is derived from teaching (from state grant and from fees) and only 12% from research. At the Adam Mickiewicz University (AMU), for example, research income has fallen from 15% of total income in 1994 to 9.5% in 2004, so that although the budget is not dominated by private tuition fee income the overall impact has been, as in other universities in transition countries, to lower the priority attached to research over the decade. Although sharing many of the characteristics of Nottingham and Lund – a comprehensive university, with long traditions, located in a provincial capital – AMU cannot compete with them in research, and its human resource management reflects none of the commitment to research that would be found in them or in other comparable institutions.

Some conclusions

The picture to be drawn from these different country groupings is mixed. It is not at all clear that additional financial reward is necessarily the spur to outstanding achievement and the evidence from the two Nordic countries makes it clear that reputational rewards can be even more important in some academic cultures. On the other hand, the more international and inter-university competition increases, the greater the role of flexibility in reward structures is likely to become. This is, however, difficult, if not impossible, to achieve when salary levels and structures are determined by central authorities and especially when they are linked to other state salary structures (e.g. through civil service or state agency processes); this also has the disadvantage of imposing systemic rigidities on universities, which, as our case studies show, may have significantly differentiated missions. Only one system, that of the UK, confers absolute legal autonomy on universities, giving them the freedom to design their human resource policies in line with their individual institutional strategies, but even here it should be noted that it has only been very recently that the universities have agreed a salary structure that offers real freedom to tailor rewards to performance related to mission. As the distance between research-intensive and teaching-intensive universities has grown wider, under the pressure of the concentration of research resources, the need to differentiate salary structures has forced change.

One overall conclusion is summed up in a comment from Umeå University that: 'There is too much comfort' in university reward structures (Umeå case study), and while it is not necessary to go to the lengths that LSHTM has gone to as a specialist research institution in limiting tenure and using the generation of external grant income as a stimulus to performance, it is nevertheless the case that human resource mechanisms do not in general offer sufficient incentives for innovation and outstanding achievement, with promotion being far too often dominated by the achievement of specific qualifications rather than being the reward for a broad range of performance. Over the decade, all the countries in the study have seen a movement from elite to mass higher education and have tried to adapt to it either by measures for institutional differentiation as in the UK or by the creation of new institutions. In the transition countries, in particular, where the impact of expansion was combined with that of sharp economic downturn, the entrenchment of a reward system based on student numbers and teaching workloads, at the expense of research, has built a structure that will be difficult in the short term to change. The steps being taken at the HSE in Moscow are reinforced by a considerable state investment and may be difficult to replicate elsewhere, and indeed in Russia itself. Where there is institutional flexibility in human resource management policies, universities can adapt their strategies to changed circumstances, but where a 'one size fits all' structure exists across a whole system, the human resource management structures become a real inhibition to institutional mission change or to recognizing entrepreneurial innovation.

Academic communities on the whole favour the application of equity in reward structures, but in a period when competition between institutions has been increased and there is a greater reliance on market principles, a balance needs to be struck between collegially based reward structures and reward structures that recognize individual excellence. Another way of putting this is to suggest that organizational cultures need to be changed so that collegial processes can recognize diversity of performance in terms of reputation as well as in more tangible benefits. An important test for human resource management structures in the modern university is the extent to which they encourage or discourage academic intrapreneurs. Most of the structures examined in our case studies fail in this respect or offer mechanical rewards such as a financial percentage of an external project grant or increased salary to reflect a larger teaching workload, so that financial incentives are not linked in any way to reputational incentives. Academic intrapreneurs thrive when their efforts are admired (the 'glory' referred to in the quotation from Tampere, above) but they also need financial incentives for themselves and confidence that the institution will invest in the academic infrastructure that supports them.

6

Governance, organizational change, and entrepreneurialism: is there a connection?

José-Ginés Mora and María-José Vieira

Introduction

In other chapters, the connections between funding, teaching, and research with the entrepreneurial character of the institutions in our sample have been analysed. In this chapter, we focus on the organizational structure of higher education institutions (HEIs), especially governance and organizational changes, in connection with entrepreneurialism. We will consider not only the internal structure of HEIs, but also other environmental characteristics that could be important for this analysis.

In the first part of this chapter, the concept of governance is discussed, and the trends in Europe and the recent recommendations of the European Commission for reforming governance are analysed. In the second part, we analyse our sample of 27 universities trying to connect the organizational characteristics of these universities with the idea of entrepreneurialism.

University governance: concepts and trends

Governance: meaning and conflicts

As Shattock (2006) states: 'Organisational governance has become of much more interest in recent years – in higher education as much as in companies and charitable bodies'. Consequently, there is relevant and recent literature on governance, and specifically on university governance (Bargh et al., 1996; Braun and Merrien, 1999; Amaral et al., 2002; Shattock, 2002, 2006; Gayle et al., 2003; Weber, 2004; Kezar, 2005; Jansen, 2007). Nevertheless, in this chapter we take a policy orientation and discuss practical facts and policy trends in university governance.

University governance refers to the structure and process of authoritative decision making across issues that are significant for external as well as internal stakeholders within a university (Gayle et al., 2003). It can be understood as the exercise of collective control over the achievement of common institutional goals. It could be defined as the way that public and private actors seek to solve university organizational problems. Governance raises questions about who decides, when, on what. Governance is also related to the institutional capacity to change and to change properly and in timely fashion to institutional needs.

Clark (1983) defined his well-known triangle of coordination with its three corners, 'the Market', 'the State', and 'Academic Oligarchy', acting as drivers for higher education systems. Each system (or each institution) could be located somewhere within the triangle depending on how much these forces dominated the system. This is a simple but extremely visual way of presenting the position of higher education systems in relation to the dominant forces on university governance. In that sense, university governance can be considered to have five dimensions. These dimensions can be found, in different proportions and with different predominant effects, in most systems or HEIs (Schimank, 2005):

- *State regulation* concerns the traditional notion of top-down authority vested in the state. This dimension refers to regulation by directives; the government prescribes institutional behaviour in detail under particular circumstances.
- *Stakeholder guidance* concerns activities that direct institutions through goal setting and advice. In public higher education systems, the government is usually an important stakeholder but certainly not the only player. It may delegate certain powers to guide other actors, such as intermediary bodies or representatives of industry, on university boards.
- *Academic self-governance* concerns the role of professional communities within higher education systems. This mechanism is institutionalized in collegial decision making within universities and the peer review-based self-steering of academic communities, for instance in decisions of funding agencies.
- *Managerial self-governance* concerns hierarchies within higher education institutions as organizations. Here the role of institutional leadership in internal goal setting, regulation, and decision making is at stake.
- *Competition for resources* within and between universities takes place mostly on the basis not of 'real' markets but of 'quasi-markets' where performance evaluations by peers substitute the demand pull from customers.

To some extent, these dimensions are in conflict in each higher education system and in each institution. Weber (2004) points out the following main types of conflicts:

- *Relationship with the state.* In many countries, the rules imposed by the state, as well as its permanent temptation to politically micro-manage the institution, are putting a serious brake on the willingness and capacity to change. However, emphasis should be placed on convincing the state that the lack of real autonomy is counter-productive in the long run.

- *Internal governance.* The traditional organizational structures and systems of university governance restrain institutions from adapting rapidly enough. The vast majority of universities have always been governed according to what is referred to as a system of collegial governance; decisions are made collectively, mainly between faculty, directors, deans, and rectors. However, this decision-making system now appears to be less and less adequate for the new environment, which requires strong leadership to realize future-orientated decisions, which cannot always count on the consensus of all involved. To make the decision process as efficient as possible, it is important to state clearly which body or person is making the decision and is responsible for it, which bodies must be consulted before the decision is made, and which body is validating the decision.
- *Management tools.* One of the main challenges of governance is to find the right means or tools to secure the effective participation of the people concerned by a policy change and to encourage them to take initiatives spontaneously in line with the general policy.

Organizational changes and governance trends in European universities

A state of flux is the only real common denominator in European higher education in the last decade. As Barnett (2000, 2003) states, universities have to cope with a high degree of uncertainty and 'supercomplexity' that stems from internal and external pressures. There is not a single European higher education system in which significant change has not been implemented in the last 5–10 years, including the structure of higher education, governance, management and control, financing, and quality assurance. Universities are challenged in all aspects of their activities: the nature of their students, the way they deliver knowledge and do research, the way they interact with the civil society, business, the state and other universities, and the manner in which they manage their human resources. Consequently, universities have to cope with new challenges and many of them are related to governance.

In response to these needs, the governance of universities is changing in most European countries. The main trends are as follows:

- *More autonomy.* Enhancing institutional autonomy has probably been the overarching governance trend in European higher education over the last two decades (Maassen and Stensaker, 2003). The degree of change varies between countries and in all respects. Generally speaking, in the areas of staff management and recruitment, particularly with respect to student selection, further progress needs to be made, whereas with block grant funding instead of line item budgeting, institutions now very clearly have more room to make their own decisions (Haug and Kirstein, 1999).
- *Less state regulation.* The rearrangement of the public sector as a whole is a central issue for the debate on university governance. There is a switch

from traditional legalistic steering mechanisms of top-down implementation of normative formulae to a more economically driven steering system based on contractual consent on objectives to be achieved. Generally speaking, the state's new role may be called 'facilitative', as it creates a viable higher education environment in which the state controls the outcomes at the national level without too much detailed interference. Key words like 'accountability' and concepts like 'New Public Management' or 'network governance' ('state supervision', 'the evaluative state') are gradually replacing the traditional focus on state control and academic collegial governance (Neave and van Vught, 1991). State control is giving way to more self-management in the name of efficiency and responsiveness to society's diverse needs. Institutions are being encouraged to increase their capacity and willingness to become engaged in the production of useful knowledge (Schimank et al., 1999). New steering devices have been introduced, while output funding and multi-year agreements with the higher education institutions provide illustrative examples. Former state responsibilities have been transferred not only to the institutions but also to intermediate organizations such as research councils.

Nevertheless, the state retains influence on university development. State oversight is evolving into sometimes elaborate systems of incentives and sanctions that allow governments to continue utilizing their higher education sectors by 'steering from a distance'. For this objective, two mechanisms are mostly used: (a) performance-based funding contracts for delivering public funds to universities, and (b) quality assurance procedures to guarantee citizens the quality of what universities are offering.

- *University leadership* is increasing and collegial models are losing relevance. Enhancing institutional autonomy has meant a strengthening of institutional leadership, particularly in those higher education systems where traditionally the institutional top level was relatively weak. In Europe, the decentralized collegial decision-making within universities is in the process of being replaced by managerial self-governance. As top-down regulation by governments decreases, university leadership is strengthened. This has led to a further rationalization in the institutions and in many cases implies putting in place new 'hierarchies' in which institutional leadership holds a central role. This also places new strains on the institutions' central administration, including the setting up of new offices in the areas of technology transfer, internationalization, and so on.

  In many countries, the introduction of new bodies has taken place at the apex of higher education institutions. Supervisory boards or 'boards of trustees' have been installed, primarily composed of 'lay members' (high-profile persons from the community and from industry). These supervisory boards are expected to give the general public a more vested interest in the institutions' processes. Another trend in this respect is that institutional leaders are being appointed rather than being elected.

  Collegial self-governance is a loser in all the changes in university governance across Europe. Traditional notions of collegiality and consensus-based decision making have increasingly come under pressure, making room for 'business-like' management and 'professionalization' of administrative structures. Borrowing instruments from the private sector, institutions have tried to enhance their possibilities to streamline the organization to cope with an increasingly complex environment.

- *More market influence.* The greater reliance on market signals brings a shift in decision-making power not just from government, but also from educational institutions to the consumer or client, whether student, business or the general public. Through competition, higher education institutions are being driven to become more sensitive to their varied consumers' demands.

- *Greater cooperation with the wider society.* Universities across Europe are more or less responsible towards society for their role in terms of autonomy and accountability. Cooperation between universities and with the private sector (industry) is enhanced (joint research) and supported by governments in all countries (public–private partnerships and/or funding). Knowledge exchange and technology transfer are instruments commonly used to link up with society.

  New actors at the national level are entering the higher education scene, especially given their interest in the emerging knowledge society and technology transfer. In this respect, the role of the state has become one of a network manager. From this point of view, a new mode of governance has emerged: multi-actor, multi-level governance. This greater stakeholder scrutiny is forcing European universities to become more innovative and entrepreneurial. Amidst the rapidly changing European environment, universities are seeking new ways of adapting to the changes they are facing. In some circumstances, this involves adopting policies or practices from other systems; in others, it involves developing creative solutions to meet each country's unique circumstances.

- *Accountability.* One of the consequences of enhanced institutional autonomy has been greater accountability as well as more stringent and detailed procedures for quality assurance ('the rise of the evaluative state'). Greater institutional autonomy has meant higher education institutions exercising greater responsibility for their own management. This means that they have to redefine the ways in which they inform their stakeholders about their performances. Additional demands are placed on academic leadership, which in turn requires new modes of communication with and assistance from the decentralized units (faculties, schools, institutes, departments). New procedures and rules are being put in place.

The changes that are occurring today represent, in part, an effort to redress 'government failures' (Wolf, 1993) of the past. At the same time, the pace and reach of the changes now taking place raise the distinct possibility that policy-makers are fixing one problem by creating another. Markets breed 'market failures' and economists are quick to point out that universities are fundamentally different from the textbook firms that shape standard theories (Winston, 1999). If Europe is to succeed in its efforts to create both a Higher Education and a Research Area that will drive its economy in the years ahead, then striking a balance between these extremes will be crucial.

University governance reforms in Europe: the Lisbon Strategy approach

Europe needs excellence in its universities to optimize the processes that underpin the knowledge society and meet the target, set out in 2000 by the European Council in Lisbon, of becoming 'the most competitive and dynamic knowledge-based economy in the world, capable of sustainable economic growth with more and better jobs and greater social cohesion'. This commitment puts pressure on European universities to transform themselves into agents for increasing the competitiveness of national and regional economies. However, despite their crucial role in achieving the Lisbon goals, European universities are not yet in a position to deliver their full potential contribution:

> Knowledge and innovation are the engines of sustainable growth in Europe today, and universities are crucial for achieving the goals set out by the ... European Council. However, ... there are important weaknesses in the performance of European higher education institutions compared to those of our main competitors, notably the USA. Although the average quality of European universities is rather good, they are not in a position to deliver their full potential to boost economic growth, social cohesion and more and better jobs. The European Commission invites national decision makers to set out measures that would enable universities to play a full role in the Lisbon strategy. (Figel, 2005)

The Lisbon Strategy's call for curricula, governance, and funding reforms reflects not only the growing recognition of how important higher education is to economic and cultural prosperity, but also the belief that maintaining the status quo threatens Europe's dominance as a global higher education competitor. Policy makers express concern that gaps in key indicators like participation rates, gross enrolment ratios, and numbers of employed researchers are not closing and in some cases even widening.

European universities are the heart of the Europe of knowledge: 'Europe must strengthen the three poles of its knowledge triangle: education, research and. innovation. Universities are essential in all three' (CEC, 2005). Future growth and social welfare will rely increasingly on knowledge-intensive industries and services, and more and more jobs will require higher qualified personnel. Europe's universities face formidable challenges and ever-growing global competition. Far-reaching reforms are needed to enable

European universities to meet the challenges of the knowledge society and of globalization. Without a change in the governance and leadership of their institutions and systems, the European universities will not be able to address all the current technological, economic, and demographic challenges. Universities need not only to be responsive (to adapt to the changing environment) but also to be responsible for the common long-term interest of society (outside and inside the institutions).

The European Commission urged that modernization of the European universities should be prioritized (CEC, 2005). Its 2005 document emphasized the need for:

- *less regulation:*
  The over-regulation of university life hinders modernization and efficiency.
- *more autonomy:*
  In an open, competitive and moving environment, autonomy is a precondition for universities to be able to respond to society's changing needs and to take full account for those responses.
- *more funding for innovation:*
  Additional funding should primarily provide incentives and means to those universities (they exist in every system) and to those groups/individuals (they exist in each university) that are willing and able to innovate, reform and deliver high quality in teaching, research and services. This requires more competition-based funding in research and more output-related funding in education.
- *better leadership:*
  Empowering universities effectively to take and implement decisions by way of a leadership team with sufficient authority and management capacity, enough time in office and ample European/international experience. This is all the more important given the positive link between the quality of universities' leadership and output.

In 2006, a new document from the Commission (CEC, 2006) reinforced the same objectives:

Without real autonomy and accountability, universities will be neither really responsive nor innovative. In return for being freed from dysfunctional over-regulation and micro-management, universities need to recognize the importance of accountability and more professional management.

The Commission therefore suggested that:

Managing a university is as complex and socially as important as managing an enterprise with thousands of staff and an annual turnover in the hundreds of millions of euros. Member States should build up and reward management and leadership capacities within universities.

Consequently, the Commission recommended to universities:

- Take on greater responsibility for their own long-term financial sustainability and be more pro-active in diversifying their research funding portfolios by securing financial resources from a variety of sources, including those beyond the public sector;
- Establish stronger and sustainable partnerships with the business community through collaboration with industry on university-based research and technology initiatives;
- Exploit knowledge by sharing it with the business community and society at large and better communicate the relevance of their research activities and identify and implement models that allow co-funding of researchers' basic salary from other sources.

The Commission recommended to Member States that they:

- Adapt their legal frameworks at national and regional levels to allow universities to develop new models for governing their research activities, including a higher degree of autonomy and new ways of ensuring internal and external accountability;
- Adapt, if necessary, their legal frameworks at national and regional levels to allow universities to diversify their funding sources, including in the domains of procurement policies; to use offset funds for research; to enjoy tax breaks for endowment funding; to encourage researchers to create university research spin-offs and to apply their research results and patents;
- Allow and support universities to develop incentive mechanisms for a better exploitation of knowledge and wider sharing of research results and activities with society and SMEs [small and medium enterprises].

Additionally, the Bologna Process has broadened its perspective and connects with the Lisbon Strategy. In Bergen (2005) and in the last Bologna ministerial meeting in London (2007), ministries underlined the importance of developing strong universities that are diverse, adequately funded, autonomous and accountable, and strengthen Europe's attractiveness and competitiveness. In summary, universities need to adopt more entrepreneurial attitudes if they are to become more responsive to the demands of the knowledge society. But this requires a deep organizational change and, to make this possible, a new approach to governance.

Governance and organization: empirical results

The trends in university governance described above are present in the sample of universities considered in this study. In our data set of 27 universities drawn from seven countries, we can identify different types of universities depending on their: ownership, autonomy, governance model, organizational change, and some other characteristics (size, age, location, and so on), which to some extent influence both governance styles and entrepreneurialism. Our purpose has been to analyse these dimensions in each institution and identify the possible connections between these characteristics and their entrepreneurial behaviour. The aim of this analysis is to arrive at an 'entrepreneurial framework' or identify the 'entrepreneurial characteristics' that will allow us to predict the entrepreneurial attitude of one institution.

Defining universities in relation to entrepreneurialism

For practical reasons, the following definitions will be considered in this chapter:

1. Entrepreneurialism *broad-sense:* an institution able to adapt with flexibility to the changing environment; able to respond quickly to the needs of society offering the services that this society demands. *Flexibility and rapid response* are the key words to define entrepreneurialism in this broad sense.
2. Entrepreneurialism *strict-sense:* institutions that are able to be flexible and adapt rapidly to the environment but, in addition, are able to transform this environment by establishing permanent links mutually beneficial to society and to the business sector in particular. *A capacity for acting in the environment* is the additional key phrase for entrepreneurial universities in this strict sense.

Ownership

There are four wholly private universities in our sample: the University of Buckingham, Cardenal Herrera University, the University of Pereslavl, and the Academy of Hotel Management and Catering Industry (WSHIG). In spite of their private character, they are completely different in their basic traits, and consequently in their approach to entrepreneurialism.

The University of Buckingham is a very small teaching-orientated institution established two decades ago as the first non-public-funded British university. In principle, the typical criteria of entrepreneurialism do not fit for this institution. They do not pretend to be entrepreneurial in a strict sense, but they need to be (and they probably are) entrepreneurial in the sense of making efforts to attract students, many from abroad, able to pay the high fees the university charges.

> You can't run an independent university on fees alone. Buckingham has no other source of income, no endowment income, and it tries to survive on fees alone. The University does not have enough income and it is

desperately struggling to survive . . . There is little money to do research. (Buckingham case study)

Cardenal Herrera University is basically a teaching university owned by a religious association. Religious motivations are behind the creation of the University. The lack of diversity in the Spanish model of higher education impels this university (and other similar institutions) to try to be active in research, but the lack of resources, both human and financial, makes it difficult to develop research entrepreneurial activities in the strict sense. Nevertheless, the complete dependence on fees makes this university 'entrepreneurial' in attracting paying students.

The strategy is changing constantly. Some of the influential factors are: competition with public universities, the academic authorizations required by government bodies, and the uncertainty about the number of prospective students. The factors which affect private universities are based on the amount of resources, i.e. it is the students themselves who guarantee the minimum amount of revenue required to survive. (Cardenal Herrera case study)

The Academy of Hotel Management and Catering Industry is a completely different case. It is basically the personal project of an individual trying to meet an important social demand, in this case training in tourism-related activities. This is without doubt an entrepreneurial project that does not fit well into the typical idea of an entrepreneurial university.

The University of Pereslavl is also quite different from the rest of the private universities. In this case, the idea of founding a new university comes from an advanced research institute in the field of information and communication technologies (ICT). The university is also located in an area of high-tech industries. It is too young and it is probably too early to assess the results, but if it is successful, the University could become an active centre of entrepreneurialism in all senses.

The rest of the case study universities are public institutions, although there is a partial exception, the Trade Cooperative University of Moldova (TCUM), which is something like a 'joint venture' between the state and the association of consumer cooperatives:

The Trade Cooperative University of Moldova is an institution with collective form of organization of private type of propriety. All its patrimony is public and indivisible; it belongs to the Consumer Cooperatives of Moldova. TCUM is a departmental institution with double subordination: in administration and management of the patrimony is under the authority of the Central Union of Consumer Cooperatives of Moldova, but in questions of organizing the educational process is under the authority of the Ministry of Education, Youth and Sports. (TCUM case study)

The first conclusion we can draw from this sample of institutions is that the type of ownership, in Europe, is not related to entrepreneurialism in the strict sense as generally understood. On the contrary, universities in the private sector are even less entrepreneurial than the public ones, mainly due to the scarce resources for developing research and for establishing connections with the business sector. They have a strong dependence on fees for survival. Nevertheless, as a consequence of this dependence, all the private universities in our sample (and probably all such universities in Europe) are entrepreneurial in the sense of being educationally innovative in having to offer attractive courses in order to increase or maintain their only source of income.

Autonomy

Obviously, the private universities in our sample are fully autonomous, but the situation of public universities with regard to autonomy is quite different. The level of autonomy depends on state regulations, but this is not the only factor as we will see later.

Among the public universities, the UK universities have the more developed level of autonomy. UK universities have a long tradition of independence. At the beginning of the nineteenth century, traditional university systems changed around Europe and institutions became in most countries 'state institutions'. This did not happen in the UK and, consequently, UK universities are still ruled by private laws, whereas other public European universities are covered by public laws. One exception, in our sample, is the University of Jönköping in Sweden. This university is owned by a public foundation instead of being directly ruled by the state. It could be said that the University of Jönköping is a private institution owned by the state, although it could be considered a public institution with a special legal status. In any case, this makes it different from other Swedish universities:

> There is no set order for how and by whom decisions are to be made as it is in other Swedish state HEIs. Instead it is corporate law which is the guiding principle. There of course exist instructions to faculty boards, boards of admission and examination but they are much simpler than in other HEIs. (Jönköping case study)

The remaining Swedish universities also enjoy a high level of autonomy:

> The major change, affecting all HEIs in Sweden, which has influenced university operations and organization, was the reform in 1993. This reform opened up for more freedom of universities to decide about their own business, internal structure, decision-making bodies etc. (Lund case study)

Nevertheless, Swedish universities are more dependent on the state than UK universities. Tradition, more than legal status, is probably the reason for continuing to have important ties with the state.

On a third level, we have most of the other public universities. Finnish, Spanish, and Polish universities have equivalent levels of autonomy. In principle, universities are granted formal autonomy but the state interferes in many details of the universities' operations. In Finland, a rector stated:

> After all, it is the government that deals with the issues of Finnish universities and their legal aspects, the number of their degrees, their funding and rules and so on. So in a commercial sense the strategic latitude that a single university has is very small. (HSE, Finland case study)

And a Head of the Finance Office from the Helsinki School of Economics added:

> Now of course there's also the fact that funding can be used more freely. But the framework, which is quite tight, does still exist. So I don't know whether autonomy has really increased. Sometimes it even seems like it has decreased. (HSE, Finland case study)

Moldovan public universities probably have even less autonomy than universities in Finland, Spain, and Poland: rectors or vice-rectors are elected but they have to be approved by the Ministry of Education. A similar situation is perceived in Russian public universities, where 'Being a state institution, the SU-HSE is subordinated to the policies of the central Ministry of Education' (HSE, Russia case study).

Nevertheless, in countries with limited university autonomy, the real autonomy of each institution is to some extent dependent on the ability of the internal governing teams to take the lead. This is the case, for example, at the University of Lapland in Finland and the Technical University of Valencia (UPV) in Spain, where strong leadership was able to provide these universities with a higher level of real autonomy than the other universities in their respective countries. The Technical University of Valencia report says:

> The general opinion of the interviewees was that national and regional policies have some influence on the mission and strategy (for example, new study plans, research financing, etc.), but it is not a key factor. This means that these policies establish frameworks for action, but that the university has a great deal of room for manoeuvre when making decisions. Many people think that the university is reasonably independent from government policies. (UPV case study).

It is clear that there is a relationship between the level of autonomy and the capacity of universities to be entrepreneurial. Nevertheless, relationships are not linear. In principle, autonomy could be considered to be a necessary condition for entrepreneurialism. This is basically true, but some universities, like the University of Lapland and the Technical University of Valencia, seem to be able to take shortcuts and to behave as relatively entrepreneurial universities in spite of legal restrictions. In the first case, a young, small, relatively isolated and regional institution uses these limitations to develop a proactive character. As the Rector of the University of Lapland said:

> We've always been quite quick to react and change, we've been able to meet the needs of the external system and our internal objectives. So, we've always tried to act in such a way that our organization maximally supports the achievement of these objectives . . . And how this organization can also have an impact on this national negotiation system in such way that it actually has some influence. And we've carried out these changes quite flexibly on several occasions. This just goes to show that we're not stuck to any single model. (Lapland case study)

The case of the Higher School of Economics in Moscow is an example of an institution trying to be entrepreneurial where a lack of autonomy is perceived as an important inhibitor.

On the other hand, some universities that enjoy a high level of autonomy are not fully entrepreneurial in the *strict sense*. In some cases, traditional structures do not allow them to be more entrepreneurial, as is the case with the University of Lund: '[some centres] could be considered as being entrepreneurial, certain individuals in particular as well, but not really the whole university' (Lund case study). In other cases, it is the special characteristics of the institution that do not allow it to be more entrepreneurial. This is the case with the London School of Hygiene and Tropical Medicine (LSHTM), where the focus on specialization and the strong research orientation do not generate the need to be entrepreneurial in the *strict sense*. As the report on this institution states:

> The School is hardly entrepreneurial at all, however, in commercial matters. Staff are not interested in exploiting their research commercially; they see the outcomes of their research as producing social good; and they reject the opportunities to undertake well financed drug trialling for pharmaceutical companies preferring instead to do development screening of drugs for neglected diseases where poverty is a major factor. Consultancy, which was once a growing component of the School's budget, has been withdrawn to concentrate on research. (LSHTM case study)

A third example of a lack of entrepreneurialism in the *strict sense*, in spite of a high level of autonomy, is the University of Plymouth (although it is an institution that is quite entrepreneurial in the *broad sense*). In this case, the strong teaching approach, the large size of the institution, and its location in an underdeveloped area inhibit the development of stronger links with the business sector.

Governance style

At least three basic governance styles can be recognized in our sample of 27 universities:

1. *The collegial model.* This model is represented by universities with different levels of autonomy (and, consequently, different levels of state interference) but where internal decisions are taken mainly by academics. The public universities of Finland, Spain, Poland, Russia, and Moldova fit this model. In Finland and Spain, there are external bodies such as the Consultative Committee in Finland: 'a dozen local influential persons: representatives of municipalities, firms and local public organizations. They assemble twice a year to discuss current cooperation schemes and developing plans. The interviewees do not think that it would have a major influence on the action of the university' (Tampere case study). In Spain, the Social Council 'is partly made up of external members, [who approve] university budgets but otherwise play a very weak role' (UPV case study). However, these external bodies have no real power.

2. *The shared governance model.* This model is represented by universities with a high level of autonomy that have a strong governing board with lay membership governing the institution but, at the same time, where academics have a central role in academic matters. This is the dominant model in UK and Swedish universities. The University of Lund, for instance, 'is governed by a university board which is made up of representatives of the academic faculty, students and a majority of external members from public society or working life. The chairperson is an external member. The Rector is responsible for the management of university activities and [is] directly responsible to the board' (Lund case study). This is also the model in the private University of Buckingham in the UK, following the British tradition, and in the private University of Pereslavl in Russia, where: 'Operational management of the University is accomplished by the Rector. The Board of Trustees can delegate part of its authority to the Rector. Decision-making on the main managerial issues of the University is done by [the] Academic Council of the University chaired by the Rector. The Academic Council is elected by a general meeting of the University staff for a term of 5 years' (Pereslavl case study).

3. *The leadership model.* This model is represented by private universities where either the governing board (Cardenal Herrera in Spain) or the rector alone (WSHIG) has a dominant position in the governance of the institution. The report on WSHIG states: 'The Academy has a stable organizational and management structure: the founder and the owner (Professor Roman Dawid Tauber) has been its rector in the whole period. All key decisions concerning WSHIG are taken by [the] rector' (WSHIG case study).

Obviously, the above classification is to some extent simplistic. All kinds of mixed situations can be found depending on the legal status, traditions, or just the ability of governing boards or rectors to take the lead. In countries where the collegial model is still dominant, as mentioned earlier in this chapter, there is a tendency for the individual power of rectors to increase. In our sample, an example of tension between collegial bodies and leaders can be observed at the University of Tampere:

The role of the rector is changing although there was no fully clear conception of that. It was stated that the power of the rector has increased in the last five to ten years. At the same time the Board has lost its significance. It is seen that the Board handles too much routine issues. (Tampere case study)

Although not everybody agrees:

On the other hand, the Chancellor sees that because the leadership system at the university is based on assent and the rector is chosen inside of the university and he has as much authority as the faculties allow, his authority cannot be that strong. (Tampere case study)

This tendency towards stronger leadership is beginning to be seen in Spanish universities. In spite of having strong collegial legal structures, the growing complexity of institutions and the day-to-day realities are transforming the role of rectors and governing teams. While they are taking a more active role, collegial bodies are becoming less active. This transformation is happening in a quite natural way because most people on both sides understand that this is the only way to manage institutions that are becoming increasingly too complex. In some cases, the rector behaves as a real leader, as at the Technical University of Valencia:

what best defines the university is the mark its previous Rector left on it during his 18-year term of office. During his term of office, the University changed from being a selective centre of higher education to an entrepreneurial university of regional, and to a certain extent international, prestige and influence. However, this change took place without a defined plan or strategy approved by the university community. The plan was the brainchild of a rector with an entrepreneurial vision which was gradually implemented via an incentive system thanks to mechanisms which allowed the plan to be created. Against a backdrop of rigid governance systems which exist in all Spanish universities, more formal mechanisms to achieve the same goals would possibly have been much less effective in transforming the university. (UPV case study)

This trend is not perceived in Polish or Moldovan universities, where collegiality appears still to be very strong. For instance, the Adam Mickiewicz University (AMU):

has been ruled by the traditional spirit of collegiality rather than by any forms of corporatization. The managerial style of running the University at any level is virtually unknown; the idea of chief executive officers is absolutely alien to the university today. The vast majority of decisions are taken in a collegial and consensual manner. The culture of collegiality involves directly each senior faculty member; it consumes a huge amount of time, in most cases a few hours a week. (AMU case study).

In the Moldovan State University (MSU):

The highest governing body is the Senate, which elects the candidature of the Rector of the University to be approved by the Ministry of Education and confirmed by the Government for a five year period. The Rector is also the chairman of the Senate and is entitled to appoint Vice-Rectors. (MSU case study)

Another exception is the University of Jönköping in Sweden (a public institution but with a special legal status), which has a governance model that can be considered as 'shared' but with a certain bias towards 'leadership': 'The collegial influence is exercised through the Faculty board, which carries out quality control tasks but which is not involved in resource allocation as in other Swedish HEIs. This is in line with the foundation-corporation model' (Jönköping case study). On the other hand, the British private University of Buckingham follows the model of shared governance instead of the leadership model. In this case, the role of tradition is more important than ownership:

Essentially, Buckingham has a very traditional UK constitutional structure – a Council as its governing body, a Senate and three Schools. The Council has been very traditional in its approach and has contributed little in terms of strategy (other than a natural concern about the financial state of the University) or, as would have been the case in a comparable private US college/university, to fundraising. The Senate is similarly a traditional academic body. (Buckingham case study)

The strongest example of a leadership model in our sample is found in the Academy of Hotel Management and Catering Industries (WSHIG), where the same person is rector, founder, and owner. Nevertheless, even in this institution there is a very special kind of collegiality based on close personal relations:

The management team is small and very effective; it comprises the rector and three vice-rectors. All senior administrative staff, including vice-rectors, have been working for WSHIG for a decade or more. There is no Senate as the Academy is too small – but key academic decisions are confirmed by WSHIG's Scientific Board, meeting 3–4 times a year. The key for the success of WSHIG is the loyalty of its staff, both administrative and academic. Staff complain but keep working for WSHIG usually for many years, sometimes changing academic or administrative units every few years. Also senior academic staff, especially core full-time professors, have been employed for many years now. (WSHIG case study)

Conclusions regarding governance models are quite similar to those with regard to autonomy. At least in our sample, there is strong concordance between a high level of autonomy and a shared model of governance. It can be said that entrepreneurial universities (whether in a *broad* or a *strict* sense) have a shared or leadership model of governance. Again, this is a necessary but not sufficient condition for being fully entrepreneurial. The cases mentioned in the previous section (Lund, Plymouth, and LSHTM) can also be included here and for the same reasons. On the other hand, some universities with a collegial model have entrepreneurial traits (Lapland, Technical University of Valencia, Higher School of Economics in Moscow), but our data show that this governance model is an inhibitor of entrepreneurialism.

Organizational change

Most European universities have significantly changed in the last decade. Ten of the 27 universities in our sample have been established in the last decade and obviously change has been part of the daily life in these institutions. In addition, six universities are public universities in countries (Poland, Russia, and Moldova) where political and sociological changes have been so important that they have deeply affected universities in practically everything. Excluding these universities, only twelve institutions have not been subject to 'special circumstances' and the pace of change has mostly been motivated by internal decisions. This is the case of the older universities in Finland, Sweden, Spain, and the UK. We will concentrate on this last group of universities to analyse to what extent change has been motivated by the objective of adapting to the new environment.

Finnish universities are in general trying to adapt to a new situation but they appear not to be able to overcome some of the organizational conflicts. Although they have a vision of becoming leading universities, as is the case at the Helsinki School of Economics ('The "next strategic leap" is to be a leading research based school of economics in Europe'), there are structural difficulties in making the necessary changes:

> in the current university administration system the possibilities to develop management system are limited. Critique towards management system is quite harsh especially among the top administration. The system is seen [to be] incoherent. The attitude becomes quite clear: leadership and administration should be strengthened, clarified and rationalized. (HSE, Finland case study)

Similar problems are found in the University of Tampere:

> it is seen that the administration system and culture at the university as a whole is too heavy, bureaucratic and controlling of formal processes. But it was also noticed that the administration system is from an era of a teaching university and there are plans and intentions to create a more flexible system also for the research task. (Tampere case study)

The situation in Swedish universities is not much different regarding the will to change, as seen at the University of Umeå: 'The University is self-determined, and competing in an international arena. There is emphasis on strategic positioning. There is competition for student recruitment'. On the other hand, there are still 'many bureaucratic and managerial obstacles' and cultural conflicts ('Culture is an inhibitor. There is too much comfort. There is a rigid academic culture in the humanities') (Umeå case study). Other Swedish universities have a more traditional and stable structure, such as the Royal Institute of Technology (KTH):

> [KTH is] often seen as grey, technical, and predominantly male with a strong relationship to large Swedish industries. While this relationship is good, it contrasts with a less developed interaction between the university and SMEs and spin-off firms. This is important because the university itself wishes to be entrepreneurial, to be more than 'a hotel for faculty', and to be an active participant in both national and regional innovation systems. Some at KTH expect that this will involve new types of competition and incentives. (KTH case study)

The University of Lund has traditionally had a decentralized model: 'The organization of Lund University is decentralized. In many ways, the separate schools or faculties function like several small universities under the umbrella of the Lund University brand' (Lund case study). Nevertheless, it is trying to build a stronger core in order to become more responsive as an institution: 'There are indications, however, that some kind of "mild centralization" is attempted at present in the effort to profile and position the university further as one organization' (Lund case study).

Changes have been more frequent in British universities in recent years. To some extent they have been the avant-garde in Europe in taking the lead in adapting to a new context. This capacity for a faster response is a consequence of the greater autonomy and more flexible governance of British universities. The three public universities in our sample have changed markedly in the last few years. It is remarkable that the only private university is the exception to this trend, which has experienced no relevant change.

The structure of the University of Plymouth 'was overhauled in 2002, a process driven by a new Vice-Chancellor'. In this teaching-orientated university, reorganization has provoked some complaints: 'There are complaints from schools that the faculties appear to add little value, as the centre involves itself in relatively minor decisions'. The managerial model is also criticized:

> Sometimes there are too many layers and bureaucracy: proposals have to go through the deans and then to the VC. The middle level sometimes gets muddled up in unnecessary bureaucracy. This makes decision-making slow. It also gets in the way of responding to client need: you might lose your clients if you are responding too slowly. (Plymouth case study)

Key changes to the management of the London School of Hygiene and Tropical Medicine (LSHTM) 'were introduced in the late 1980s by a Dean who operated very much in a chief executive mode. He introduced the concept of a Senior Management Team (SMT), which has continued to be the decision-making body in the School' (LSHTM case study). These changes allowed the LSHTM to be flexible and proactive in responding to a changing external environment, and to respond effectively to external pressures. The role of the SMT has been a key aspect in implementing change:

> The SMT is the major strategic driver in the School though it consults widely. The SMT generally works in a strongly consensual way. Above the SMT is a Board of Management, a primarily lay body which stops us becoming too introverted and instead looks at changes that might be coming up externally. (LSHTM case study)

Extensive reforms in British higher education and the appointment of a new vice-chancellor in 1988 were the sparks that initiated a profound process to transform the University of Nottingham:

> from being a middle of the road, slightly unambitious institution and drive it up the then emerging university 'league tables' by increasing its size and scope and national and international visibility. The first step was to create an internal organizational structure that would enable the university to meet the challenges of increasing stringency in core funding from the HEFCE and to respond positively to the opportunities being created in the national higher education system. In 1995 a new streamlined committee and management structure was introduced. Day to day management issues at the University are the responsibility of the Management Board, which meets weekly. The Management Board is a sub-committee of the Strategy and Planning Committee. The University planning processes aim to strike a balance between consultation, bottom-up initiative and top-down strategic guidance, with emphasis on a team approach. Once the central management group has set policies and budgets, a high degree of discretionary authority is devolved to local managers to deliver their aims within available resources and University policies and quality control procedures. (Nottingham case study)

Another key to success has been the policy of 'grouping together of members of academic staff from different disciplines but with shared research interests [which] has been a major feature and key aim of Nottingham's research development'. (Nottingham case study)

The situation in Spanish universities is comparable to that of universities in Finland. In both countries, there were important changes and improvements in higher education; universities are on the right track towards more independence, autonomy, and entrepreneurialism but they still have strong links with old governance models, which prevents them from taking off. Complaints are also similar in the two countries. The Technical University of Valencia (UPV) considers itself as a modern university with an entrepreneurial attitude and very dynamic in its relationships with the external world. Generally speaking, this is true, but as examples of 'the old links', people in the University made the following statements: 'There is a lot of bureaucracy within the system, it is an important obstacle'; 'The governing team cannot take decisions. It has always to convince everybody, but people always ask for something in exchange. Everything could be speeded up if this situation changed'; and 'The university has many rules but no procedures'. Someone with academic staff status wished for 'modifications in the civil servant status of the academic staff'. Graduates criticize the old-fashioned pedagogical model: 'Teaching is very theoretically oriented and out of touch with the real world. Teaching should be more oriented to the labour market, especially in the long-cycle studies' (UPV case study). Opinions in other, less dynamic universities are similar but are even more critical. In conclusion, universities are moving in the right direction but old traditions are still very strong.

Other institutional specificities

We have considered above governance and organizational factors that affect entrepreneurialism. Reviewing the reports of the 27 universities we can also identify particular characteristics in some universities that are the spark or the inhibitor to developing entrepreneurial behaviour (see Table 2).

1. *Size and age.* In some cases, it appears that the size and age of an institution, which are to some extent connected, can be relevant in defining institutional attitudes. For instance, the Universities of Lapland, Jönköping, Jaume I, Miguel Hernandez, Pereslavl, and WSHIG have a very proactive approach. They are new universities, relatively small, and with the dominant requirement of finding a niche. On the other hand, old and large universities find it more difficult to develop dynamic behaviour. The University of Valencia and the University of Lund are the oldest universities in our sample. This is an inhibitor to entrepreneurialism in both institutions. In the case of the University of Valencia, together with the Adam Mickiewicz University, size (around 50,000 students) is probably an additional reason for being slow to respond to the changing environment.

2. *Location.* The universities in our sample are very diverse in terms of location. There are two interesting cases in this sense: the Universities of Lapland and Umeå. Both are universities located in the very north of these Nordic countries. Isolation has provoked in these universities a special strength in looking for a niche, and it seems that both have found one: 'Umeå University perhaps has been more entrepreneurial than many of its fellow Swedish universities due in part to its geographic isolation. On the northern frontier of Europe, they need to work hard or they will be forgotten' (Umeå case study). Other cases are perhaps not so extreme, but location also plays an important role. New universities in middle-size towns, such as the Universities of Jaume I (in Castellón, Spain), Miguel Hernandez (in Elche, Spain), and Jönköping (in Sweden), probably receive a special impulse from the local environment that encourages them to take a proactive attitude as engines of regional development. A different case is the University of Pereslavl. Here, a high-tech industry environment is one of the decisive factors for its more dynamic approach than many other Russian universities.

Table 2 Analysis of the case study universities' typologies

Name	Status	Age	Size	Location	Research Ranking	Focus	Scope	Autonomy	Governance	Change	Entrepreneurial
Helsinki School of Economics	Public	Old	4 000	City	>500	**Business**	**National/International**	Formal-medium	Collegial	Medium	Attempting to be
University of Tampere	Public	Modern	15 000	Town	>500	Comprehensive	Regional	Formal-medium	Collegial	Medium	Attempting to be
University of Lapland	Public	**Young**	4 500	**Isolated**	>500	**Multidisciplinary**	**Regional**	**Formal-high**	Collegial	New	To some extent
University of Lund	Public	**Very old**	30 000	Town	**90**	Comprehensive	**National/International**	Wide	**Shared**	Strong	Some parts
University of Umeå	Public	**Modern**	19 000	**Isolated**	**201–300**	Comprehensive	**Regional/National**	Wide	**Shared**	Strong	To some extent
Royal Institute of Technology, KTH	Public	Old	14 000	City	**201–300**	**Technical**	**National/International**	Wide	**Shared**	Strong	To some extent
University of Jönköping	**Foundation**	**Young**	8 000	**Town**	>500	Comprehensive	**Regional/National**	Full	**Shared-Leadership**	New	**Strict sense**
Technical University of Valencia	Public	Modern	36 000	City	**301–400**	**Technical**	**Regional/International**	**Formal-high**	Collegial	Strong	Some parts
University of Valencia	Public	**Very old**	**52 000**	City	**301–400**	Comprehensive	Regional	Formal-medium	Collegial	Medium	Weak
University of Alicante	Public	Modern	26 000	Town	>500	Comprehensive	Regional	Formal-medium	Collegial	Medium	Weak
University Jaume I	Public	**Young**	13 000	**Town**	>500	Comprehensive	Regional	Formal-medium	Collegial	New	Attempting to be
University Miguel Hernandez	Public	**Young**	12 000	**Town**	>500	Comprehensive	Regional	Formal-medium	Collegial	New	Attempting to be
University Cardenal Herrera	**Private**	Young	6 500	City	>500	Comprehensive	Regional	Full	Leadership	New	Broad sense
University of Nottingham	Public	Old	30 000	Town	**79**	Comprehensive	**National/International**	Full	**Shared**	Strong	**Strict sense**

University of Plymouth	Public	Modern	29 000	Town	>500	Comprehensive	Regional	Full	**Shared**	Strong	Broad sense
LSHTM	Public	Old	1 700	City	**201–300**	**Medical**	**International**	Full	**Shared**	Strong	Broad sense
University of Buckingham	**Private**	Modern	**700**	Town	>500	Comprehensive	**International**	Full	**Shared**	Weak	Broad sense
Poznan University of Economics	Public	Old	13 000	City	>500	Business	Regional	No data	No data	Medium	Weak
Adam Mickiewicz University	Public	Old	**53 000**	City	>500	Comprehensive	Regional	Formal-medium	Collegial	Medium	Weak
WSHIG	**Private**	**Young**	1 500	City	>500	**Hotel Manage.**	Regional	Full	**Leadership**	New	Broad sense
BIBIM-Irkutsk State University	Public	Young-Old	2 300	City	>500	Business	Regional	Scarce	Collegial	Strong	Attempting to be
Higher School of Economics	**Private**	**Young**		City	>500	Business		Scarce	Collegial	New	Attempting to be
University of Pereslavl	**Private**	**Young**	**Small**	**Town**	>500	**ICT**		**Full**	**Shared**	New	Broad sense
Moldova State University	Public	Modern	23 000	City	>500	Comprehensive		Scarce	Collegial	Medium	Weak
Trade Cooperative Univ. Moldova	**Found-ation**	Young	2 700	City	>500	Business		Scarce	Collegial	New	Weak
Academy of Economic Studies	Public	Young	14 000	City	>500	Business		Scarce	Collegial	New	Weak
State University of Bălţi	Public	Modern	10 000	Town	>500	Comprehensive	Regional	Scarce	Collegial	Strong	Weak

Note:
The bold type face indicates the particular characteristics 'that are the spark or the inhibitor to developing entrepreneurial behaviour' in an instituution.

3. *Prestige, scope, and focus.* There are also external factors that may influence institutional attitudes. These factors may not be precise: their borders are blurred and they can be both a cause and effect of entrepreneurial behaviour. With all these reservations, let us discuss some of these factors in relation to our case study universities.

The Shanghai Jiao Tong Ranking is a list of the 500 most productive research universities in the world. With all the caution with which such rankings should be considered, this list provides a simple view of research capacity and consequently of institutional prestige. Not surprisingly, probably the most entrepreneurial university in our sample, the University of Nottingham, is also the highest ranked (position 79). The University of Lund (position 90) is also in the top 100. The University of Umeå, the Royal Institute of Technology (KTH), and the London School of Hygiene and Tropical Medicine are in the top 300. Finally, both universities of the city of Valencia are in the top 400. No other university in our sample is included in the list. Research productivity does not necessarily make these universities more active but it is an indicator of the potential that these universities have for becoming active agents in the production and dissemination of research.

In addition to research potential, the particular institutional focus may also be relevant. The Royal Institute of Technology and the Technical University of Valencia, both of which have a focus on engineering, have a unique advantage in having closer relationships with industries and in being agents in economic development. Something similar may be happening in the Helsinki School of Economics, the Poznan University of Economics, the BIBIM-Irkutsk State University, the Higher School of Economics in Moscow, WSHIG, and the Trade Cooperative University of Moldova. Universities focused on business studies have, in principle, a greater chance of having links with the outside world. The LSHTM is an interesting case of how a high level of specialization, combined with a high academic level, can provide excellent opportunities for developing a specific and beneficial niche. WSHIG's focus on the hospitality industry also offers the opportunity to find an entrepreneurial niche. In a similar sense, the University of Pereslavl, which focuses on ICT, is building a special platform full of possibilities. An innovative way of developing a special character is provided by the University of Lapland, where 'there are no specified disciplinary focus areas. The university has concentrated on thematic approach. The research strategy which is under construction will also emphasize the multi-disciplinarity and the north theme'. (Lapland case study)

The universities in our sample have a regional, national, or international scope. In most cases, having a regional scope is not an intended objective of the institution but a consequence of its own reality. In others, such as the Universities of Lapland, Plymouth, Jaume I, and Miguel Hernandez, it seems that the regional scope forms the challenge for institutional development. Other universities have an international orientation, although for different reasons: Nottingham and Lund because of their recognized research capacity, LSHTM because of its intrinsically international focus, and Buckingham because of its need to look for international students. Others, such as the Technical University of Valencia, the Royal Institute of Technology in Stockholm, and the Helsinki School of Economics use their specific focus and prestige to try to be active in the international arena, both in research and consultancy and in attracting international students.

The entrepreneurial framework: some conclusions

In the previous sections, we have analysed the organizational and governance structure of 27 European universities with the aim of identifying a framework to define the structural conditions that facilitate entrepreneurialism in universities – that is, to create a framework that is able to predict the entrepreneurial character of an institution.

In analysing the 27 universities in our sample, we found the following:

1. *Full autonomy* is a condition *sine qua non* for entrepreneurialism in the *broad sense*, but it is not sufficient of itself to generate entrepreneurialism in the *strict sense*. All the fully autonomous universities in our sample (private universities, the UK public universities, and the University of Jönköping) are entrepreneurial in the *broad sense*. Private universities need to be entrepreneurial in the *broad sense* because their survival depends on their capacity to be flexible, to offer 'clients' what they need, even to have a vision for anticipating what is going to be demanded in the future. The University of Pereslavl and WSHIG are good examples. The University of Buckingham and Cardenal Herrera University are in a slightly different position, perhaps due to their having a more ideological background, but in any case they have to fight to get students and offer them the best services. Among the public universities of this group, the University of Plymouth could also be considered entrepreneurial only in the *broad sense*. This university has been very active in teaching and learning and it is attracting many students, but the lack of a robust research orientation impedes its becoming an entrepreneurial university in the *strict sense*. The remaining universities that enjoy full autonomy – Nottingham, Jönköping, and LSHTM – are, without doubt, entrepreneurial universities. The case of the LSHTM is peculiar and deserves some reflection. This institution is not very interested in commercial links, probably because it does not need them. Research and charitable funds make this a very well-financed institution. Bearing in mind the focus of this institution (medical studies for poor countries), this is probably the smartest way of being entrepreneurial. Perhaps the proclivity of charities and foundations to provide generous support to this university is due to the lack of commercial entrepreneurialism.

2. *Shared governance* is an important condition for entrepreneurialism in both senses but it is not sufficient of itself. Not all of the universities with

these models of governance can be considered fully entrepreneurial. The three Swedish universities are a good example. They have shared governance like the UK universities and they have wide autonomy but less than in the UK. The three universities claim that they are just becoming entrepreneurial, as in Umeå ('Entrepreneurialism is not yet general but it is growing'), or that some parts of the university are entrepreneurial, as in Lund.

3. Universities without full autonomy and with collegial models of governance are not (and probably cannot be) fully entrepreneurial. In our sample, the Finnish and Spanish universities, which share a governance model and limited autonomy, are in a similar position with regard to entrepreneurialism. On the one hand, all of them have accepted that entrepreneurialism is a goal to be reached. At least, at institutional level there is no reluctance towards entrepreneurialism. Nevertheless, there are still two kinds of impediments to developing a more entrepreneurial behaviour. On the other hand, links with the state are still too strong: 'We have more prohibitions to make revenues than instruments to make revenues. You can pretend to act entrepreneurially, but if it is unclear who has the power and responsibility within the higher education system, entrepreneurialism is impossible' (HSE, Finland case study). In addition, the culture has not changed enough, especially at the academic staff level: 'The structures of the system and the university can be barriers but the real reasons and conditions behind that [the lack of entrepreneurialism] are attitudinal' (Tampere case study). In spite of these limitations, the Finnish and Spanish universities are moving more or less quickly towards becoming entrepreneurial.

4. Finally, in some other cases the confluence of several factors, such as a lack of full autonomy, the predominance of collegial models of governance, and a tremendous increase in teaching activities as a consequence of a dramatic increase in student numbers, does not permit universities to develop entrepreneurial activities, either in a broad or in a strict sense. The public Polish and Moldovan universities conform to this situation.

What happens when there is no entrepreneurial framework? What happens when institutions as a whole are not entrepreneurial because the legal frameworks are too restrictive, the external conditions are not favourable or just because the their traditions do not encourage entrepreneurialism? Universities respond to these situations in at least two, sometimes complementary, ways:

1. *Entrepreneurialism through satellites.* Universities with a very traditional core, without a favourable legal framework for entrepreneurialism but with a strong potential (due to their particular approach, their research capacity, and so on), can adopt the solution of not changing the institutional core (because it is legally or culturally difficult, even impossible in the short term), instead creating satellites around the university that can adopt an entrepreneurial outlook. This is the case, for instance, with the Technical University of Valencia:

It could be said that the UPV is not an entrepreneurial institution (this is, in fact, true of any Spanish university). However, it is full of entrepreneurs who are relatively free to work as they wish within the UPV. They have been helped by the creation of independent satellite centres which have become the driving force behind entrepreneurial activity at the UPV, yet the institution's core, and to a great extent, the university's formal teaching methods, are still highly conventional and insist on using outdated practices. This is a clear case of 'institutional schizophrenia', i.e. the two live together in harmony as long as there are no clashes between the two cultures. This balance has been maintained up until now thanks to the previous rector's leadership. (UPV case study)

To give an example of such satellites, the Centre for Continuing Education in this university is like a private university within a public one, delivering all kinds of short courses (shorter than one year) to more than 35,000 students and charging the full cost to them.

2. *Entrepreneurialism through individuals*. Another alternative that non-entrepreneurial universities adopt when the potential exists in some individuals is to develop individual entrepreneurialism. This behaviour (which can also be found in the model of satellite entrepreneurialism) requires that individuals who have the capacity to undertake entrepreneurial activities be granted some level of freedom from the institution. The case of the Adam Mickiewicz University is a good example: 'entrepreneurial behaviour takes place mostly at the level of particular professors, governance structures seem to have no influence on entrepreneurialism' (AMU case study). The case of the LSHTM is similar:

The School provides a very clear example of academic entrepreneurialism: it generates 79% of its income from non-HEFCE sources and 63% from research; its academic community is highly innovative in winning research grants and contracts and engaging in wide ranging partnerships with external bodies; it takes financial and academic risks in tackling research projects on important and high profile public issues. (LSHTM case study)

It is evident from our analysis that the trend towards a more entrepreneurial attitude of universities is unstoppable. In all types of universities and in all countries the trend is clear – universities are increasingly becoming more responsive to social and economic demands. They are transforming their structures to be more flexible and faster to respond to these demands. When the circumstances, legal or economic, do not allow them to better adapt to the new situation, new ways of entrepreneurialism are embraced. The creation of 'entrepreneurial units' inside the university and the individual initiative of the most active members of the academia are classic examples. Probably, in the future these different paths will converge towards similar ends.

7
Entrepreneurialism and private higher education in Europe

Marek Kwiek

Introduction

It is difficult to analyse private universities in Europe (including those that are part of the EUEREK case studies) in the context of entrepreneurialism in the form the concept has emerged in the basic literature on the subject and available case studies. The private sector in higher education in Europe, with several exceptions (e.g. Portugal and Spain) – from the point of view of both numbers of institutions, share of enrolments in the sector, and study areas offered – has been an educational phenomenon of the transition countries. In some countries (e.g. Sweden, Belgium, and the Netherlands), nominally private institutions are funded in practice with public money, in various forms and under different umbrellas.

At the same time, the conceptual framework currently used to analyse entrepreneurialism in higher education seems somehow restricted in use to public sector institutions, and rightly so. Very few scholars ever refer to private institutions in their discussions of academic entrepreneurship. And if they do, they often mean selected top US universities (as Clark refers to Stanford and MIT in *Sustaining Change in Universities* – but in the context of public institutions briefly studied, such as the University of Michigan at Ann Arbor, UCLA, North Carolina State University, and Georgia Institute of Technology: Clark, 2004a: 133–66; Clark discusses also the Catholic University of Chile, *ibid*.: 110–21). Clark's (1998) classic five case studies in *Creating Entrepreneurial Universities* were all about European *public* universities and the only one that stood out – Chalmers University of Technology in Sweden – had indeed 'opted-out' of the Swedish public education system but has remained funded by the state. In Europe, not only is the experience of private higher education very limited, but the emergent concepts related to entrepreneurialism have derived from analytical work on the public sector and have rarely touched on the private sector. Shattock (2004b) and Williams (2004b) applied a concept of 'entrepreneurialism' to (somehow alien) universities in transition countries – in Russia. But again they were public universities. Sporn (2001), while analysing 'adaptive universities', focused on four public (the University of Michigan at Ann Arbor, UC Berkeley, St. Gallen Universität in Switzerland, and Wirtschaftsuniversität Wien in Austria) but also on two private institutions, including New York University and a vocationally orientated university in Europe, Università Bocconi in Milan.

This chapter is based, in more theoretical terms, on the conceptual work on 'entrepreneurial', 'enterprising', and 'proactive' universities by Clark (1998, 2001, 2004a, 2004b, 2005), 'self-reliant' and 'enterprising' – as well as, more generally, 'successful' – universities by Shattock (2000, 2003, 2004a, 2004b, 2005) and Williams (2004b), and Sporn's (1999a, 1999b, 2001) notion of 'adaptive' universities. In empirical terms, it is based on case studies of entrepreneurialism in universities drawn from the EUEREK study on entrepreneurialism in private institutions within the context of what Clark, Shattock, Williams, and Sporn suggest for the study of public institutions[1].

The EUEREK case studies of private institutions included the University of Buckingham (UK), Jönköping University (Sweden), TCUM – Trade Cooperative University of Moldova (Moldova), UCH – the Cardenal Herrera University (Spain), WSHIG – the Academy of Hotel Management and Catering Industry (Poland), and the University of Pereslavl (Russia). They are all relatively new institutions, with almost all of them being founded in the 1990s – in the UK (1976), Poland (1993), Russia (1993, transformed from a state-funded think tank founded in 1984), Sweden (1994, one of three 'foundation' universities), Moldova (1993), and Spain (2000). Almost all are located outside of capital cities. The reasons for founding them varied, from being political/ideological (UK), an individual's passion (Poland), political/regional considerations (Sweden, Russia), and religious interests (Spain). What is crucial from the perspective of entrepreneurialism is that they represent, in general, a fundamental reliance on tuition fees as a source of income and a limited reliance on, and access to, external research funding (the exception is Sweden)[2]. Small research groups are formed in the UK and Spanish examples but no major financial impact attributable to them is actually reported. Also no endowment income is reported, and sometimes there is a strong reliance on bank loans (Poland, UK). In almost all cases (especially in interviews), such characteristic expressions as 'to survive', 'survival', 'uncertainty about the future', occur. The Spanish EUEREK case study confirms that private institutions can regard themselves as entrepreneurial but there are discrepancies between descriptions (and feelings) expressed by academic staff on the one hand and managers, rectors, or deans on the other. With such small exceptions, private institutions view themselves as less entrepreneurial than public ones. In Poland, Russia, and Moldova, no feelings about being specifically entrepreneurial were reported – instead, there are references to being 'innovative', 'unique', and so on (especially in comparison with some old-style public institutions). Another common feature is that they are very small or relatively small institutions within their respective national higher education systems (of a size from a few hundred students in the UK and Russia to a few thousand students in Moldova, Poland, Sweden, and Spain). In most of the case studies, they are vocationally orientated and have small research ambitions (and, at the same time, small research funding opportunities). Often, they are born out of visions and ambitions of entrepreneurial individuals (academics and non-academics alike in Poland and Russia).

Regarding the growth of the private sector generally, as Levy notes, the twentieth century norm and persisting public norm is state funding of public universities (and overwhelmingly private sources of funding for private institutions). State subsidies for private institutions are rare and the examples of India, Belgium, and the Netherlands (as well as Swedish 'foundation universities') may call into question the designation of private (Levy, 2006: 10). The global demographics of private higher education is such that the major centre of the sector is East Asia, with about 80% of all students enrolled in private universities in Japan, South Korea, Taiwan, and the Philippines; in the United States, surprisingly, only 20%; in Western Europe, on average 10% or much less; in Latin America, over 50% in Brazil, Mexico, Colombia, Peru, and Venezuela; and finally in the transition countries, and some post-Soviet republics – where the most rapid growth took place after 1989 – up to 30% (on the private sector in Europe, see in particular two recent fundamental edited volumes: *The Rising Role and Relevance of Private Higher Education in Europe*, edited by Wells et al., 2007; and *Private Higher Education in Post-Communist Europe: In Search of Legitimacy*, edited by Slantcheva and Levy, 2007). As Levy puts it, 'where public budgets do not meet the still rapidly growing demand for higher education, students pay for alternatives' (Levy, 2002: 4) – and this is what happened in several transition countries. In most of them, both public and private higher education enrolments in general, and the share of the private sector in overall enrolments in particular, have changed dramatically over the last 15 years. While Western Europe has not in general witnessed the emergence (or substantial strengthening, depending on the country) of the private sector in higher education, in several post-communist transition countries in Europe, for a variety of reasons, the private sector emerged as a tough competitor to the most often traditional, elitist, faculty-centred, and quite often inaccessible public sector. The differences between the transition countries are significant, however; while in Croatia and the Slovak Republic private institutions enrol as few as 3.0–4.6% of the countries' student bodies, the private sectors in Estonia, Poland, and Romania enrol almost one-third of all students. Other countries such as Bulgaria, Hungary, and Russia have enrolments of about 15% (Slantcheva and Levy, 2007: 3)[3].

The diversified funding base: possible sources of income

There are several ways in which the case studies can be considered. Sporn discusses five factors enhancing adaptation at specialized European universities that lead in five directions: externally focused mission, differentiated structure, collegial management, institutional autonomy, and diversified funding (Sporn, 2001: 27); Shattock discusses six key words highlighting the characteristics that successful universities have to demonstrate: they are competitiveness, opportunism, income generation and cost reduction, relevance, excellence, and reputation (Shattock, 2000: 96–103). We could discuss the private sector represented in the case studies in the context of the two above sets of features, but we will base our further analysis on Clark's 'pathways to transformation', revisiting his classic formulations. Clark analysed five (entrepreneurial, innovative, enterprising) European universities in action, transforming themselves over a period of 10–15 years, within a common conceptual structure. In brief, according to Clark (1998, 2004a), the entrepreneurial universities studied – universities systematically seeking to transform themselves – show five elements that differentiate them from others and which form an 'irreducible minimum': a strengthened steering core, an expanded developmental periphery, a diversified funding base, a stimulated academic heartland, and an integrated entrepreneurial culture (Clark, 1998: 5). Clark's criteria are organizational characteristics rather than definitions. The five elements, or generalized pathways of university transformations, according to Clark:

> rise up from the realities of particular institutions to highlight features shared across a set of universities, but at the same time they still allow for local variation . . . Four elements are highly structural: we observe them in tangible offices, budgets, outreach centres, and departments. Only the more ephemeral element of institutional idea, floating in the intangible realm of intention, belief, and culture, is hard to pin down. Emphasizing manifest structures helps greatly in explaining the development of organized social systems . . . Significant change in universities has definite organizational footing. (Clark, 1998: 128)

Let us begin with the diversified funding base of entrepreneurial universities. There are three streams of income: mainline support from government, funds from governmental research councils, and all other sources lumped together by Clark as 'third-stream income' (Clark, 2004a: 77). A widening of the financial base becomes essential for public universities, and discretionary funds are particularly important for university transformations (Clark, 1998: 6).

Transformations in funding at public universities in the last twenty years have been towards the second and the third streams of income. In the specific case of European private institutions, it is crucial to underscore the role of the third stream (all other, largely non-governmental, sources of income), as most of them in Europe are cut off from major forms of governmental funds. Private institutions in Europe find it hard to be entrepreneurial, and to have entrepreneurially minded academics – because their faculty and academic units do not compete globally or nationally for outside research funding. And the role of competition with others – institutions and individual academics alike – is fundamental to the entrepreneurial character of an academic institution. We mean here both internal competition (for research and other development funds) and external competition for other outside funds. At entrepreneurial universities, a considerable element of managerial practice is devoted to managing competing units (and academics) in terms of human resources, non-core external finance, and the resulting tensions between academic units, between the centre and departments, through resource allocation utilizing, for example, various top-slicing and cross-subsidizing techniques. With competitive research funding available in entrepreneurial universities, as most case studies confirm, there are no limits to the academic financial expectations, and inventing and re-inventing fair and transparent funding formulae for departments and the centre are critical: if procedures are non-transparent, or unfair to some academic units, management loses a lot of time and energy in managing tensions which in other circumstances would not appear.

From the perspective of entrepreneurialism, a negative aspect to the development of the private institutions studied is their status as teaching institutions only. Case studies of Polish and Russian (as well as Macedonian and Ukrainian, outside of the EUEREK project) – private – entrepreneurially minded universities show that the road to excellence in research is difficult to follow, especially with external funding being scarce at the beginning, but the prestige and reputation of an institution accumulates when significant research is being done, including especially internationally relevant research. Only a few private institutions in Poland have reached that level – but today they have the best graduates and the top PhD students (in the Polish context, these institutions are allowed to offer PhD studies in selected areas, in acknowledgement of the quality of the core staff they employ and the high national rating of their research output; WSHIG, being a vocational institution, does not have research ambitions). Not surprisingly, investing in research brings more, and especially better, students to these institutions. The access of these private institutions to public subsidies is very limited and private R&D investments in private higher education institutions are marginal (again the Swedish case is exceptional and testifies to different senses of 'privateness' of higher education – at Jönköping University, the level of public subsidies is equal to that of public universities; in the Russian case of Pereslavl, public research funding is provided for its research part, the Institute of Programming Systems of the Russian Academy of Sciences).

In more general terms, the financial diversification of an institution is also healthy academically: the general rule is simple – as Clark put it, 'it is better to have more money than less', or elsewhere: 'more income is always needed:

universities are expensive and good universities are very expensive' (Clark, 1998: 26). The diversified funding base of an entrepreneurial university means a portfolio of patrons (national and international, private and public, long- and short-term) to share inevitable rising costs. Entrepreneurial universities aggressively seek third-stream sources, and it has become a very powerful trend in the Netherlands, the UK, Sweden, and Finland, as well as in several transition countries including Poland. Internal university reforms and restructuring, including closures and mergers of academic units, are increasingly 'finance-driven' (rather than, for example, 'equity driven'). Third-stream income is becoming crucial for public institutions; some components are also fundamental for the vitality (development or survival) of private institutions.

The case studies in Clark (1998) from the University of Warwick in the UK, including Shattock's 'earned income policy', and from Twente University in the Netherlands, are crucial to understanding the phenomenon of entrepreneurialism because they demonstrate the importance of all academic units being involved in seeking external funding for research (consulting, patents and licences, short courses, and from fees paid by international students). Separate units increasingly become separate small academic and business units, 'rewarded' and 'punished' for their entrepreneurialism (as Williams noted, 'managers who take risks and are successful are rewarded. Failure and passivity are penalized' (Williams, 2004a: 87)). The culture of entrepreneurialism, an irreducible element of entrepreneurial organizations according to Clark, means that virtually all units are involved, including the social sciences and the humanities. In Poland and other transition countries, by contrast, most entrepreneurial units were social science departments only – especially political sciences, sociology, psychology, and business-related (but not strictly economic) areas. The number of private institutions rose from 3 in 1991 to 250 in 2002, 301 in 2005, and 315 in 2006 (GUS, 2006: 20), of which the vast majority were economics related. Since the beginning of the 1990s, the private sector has changed the educational landscape in Poland beyond recognition: in the academic year 2006/07, almost one-third of the 2 million student body (32%) chose private higher education institutions[4]. The Warwick example of financial management shows that what is crucial is to look outside the university for opportunities and to regard academic units from a financial as well as an academic perspective as if they were small business units.

The possible new sources of income for entrepreneurial universities in Europe include support from other public agencies, support from large business firms, engagement with small- and medium-sized firms, philanthropic foundations, professional associations, university endowment income, university fundraising from alumni and willing supporters, student tuition and fees for foreign students, graduate students, and continuing education students. In the entrepreneurial framework of academic thinking, customer-students of the emergent private sector are happier to pay what is required and get what they want than to pay less and get less. Private institutions as providers of services appear to have a better reputation if they do not under-price and undercharge for their services, such as renting conference centres, sports facilities, and so on (in the UK, the phenomenon is called the academic 'low price culture'). This is prevalent at most public, even entrepreneurially minded, universities in Europe; on the other hand, many private universities charge full recovery costs plus a substantial surplus, both for teaching students and for renting their facilities to outsiders. The Polish case where there were 315 private universities in 2006 but where only a few have gone bankrupt in the past few years and where private universities are aggressively developing their infrastructure and their study offers, confirms that the phenomenon of underpricing is absent in the private sector. In Russia, as Shattock stresses, 'an extremely important contribution to Russian university entrepreneuria-lism was the central government's decision to allow universities to admit fee-paying students' (Shattock, 2004a: 31); it is like the Polish case, with some differences (such as legal limitations in the number of part-time fee-paying students: up to 50% of all non-fee-paying regular students at an institution as a whole).

Other sources of new income for Clark's entrepreneurial universities included earned income from campus operations, academically driven activities plus spin-off companies and self-financing activities, and royalty income from patented and licensed inventions and intellectual property. Incentives for staff and academic units to be entrepreneurial rather than to be traditionalist are crucial – this is confirmed by numerous examples in Europe. Incentives do not have to be financial only; they can be reputational (individual distinction), academic career-related, and time-related (e.g. smaller teaching loads for those successful in research). Certainly, too heavy top-slicing of additional outside income is an inhibitor to entrepreneurialism of both units and academics. As stressed by Williams and Kitaev (2005: 139), there is a balance between an individual's gains and an institution's gains, both in financial and in reputational terms.

Thus, in general, the fundamental dimension of an entrepreneurial university – having a diversified funding base – does not seem to work for the private institutions studied. Their ability (and opportunities) to use the 'third source' of income, especially (perhaps most welcome) 'university-generated' income, is very limited, as confirmed by detailed statistical data in the relevant case studies. Their high degree of financial dependence on a single source of income (namely, student fees) makes them easily prone to financial problems (Buckingham University differs in this respect from the other private institutions studied and is closer to public universities: while its income from fees in 2004 was 70%, its income from research reached 11%). At the same time, it is critical to note the dependence of public institutions on fees in the transition countries as well: from among the case study institutions, in Poland fees were between 18% of income for Poznan University and 41% for Poznan University of Economics, while in Moldova, the structure of funding of public universities make them quite similar to private institutions (and makes the very public/private distinction blurred): the percentage of income from fees in the three public institutions in Moldova is between 71% and 83%. Not surprisingly, a high or very high reliance of private institutions on fees is inversely proportional to their reliance on research funds. While they lead the list for the highest percentage of income from fees (in 2004, UCH in Spain 99%, WSHIG in Poland 94%, Moldova State University 83%, AESM in Moldova 77%, Balti in Moldova 71%, Buckingham in the UK 70%, PUE in Poland 42%), they are also lowest on the list for external research income (between 0% and 1% for Polish public and private, Moldavian public and private, and all other private case studies except for Buckingham at 11%). This income structure determines the mission of institutions studied: teaching, in real rather than declarative terms, is becoming more important than research (except for promotion and career ladder reasons in the public sector)[5].

In general, private institutions are able to compete for public or private research funds to a very limited degree; being largely teaching institutions (except for the two unique cases of Jönköping and Pereslavl), even if they are permitted by national laws to be state-subsidized in research, they are not able in practice to compete for funds with public universities. Separate units are rarely rewarded (or punished) for their entrepreneurialism and rarely act as separate business units, as is often the case with most successful public entrepreneurial universities.

The strengthened steering core

The role of the 'strengthened steering core' in entrepreneurialism of the private institutions studied is important. Clark's 'notoriously weak capacity to steer themselves', exhibited by traditional European universities (Clark, 1998: 5), is not observable in the private sector studied. There does not appear to be any need for balancing influences across multiple levels of these institutions, or a need to keep a constant balance between particular departments through the intervention of the centre. In contrast to public entrepreneurial institutions (and even more, in contrast to the whole public sector in higher education), the role of faculty participation in central councils is severely reduced (here Buckingham is an exception). But, in general, collegial management is non-existent, and connections between academics and administrators/management/founders/owners are limited. As Clark observed about ambitious universities concerned about their 'marginality' and even 'survivability', they 'cannot depend on old habits of weak steering'. They need to become 'quicker, more flexible, and especially more focused in reactions to expanding and changing demands'. A strengthened steering core is a necessity – and it is prevalent in the private sector.

The university centre is constantly dealing with risk, the management and understanding of which is crucial; and *the* risk, to manage on a daily basis, is the financial one (as the rector in the Russian case study of the University of Pereslavl put it, 'the university constantly encounters difficulties securing basic daily needs . . . which demoralizes staff and distracts it from its mission'). The role of obtaining resources (through retaining or increasing the number of students) seems more important than the role of building reputation for the private institutions studied. In terms of management structures, as in public entrepreneurial universities, private institutions have powerful centres, strong management groups, usually comprising a few administrators. In decision making, the role of collegial bodies appears, in most cases, marginal (most often, if they nominally exist but only their formal approval of decisions taken is sought). Most private institutions do not use resource allocation procedures to make strategic choices about their future direction. Also, no major impact of a new bureaucracy is reported: both the number, and the role, of development officers, technology transfer experts, special staff managers, and fundraising officers is small. The role of strategic committees, so fundamental to managing the entrepreneurial universities studied (especially at Warwick and Nottingham), is minimal. In transition countries, a unique feature is that management in the private sector is dealing, to a large extent, with academics also working (in a parallel manner) in the public sector (the Russian case of the small, regional, and private University of Pereslavl is a counter-example to this, as most academics working there are full-time professors – but this institution was born out of a former state-funded think tank of the Russian Academy of Sciences). Consequently, the fusion of managerial and academic values is both more and less feasible: more, because academics bring with them the traditional collegial attitudes prevalent in public institutions; less, because most of them come to the private sector not for research and teaching satisfaction but for financial reasons, and they can quit any time. In the other countries studied, this could not happen (the UK, Spain). The management structures are nominally three-level arrangements (centre–faculties–departments) but in practice they seem to be flat (centre–departments, as at Buckingham), and in smaller institutions, even centre–academics, with no intermediaries (WSHIG in Poland).

In small private institutions, which have sometimes appeared out of nowhere, with no international investments or public subsidies involved, and which in their first years of operation had been constantly in danger of financial collapse (WSHIG in Poznan being a perfect example), both governance and management structures and procedures may be simplified to the extreme. The culture of financial survival, as reported in Spain, Russia, Moldova, and Poland, has been very strong in these institutions. The consequences for management styles and managerial practices are significant: most often, decisions are taken by one to five people only, there is almost no spirit of collegiality, and all major (and sometimes even most minor) decisions are actually taken by rectors/owners/founders; sometimes, as reported in the Russian case of Pereslavl, some collegiality is still reported, combined with what its rector calls:

> overall management ineffectiveness . . . in its purest sense, to connote
> weakness in organization of university activities. The development of

effectively operating offices is in process, while ill-prepared documents, inability to effectively process data and chaotic scheduling still chronically undermine the effectiveness of university management. (Pereslavl case study)

These simplified management structures in most institutions studied seem to be possible only in relatively small institutions, with limited research ambitions and those which are relatively non-competitive workplaces for the staff. There are virtually no research funds available to these institutions (either from private or from public sources) and consequently most academic decisions are relatively non-controversial and teaching-related. As in the Polish case of WSHIG:

> The Academy has a very stable organizational and management structure: the founder and the owner (Professor Roman Dawid Tauber) has been its rector in the whole period. All key decisions concerning WSHIG are taken by the rector. There is no Senate as the Academy is too small – but key academic decisions are confirmed by WSHIG's Scientific Board, meeting 3–4 times a year . . . The management team is small and very effective; it comprises rector and the three vice-rectors. All senior administrative staff, including vice-rectors, has been working for WSHIG for a decade or more. The key for the success of WSHIG is the loyalty of its staff, both administrative and academic . . . In a small-size academic institution like WSHIG it is still possible for its rector to make all major decisions; and to make many minor decisions. (WSHIG case study)

The role of strong core administrators – accompanied by strong strategic committees – is emphasized in many EUEREK (and other) case studies of European universities. Managing structures and decision-making processes at a small private university (University of Buckingham) are substantially different from those at bigger institutions (such as Warwick and Nottingham Universities in the UK or Twente University in the Netherlands). For example, each of the three schools at Buckingham is treated as a business division, with each responsible for maximizing its financial return (derived largely from teaching). The decision-making process at Buckingham is quick but there is also considerable space for collegiality – which makes it different from other private institutions. As the Director of Finance puts it:

> Buckingham has three academic Schools, and we look at them as three business divisions. Each is responsible for making the maximum financial return and growing their business. The decision-making process at the University is quick and comprises five people: the VC, his deputy and the three Deans. We meet every week for two to three hours, so we do make good progress and good academic decisions in that sense. We get on very well. (Buckingham case study)

Academic entrepreneurialism involves risk-taking (Shattock, 2003; Williams, 2004a: 19); in most of the EUEREK case studies, institutions have to deal with a high level of risk on a daily basis; in private institutions, *the* major risk studied is a financial one, related to student numbers (and student fees). But as Shattock explains, 'risks [in universities] may be academic or reputational as well as financial' (Shattock, 2005: 19). The Polish case study of a medium-sized, vocationally orientated private institution (WSHIG – Academy of Hotel Management in Poznan) explains:

> WSHIG has been operating under constant risk in recent years. The major risk has been financial – will the income from student fees cover the expenditures, especially including debt instalments to the banks. WSHIG has been investing heavily in its infrastructure. As other private institutions, only from its own sources, with no state subsidies. WSHIG's rector was doing wonders to be able to pay back the bank loans in time (also using his private assets). The second risk has been student enrolments. (WSHIG case study)

At Buckingham, in a similar vein, what is meant by risk is financial risk:

> The most important risk to the University is financial. With a small research portfolio, academic risk is restricted to the student take up of degree programmes. In that sense the University is operating on a knife edge of risk. (Buckingham case study)

There are also other forms of risk: competition in the areas of studies (public institutions suddenly opening the same specializations/programmes or modifying existing ones – and running them without charging student fees), state regulations, and prestige (reputation). As reported in Russia, the most important risk at Pereslavl is the possible future shortage of qualified professors, followed by the possibility of losing existing public funding for its research centre run by the Russian Academy of Sciences (the University itself lost its public funding in 2001). As the case study reveals, 'the university is in constant talks with the local administration and enterprises for extra funding but their support normally comes in kind' (Pereslavl case study). Finally, the risk for both public and private institutions can also be reputational.

The extended developmental periphery

The third element of entrepreneurial universities in Clark's formulation is their extended developmental periphery, units that 'more readily than traditional academic departments, reach across university boundaries to link up with outside organizations and groups' (Clark, 1998: 6). This element appears quite limited in scope, operations, and importance at traditional universities. In the private sector studied, academic peripheries also play a very limited role: most case studies do not mention them at all.

In universities generally, there is an increasing number of operating units that are not traditional, discipline-centred departments. These units in particular take the form of interdisciplinary and transdisciplinary research centres focusing on a wide range of societal problems. The extended periphery can also be units of teaching outreach, under such labels as continuing education, lifelong education, distance education, and professional development. These research and teaching instruments cross old university boundaries to bring in new students and new kinds of research. Clark (1998) suggests that such base units have natural allies in the steering core – among agents of change located in the centre. These new entrepreneurial units fundamentally change the character of the university, adding new dimensions to traditional (departments–faculties–the centre) or newer, flatter structures (departments–centre). They require different management styles as they are often non-permanent, contract-funded units, staffed by non-tenured contracted academics. These styles are more flexible and relationships between the centre and peripheral units become much less formal and less bureaucratic – one of the reasons is that these units at the peripheries are often where most outside research funds are being invested.

The crucial role of these new research centres is overwhelming and universally reported. Research centres increasingly attract more outside funding in the form of grants and contracts. Their existence confirms a dual structure of most entrepreneurial institutions: traditional academic departments (and disciplines of teaching and research) and transdisciplinary and non-traditional research centres (and transdisciplinary research; sometimes teaching – but then mostly postgraduate programmes and short courses). These academic peripheries can come under the structure of departments, or be accountable directly to the centre (as is the case in Poland where most new research centres are accountable academically and financially directly to vice-rectors for research, avoiding hierarchies of departments and faculties, and deans and heads of departments, for example at AMU).

The new peripheries take two basic forms: (a) new administrative offices and (b) new academic units. The appearance of new specialized administrative offices is closely related to new tasks being undertaken and unknown to the institution in its traditional structures and funding opportunities. New offices (and posts) include: grants and contracts office, research and innovation offices, and various offices related to new academic programmes, such as entrepreneurship support programmes as described below. Other new units mentioned by Clark (2004a: 86) include the office of industrial relations, the alumni offices, the retail services office, the conference and special events office, the continuing education office, and the capital projects office. They all make sense at entrepreneurial universities where they are all closely related to the third stream of university funding discussed above. Clark calls them 'new bureaucrats of change' – who increasingly replace old traditional civil servants in transforming public universities. New funding opportunities contribute to the emergence of new peripheral support units. The academic structure as reported by case studies on entrepreneurial universities is changing substantially owing to these new peripheries, both academic and administrative. New boundary-spanning academic units (research centres and institutes) link themselves much more easily to the outside world (and outside funding), in contrast to the traditional, disciplinary-centred departments.

To summarize, the role of extended developmental peripheries in the private institutions studied is marginal; new transdisciplinary research centres are sometimes reported but they do not change the character of these institutions and their (rare as it is) existence does not lead to the introduction of new management styles or new internal resource allocation procedures. They do not form parallel, increasingly powerful university structures. They do not seem to attract new sources of funding and they are not engaged in an aggressive search for new research areas, as in the public sector. Also, the role of new administrative units, so crucial to the public entrepreneurial institutions studied, by comparison, is marginal. Most new posts and new units in the public sector are related to new opportunities for research funding, or the exploitation of research results, innovation, international off-campus teaching, or royalty rights. In the private institutions studied, the need for these units is still very limited, although they do sometimes appear (offices for EU structural funds in Poland, EU research or Tempus officers in Russia and Ukraine, etc.). The balance of power in management is not changed by new peripheral research (or teaching) units. There are few people working on research grants, without employment contracts, and there is no need to have bridging policies ready for this staff category. They do not have major (or, in most cases, any) problems with managing intellectual property issues or consultancies. There do not seem to exist clear research targets and funding for particular units does not seem to be based on meeting the targets, or bringing additional research-related revenue to the institution. Consequently, at the moment, the extended developmental periphery is almost absent in the private sector in Europe, at least as revealed in our case studies.

The stimulated academic heartland

The fourth element of Clark's entrepreneurial universities recognizes that strong universities are built on strong academic departments. The acceptance of change by departments is critical. As Clark put it, 'for change to take hold, one department and faculty after another needs itself to become an entrepreneurial unit, reaching more strongly to the outside with new programs and relationships and promoting third-stream income' (Clark, 1998: 7). Entrepreneurial universities become based on entrepreneurial departments. Research centres and institutes proliferate and may change the balance of power at an institution – they usually have greater opportunities for outside funding, and are directly related to the university management centre (also owing to their successes in attracting funding; this proximity to the centre, as reported by case studies, is most often informal). But apart from academic peripheries, traditional departments do count, and this is where most teaching and research is reported to be taking place.

The issues of developing new knowledge from entrepreneurial activities, the dissemination of new knowledge, and knowledge exploitation and technology transfer mechanisms look quite similar in most of the private institution case studies. Except for the Swedish case of Jönköping, none of the institutions have science parks or significant (either public or private) research funds. Interviewees mention teaching, seminars, and books as their contribution to knowledge transfer. There is no major difference in this context between WSHIG in Poland, UCH in Spain, or the TCUM in Moldova: they are mostly teaching institutions, with a strong vocational component of studies. In the Spanish case, though, there is an idea to set up an Office for the Transfer of Research Results – and there are already two institutes where the dissemination of research work is located (Buckingham also intends to go in the same direction). In the Russian case, the strong research inclination of the Pereslavl faculty is emphasized, following its origins in the fundamental research of the local branch of the Russian Academy of Sciences. As the Polish case study explains about the role of research and teaching:

> WSHIG is a special case of fully professionally-oriented educational institution. Being both a private institution and an almost completely teaching (as opposed to teaching and research) institution, WSHIG does not intend – by its mission – to develop or disseminate new knowledge or intend to get involved in knowledge transfer ... If any knowledge transfer could be mentioned, it would be the knowledge provided through short-term courses to professionals already working in the areas of studies represented by WSHIG. The role of research at WSHIG, both according to its mission and in practice, is marginal. But nevertheless WSHIG has published a few dozen books and collective volumes in its areas of interest. As a vocationally-oriented teaching institution, WSHIG does not see the reason to get involved in research not related to its major areas. (WSHIG case study)

The private institutions studied do not have a strong 'academic heartland', as they are predominantly teaching institutions.

In more general terms, and with respect to the public sector, entrepreneurship is reported not to belong to a few disciplines or subject areas – it has come to characterize virtually all academic fields (and such universities as Twente and Warwick are the best examples here, even though they represent two extreme poles in management structures: decentralization and centralization). The following features from academic departments are reported to reveal their growing entrepreneurialism (the Warwick case): the melting of the periphery into the core; the extensive building of research centres under departments; the construction of a university-wide graduate school; and the introduction of an imaginative and highly attractive research fellowship scheme (Clark, 1998: 27).

Both Clark's case studies and other European case studies of entrepreneurial universities show that there is an uneven spread of entrepreneurialism within an institution, with various rates of change, most often depending on external opportunities. While in Western Europe and the United States, apparently the most enterprising parts of traditional academia ('academic heartland') are in the science and technology areas; in most transition countries, as confirmed by the case studies, the most entrepreneurially minded units, departments, and institutions, as well as academics, are those 'soft' areas: economics, law and business, management, marketing, sociology, political sciences. These are the areas in which the largest part of the private sector operates, and in which the public sector runs its most enterprising study programmes for fee-paying students (all the Polish, Russian, and Moldovan EUEREK case studies confirm this tendency). Also, the availability of grants, including international research grants, in these areas is considerable. In transition economies, 'soft' disciplines, including economics and business and social sciences in particular, are much more easily fundable, and consequently are much more agents of entrepreneurial change in academic institutions.

In the private institutions studied, a variety of forms of study are available (full-time, part-time, weekends). Despite, at least in some countries, flexibility in opening new programmes wherever necessary, the content of study on offer seems to have been stable over the last 10 years, despite the frequently proposed need to expand the institutional profile. Thus WSHIG continues to teach mostly hospitality management and culinary arts, and Pereslavl continues to concentrate teaching on computing and mathematics; as the Pereslav's case study explains, 'more than ten years after the opening of the university, it did not expand dramatically in terms of enrolment or courses', and its rector mentions 'the most common feature of the Pereslavl university is single-sector orientation'). No major changes in governance and organizational structures in the last 10 years were reported in the majority of institutions studied. They provide wide opportunities for on-the-job training and work experience for a large proportion of students (especially in Poland, UK, Russia, and Spain). There are often people with professional prestige (non-academics) among part-time staff. The feeling of being disadvantaged compared with the public institutions is reported in interviews (especially with respect to research funding). They have a record of appointing their own graduates to staff or faculty positions: in 2005, 80% of administrative staff in WSHIG and 30% of academic faculty at the University of Pereslavl were their own graduates. The institutions are most often ineligible for public funding: Poland (both for teaching and research), UK (for teaching), Russia (both for teaching and research), and Spain (for teaching). Jönköping is exceptional in being eligible for public funds both for teaching and research. Often, eligibility for public research grants in theory does not mean that research grants are awarded in practice, because of losing out in competition with elite public research universities.

Institution-wide, integrated entrepreneurial culture

The last element of the entrepreneurial university within Clark's framework is the 'entrepreneurial culture'. 'Enterprising universities ... develop a work culture that embraces change' (Clark, 1998: 7). Organizational culture, seen as the realm of ideas, beliefs, and asserted values, is the symbolic side of the material components featured in the first four elements, Clark claims. It may start as a (relatively simple) institutional idea that is later elaborated into a set of beliefs and finally becomes the culture of the institution. It is a crucial component for entrepreneurial transformations, the first four elements being merely the means. In the case studies analysed, the founding idea was 'the earned income' concept as conceived at the University of Warwick after the Thatcher financial cuts over 20 years ago; the idea of 'the entrepreneurial university' as conceived vaguely at Twente; the idea of commitment to 'innovation' back in the 1980s at Chalmers University of Technology in Sweden (and its opting-out of the Swedish state system in 1994); the idea of following 'northern issues' at Lapland University, as reported in the case study; and the idea of rejecting state funds and state bureaucracy at the foundation of Buckingham University. Sometimes the emergent culture stems from individual visions, as reported in many institutions in the transition countries. WSHIG in Poland, whose founder and owner wished education in the catering industry, the culinary arts, and hospitality management to be made available at a higher education level, which was not available when he was getting his education in Poland, is a good example of how an individual's idea can be transformed into a complete institutional culture within a decade a half. Another example comes from the University of Pereslavl in Russia, where strong leadership and the idea of its first rector (after whom the university is named today) to transform a state research centre in software and computing founded back in 1984 led to the opening of a small private university answering to the demands of the city and its enterprises in 1993, following Russian market reforms in other areas. The importance of sharing a vision for an institution is reported in the case studies as being very important. The role of sharing a vision is confirmed at LSHTM at London University:

> Many people in this School are very altruistic, they are interested in the School's mission, *improvement of health worldwide. They really believe in it, that's what motivates them.* You have to be creative and inventive to be able to do that, you have to keep your research and funding going. If that is entrepreneurialism, then we are good at that. (LSHTM case study, emphasis added)

Conclusions

Let us summarize our conclusions about the academic entrepreneurialism of private higher education institutions point by point.

1. The case study private institutions generally view themselves as less entrepreneurial than the public ones. Their access to research funds (especially public) – which most often heralds the appearance of the entrepreneurial culture – is very limited. But they are often very successful teaching institutions. Their major concern is to survive financially as they are heavily dependent on student fees and they experience fluctuations in enrolments. Their mission and strategy are self-determined rather than influenced by state policies, and it is usually difficult to embark on institutional transformations. No major relationships between changes in governance and organizational structures and the emergence of entrepreneurialism were reported. The major source of non-core/non-state funding in almost all cases is student fees; no major changes in income structures were reported in recent years (Buckingham is exceptional here because of its higher level of research funding and recent focus on third mission activities). No major academic risks are being taken by staff and institutions, but often financial risks are taken by institutions. Compared with the public sector, few examples of the development of new knowledge from entrepreneurial activities are reported. Apart from teaching, few examples of other major kinds of dissemination of knowledge are reported. Also, only a limited number of mechanisms of knowledge transfer/knowledge exploitation are reported. Generally, there is a non-supportive climate for developing knowledge exploitation (additionally, they are mostly teaching institutions). There is competition with other institutions mostly for students (and for their fees) and not in research. Financial incentives or award systems for staff are generally marginal. Inhibitors to entrepreneurialism have clearly national dimensions (different history and tradition, reasons to found an institution, funding regimes).

2. In general, having a diversified funding base does not seem to work for the private institutions studied. Their ability (and opportunities) to use the 'third source' of income, especially (perhaps most welcome) 'university-generated' income, are very limited (and these characteristics bring them close to public institutions in the transition countries). Their high financial dependence on a single source of income makes them easily prone to financial problems. In general, they are able to compete for public or private research funds in a very limited way; being largely teaching institutions, they are not able in practice to compete with public universities. Separate units are rarely rewarded (or punished) for their entrepreneurialism and rarely act as separate business units, as is often the case with most successful public entrepreneurial universities. They do not seem to have incentive policies to support their staff in seeking non-core sources of income – income other than student fees. They do not have access to government funds – but also most often do not have access to government agencies as sources of third-stream

income or to private organized sources (such as business firms, philanthropic foundations, etc.) and do not use policies to support university-generated income. The share of their income from alumni fundraising, research contracts, patents, endowments, or earned income from campus operations is negligible, in most cases not even marginal. There is no mutual feeding and encouragement between non-core sources of income. There is also no major need to keep complicated resource allocation formulae in funding particular departments, or the need to keep a fair balance between the centre and the units through elaborate top-slicing and cross-subsidizing techniques. In the context of a diversified funding base, if entrepreneurialism is to be taken seriously in the private sector, the non-core income would be the income from any other sources than student fees, leading to a lower dependence on this currently single most important source.

3. The role of the 'strengthened steering core' in entrepreneurialism in private institutions is significant but there does not seem to be the need for balancing influences across multiple levels of these institutions, and there does not appear to be a need to keep a constant balance between particular departments through the intervention of the centre. In contrast to public entrepreneurial institutions, the role of faculty participation in central councils is severely reduced. Collegial management is rare, and connections between academics and administrators/management/founders/owners are limited. The centre is constantly dealing with risk, the management and understanding of which is crucial; and the risk, to manage on a daily basis, is the financial one. The role of attracting resources (through retaining or increasing the number of students) is more important than the role of building a reputation for the private institutions studied. In terms of management structures, as in public entrepreneurial universities, private institutions have powerful centres, strong management groups, usually comprising a small group of administrators. In decision-making, the role of collegial bodies is, in most cases, marginal. Most private institutions do not use resource allocation procedures to make strategic choices about their future direction. Also, no major impact of a new bureaucracy is reported: both the number and the role of development officers, technology transfer experts, special staff managers, and fundraising officers is small. The role of strategic committees, so fundamental for managing entrepreneurial universities, seems minimal. In the transition countries, a unique feature is that management in the private sector is concerned, to a large extent, with academics working (in a parallel manner) in the public sector. The management structures are nominally three-level arrangements (centre–faculties–departments) but in practice they seem to be flat (centre–departments), and in smaller institutions even centre–academics, with no intermediaries.

4. The role of 'extended developmental peripheries' in the EUEREK private institutions studied is marginal; new transdisciplinary research centres are sometimes reported but they do not change the character of these institutions and their existence does not lead to the introduction of new management styles or new internal resource allocation procedures.

They do not form parallel, increasingly powerful university structures. They do not seem to attract new sources of funding and are not engaged in aggressively searching for new research areas. Also, the role of new administrative units, so crucial to public entrepreneurial institutions studied, is marginal in comparison. Most new posts and new units in the public sector are related to new opportunities for research funding, the exploitation of research results, innovation, international off-campus teaching, royalty rights, and so on. In the private institutions studied, the need for these units is still very small. The balance of power in management is not changed by new peripheral research (or teaching) units. There are few people working on research grants, without employment contracts, and there is no need to have bridging policies (as, for example, at LSHTM) ready for this staff category. They do not have major (or, in most cases, any) problems with managing intellectual property issues or consultancies. There do not seem to be clear research targets and funding for particular units does not appear to be based on meeting targets, or bringing additional research-related revenue to the institution. Consequently, at the moment, the extended developmental periphery appears almost absent from the private sector in Europe, at least as regards the EUEREK case studies.

5. Almost all private institutions studied are involved only marginally in research. Competition with public institutions, in the context of a general lack of access (in theory or in practice) to public research funds, means competition for students and their fees. The second factor relevant for the mission and strategy of the private institutions studied is uncertainty about student enrolments – as enrolments may be going down or be fluctuating. Among the public institutions, despite internal competition, entrepreneurial universities report a high degree of internal cooperation, especially in grant applications, which appears not to be the case in private institutions. Because access to research funds is very limited, so is both internal and external competition. Cooperation seems to concern teaching rather than any other activities. The role of competition at public entrepreneurial universities is widely reported to be crucial. The competition is mostly for research funds, especially external sources of income. The overall effect of growing competition in sciences and the humanities alike is reported in the case studies as extremely positive, even though the picture for universities that are the most successful in this differs substantially from that of traditional, non-competitive academic institutions. There is a strong implication from the vast majority of the case studies that without competition for funds, entrepreneurial universities would not become entrepreneurial, even though they could be top in their respective disciplines and excellent in research and teaching. Private institutions do not take part in this race for external funding.

6. The use of the concept of 'entrepreneurialism' for the study of private institutions requires further adaptations. In the case studies analysed, of Clark's five constitutive elements of the entrepreneurial university, perhaps two or three could be said to exist: the strengthened steering core, the

integrated entrepreneurial culture, and perhaps, in some cases only, the stimulated academic heartland. No diversified funding appears to have been reported, and no extended peripheries were observed.

Notes

1. I wish to express my gratitude to Professor Michael Shattock for the extended comments he made on the draft of this chapter. All limitations are my sole responsibility, however.
2. Throughout the text, and especially in its conclusions, two exceptional cases need to be borne in mind: Pereslavl is not a standard teaching-orientated private university in Russia due to its historical origins in, and current affiliation with, the Russian Academy of Sciences; and Jönköping University has been a nominally non-state – foundation-based – Swedish university with equal access to public funding. Thus in the majority of generalizations about private institutions, Jönköping University does not fit, so unless otherwise stated, the Swedish case is separate – the most important difference is that Jönköping University does not charge student fees and has full access to public research and teaching funds, which, from a comparative perspective, makes it similar to public sector institutions. It has a similar status to Chalmers University of Technology in Sweden as analysed by Clark: nominally a private institution, with full access to public funding on equal terms with other public universities (Clark, 1998: 84–102 and Clark, 2004a: 61–70).
3. The public sector, to a large extent, has produced the private sector there (through academic faculty using parallel employment opportunities), at least initially, instead of reforming itself. The privatization of higher education often meant the creation of (new) private institutions by the faculty from the public sector (and Poland, Russia, and Moldova are good examples). Questions concerning the legitimacy of new arrivals to the educational arena have been raised from the very beginning, especially in some transition countries where private universities were born in a sort of post-1989 legal vacuum. But the common feature in most of those transition countries with substantial enrolments in the private sector is the interplay of cooperation and competition: even though private institutions themselves compete with public ones, they most often share with their competitors the majority of their faculty.
4. In Poland, both the public and private sectors rely heavily on student fees; from a comparative perspective, fees constitute about 20% of the overall budget of the public sector institutions and 95% of the overall budget of the private sector institutions. For the public sector, the other sources of income include state subsidies for teaching (50–60% on average in 2002) and research subsidies (about 15%). Consequently, private institutions are almost wholly dependent on student fees,
5. To explain the Polish example: the proportion of income by source of income is highly diversified according to the type of institution. In 2004, in public technical institutions, the proportion of income from teaching was 75.1% and from research 20.5%; for universities it was 85.2% and 10.6%, and for universities of economics 90.0% and 5.1%. Public institutions are much more deeply involved in research activities than are private institutions, for most of which research is a side activity

both in terms of academic mission and in terms of funding. The structure of income from teaching activities according to sources of funding for teaching shows that the main source of funding in public institutions is from the state budget (71.2%), followed by tuition fees (21.8%) and other sources (6.9%). In private institutions, the main source of income from teaching activities is tuition fees (97%). Generally, over 80% of all income from teaching goes to public institutions (82.1%); also, all state subsidies (100%) go to public institutions and slightly more than a half (50.7%) of all income from student fees goes to public institutions as well.

8

Entrepreneurialism and the internationalization of higher education in a knowledge society

Raphaelle Martinez in collaboration with Igor Kitaev

Introduction

The research assumption linking internationalization with entrepreneurship is that the activities described under headings like the impact of globalization on higher education, cross-border higher education, and the global higher education market may lead to more entrepreneurialism through related international openness, exposure, visibility, competition, partnerships, ventures, and risk-taking. Growing and diversifying international activities may be seen as a sign of entrepreneurial behaviour but also as a driver for entrepreneurialism. 'Amongst state institutions generally universities are perhaps unique in the extent to which they are subject to supranational global influences – intellectual, in relation to the movement of staff and students, and in ideas about the role of universities themselves' (Shattock, 2005). However, even in Europe (together with the supranational Bologna process), higher education remains at present the responsibility of national governments that certainly have different views about the degree of integration into the supranational processes. Often it is the entrepreneurial initiative of individual universities that makes it possible to explore and find new opportunities via international cooperation.

An important distinction should be made about the universities in Western Europe and those in the transitional countries (such as Poland, Moldova, and Russia). For historical (or rather ideological) reasons, universities in Eastern Europe (Poland) and the former Soviet Union (Russia and Moldova) had fewer contacts with foreign countries and universities after the Second World War, and this backlog still matters because it explains a certain lack of institutional foundations and traditions for long-standing partnerships with foreign universities.

One of the most commonly used definitions of internationalization of higher education was initially elaborated and subsequently adapted by Jane Knight (1997) and in its most recent iteration reads as follows: 'the process of integrating an international, intercultural and/or global dimension into the goals, functions (teaching/learning, research, services) and delivery of higher education' (Knight, 2005). If such a definition is accepted, then internationalization may be analysed through stages, each corresponding to a certain level of internationalization

Looking at the case studies, three different stages of internationalization can be identified:

- The first stage constitutes the first steps towards internationalization when international activities are marginal or underdeveloped.
- In the second stage, international activities are more developed and diversified. International elements are incorporated into a university's management and administrative processes, which leads to internationalization being institutionalized.
- The third stage demonstrates the most challenging activities in attaining a highly developed level of internationalization.

It must be pointed out that the process of internationalization is not linear. The process is accumulative but there is no strict hierarchy between the elements. The only thing that can be observed is that the internationalization process ideally should not be made up of isolated *ad hoc* activities but should be a process that combines various international activities and projects, with organizational features such as sustainable and systematic strategies and mechanisms that incorporate a wide range of ideas, risks, and results. That is why this chapter focuses not only on activities (although they constitute a large part of it) but also on the organizational elements, policies, and strategies as identified in Table 3.

An institution will choose to develop its international activities on the basis of its own situation, resources, priorities, and its country's position in Europe and in the world. This means that one university could have developed some of the activities related to stage 2 or 3 without having developed all activities of stage 1 or 2, and vice versa. But it is important to review whether the different activities reinforce each other so that they become sustainable and make a whole that is consistent with the university's mission and policy. It is thus not worthwhile categorizing the case study universities according to whether they have achieved stage 1, 2, or 3. Nevertheless, it is possible to determine which institutions are already proactive in the internationalization process and considered as players in the higher education global market, and those that see internationalization as a potential internal opportunity, a means for self-development.

Institutional policies and frameworks

Although the Lisbon and Bologna pan-European processes will gradually impact on the European scene, it is national and mainly institutional policy making that is still the most important in decision-making about international activities and often explains the reason why an institution is more or

Table 3 The three stages of the process of internationalization

	Category	Indicators	Details
Common basis	Organizational features	Official statement, mission, and goals (institutional policies) Decision, responsible, and management structure	Consistency between the mission, the strategic plan, and the budget High-level decision maker International Office International Service Unit
Stage 1: Internationalization process	Creation of a multicultural environment	Foreign languages Student and staff mobility	Foreign language courses Analysis of student flows
	Curriculum internationalization	Partnerships	Student exchange programmes Staff exchange programmes
	Research internationalization	Partnerships	Participation in and organization of international research events Joint research projects
Stage 2: Advanced internationalization	Creation of a multicultural environment	Foreign languages Student and staff mobility	Regular programmes taught in foreign languages Analysis of student flows
	Curriculum internationalization	Partnerships Summer school	Joint academic programmes International schools Employment of foreign teachers or lecturers Incoming students and staff
	Research internationalization	Partnerships	Joint research centres Joint postgraduate programmes International researchers are hosted
Stage 3: Internationalization challenges		Foreign campuses Distance learning	

less involved in international activities. Many distinctive national features remain, such as strong academic traditions (the UK), over-reliance on the state (the Nordic countries), inertia in systemic change (Spain, Poland), or an unstable policy environment (Russia, Moldova). For example, the Rector of the Helsinki School of Economics believes that the university sector in Finland is living in a command economy: the planning machinery of the state defines how many students are educated, in which fields, who trains them, with what resources, and in line with what regulations. This system is seen as being continuously in collision with the pressures of internationalization and of the signals given by the global education market. He sees that the most significant change facing the university system is globalization [*sic*] and the emancipation of business life from a command economy (HSE, Finland case study). In Moldova, there are mixed feelings. As far as the external climate is concerned, the case studies do not offer a clear opinion whether it has or has not encouraged knowledge transfer: some institutions consider that it does, and others that it does not. In the case of Cardenal Herrera University in Spain, the General Manager uses an example from the United States to describe the model of his university development. He says, 'It is a model which is based on providing students with personalized attention which tries to imitate that of Harvard' (Cardenal Herrera case study).

In most of the case studies, the universities' missions have a clear internationalization perspective. The mission statement specifies the internationalization policy framework and includes some information on its expected scope and internal impact. For example, Polish and Moldovan universities have ambitions to network and increase cooperation in Europe. The overall aim of the Poznan University of Economic's internationalization strategy is 'to enable staff members and students to build stronger international links with European countries in the field of education, research and culture' (PUE case study). According to its statute, the Balti State University has a mission to participate 'in inter-university cooperation and building of the European space in Higher Education' (BSU case study). In other cases, the focus is on a particular region. For instance, as part of the Tampere University strategy, the institution has a strong regional mission: 'its aims are to contribute to the development of livelihoods and culture in Northern Finland and to further international cooperation between universities and research institutes in the northern regions' (Tampere case study). Others, like the UK institutions, Nottingham and the London School of Hygiene and Tropical Medicine (LSHTM), are clearly internationally orientated and wish to be recognized as international examples in the market competition framework. LSHTM wishes to be 'a leading institution in Europe, and an international centre of excellence' (LSHTM case study). Others can also expand their ambitions: 'internationalization is one important goal for the HSE and it wished to be seen primarily as an international institution' but 'at the middle of the 1990s, the university set as its aim to strengthen its position as a recognized European university' (HSE, Finland case study).

In this context, it is interesting to observe to what extent universities pay attention to their international ranking or the accreditations received:

> We have these international accreditations, we've done well in these different international and European rankings and we've usually been successful quite consistently; we've usually been place around the 20th place, or let's say between places 10 and 20, 20 on the average, so you can say that we've been internationally accredited and in this way we're part of these European networks. (HSE, Finland case study)

Nevertheless, being highly internationalized for natural reasons may not be enough to be continuously entrepreneurial. Internationalization can also be seen as a means of evaluation and internal development such as in enhancing quality and measuring oneself against international quality standard achievements. In some cases, especially in the transition countries, internationalization is strongly related to the aim of improving the quality of university programmes, research, and governance, and thus has an internal impact. Internationalization helps to 'answer international standards of quality: faculty and students, both, must conform to those standards, curricula and educational technologies must correspond to the internationally accepted level' (Pereslavl case study). To do so, most of the transition country universities as well as the Spanish universities recently launched an Internationalization Quality Review System. This distinctive part of the internationalization process (a) for enhancing institutional quality and then (b) for establishing a reputation that enables universities to be more competitive in the global market is clear from university strategic plans.

At the Poznan University of Economics, it is obvious that internationalization is considered as a way of improving the quality of the university and is not necessarily seen as a way of winning a strong international reputation:

> considering the strengths and weaknesses of the University's present situation, the authorities of the University have set the following priorities for the years 2003/4–2006/7: a) Further internationalization of teaching and research; c) development of student exchange; b) improvement in teaching quality; d) expansion of staff training. (PUE case study)

In the case of Russia, internationalization is expected to 'train a new generation of teachers from the best graduates' in order to address the 'heavy deficit of highly skilled teachers' (BIBIM case study). It is important to review the mission against the strategy plan to determine to what extent such a plan is being implemented and represents more than simply a public and official commitment. Further investigations would be necessary to observe if universities have the tools (budget, monitoring plan, organizational structures, etc.) to support the implementation of such international orientations.

This could lead one to think that once quality is enhanced, the university is likely to develop its international reputation to be considered as a global player in a competitive framework. But other factors and rationales intervene and some high-quality institutions prefer to develop a regional influence with no interest in the international one. The University of Lapland (Finland) is a good example of this trend: internationalization serves to improve the already good quality of its teaching with an altruistic regional objective contributing to 'the development of livelihoods and culture in Northern Finland' (Lapland case study). Internationalization is thus seen as an extension of the traditional university commitment to learning.

Organizational structures for conducting international activities

A common policy is to appoint a high-level decision maker to take charge of international affairs. In the UK cases, a pro-vice-chancellor is responsible for international relations and European integration. In Spain, similar responsibilities are given to a vice-rector. In the Moldova cases, it seems that giving international responsibilities to a prime vice-rector is a new initiative and shows their willingness to become more involved in the process of internationalization: 'The position of Prime Vice-Rector, responsible for international relations and European integration was introduced' (BSU case study). This kind of high-level decision maker orientates the university's vision and policies for internationalization, and can also represent the University across the world as the prime vice-rector does in the Balti State University (BSU), or the rector does for the Academy of Economic Studies of Moldova (AESM). In the UK, the pro-vice-chancellor decides on and signs agreements, and acts as the university's spokesman on international activities through speeches and so on. In the LSHTM case study, one can see that the level of integration of the School's leaders within an active international network is important for the institution. The personal capital is transferred to the institutional capital:

> Through a range of sources. One is obviously I and other senior members of staff interact at the global level, e.g. I am on a number of WHO committees, the former dean of the School is head of the Global Fund on aids, TB and malaria, an alumnus of the School is head of the Global Alliance of vaccines and immunization. So we have links into other global institutions. Another way of keeping track of where these opportunities come from is that many people sit on various grant-giving bodies or research committees. (LSHTM case study)

But, when the institution is less internationalized, some decentralized and individual initiatives can lead to one department or unit becoming more internationalized than the whole university, particularly in raising foreign funds to finance a department's research. In Finland, the Ministry of Education strongly influences the universities' actions through its policies. But this situation does not prevent a bottom-up approach where individual initiatives try to make their units more internationalized.

There are over fifty different units within the University of Tampere. They of course lead their own lives and have their own situations in terms of the surrounding society. You could say that we have a lot of units, like the hyper lab for example, that live under constant change and uncertainty, but are proactive and establish national co-operation and networks. Then we also have these traditional departments that have strong established teaching and research traditions and quite clear paradigms. They haven't really had to think about these up until now. They've settled with this traditional idea of university as an institution of civilization and with the Humboldtian identity and they've functioned under these principles. Now this is being questioned and challenged. So I guess you could say that others have operated under these new trends for almost a decade now, whereas others are just starting to do so. (Tampere case study)

Besides individual initiatives, there are bodies that oversee international policy implementation like the Department of External Exchanges (HSE, Moscow), the Consultative Committee (Finland) that is seen to enhance communication and cooperation with the external environment, the International Relations Office (Spain), and the International Office (Sweden, UK): 'The International Office [of Nottingham University] now has 38 members and is involved in everything that is not British – consultancy, research collaboration, inward and outward student mobility, foreign campuses, e-learning through U21, global collaboration, student support, and Europe' (Nottingham case study). Nottingham has, in common with most UK universities, a powerful International Office headed by a director who really drives the process in terms of international student recruitment, relations with foreign recruiting agents, and international student life management. This could be seen as a consequence of the UK universities' dependence on foreign students' fees, which implies that activities and duties related to internationalization are professionalized and entrepreneurial.

At the Miguel Hernandez University (Spain), an Institutional Relations Office is in charge of the international activities and of providing the foreign students with information, Spanish lessons, accommodation, and so on. At the AESM (Moldova) and the Higher School of Economics in Moscow (HSE, Russia), the International Relations and Services Departments spend much of their time on the resolution of foreign student-related problems. This kind of service reflects the growing trend in the transitional countries to recruit/ attract foreign students and integrate them into the university system. The number of foreign students fell in these countries after the collapse of the Soviet Union, but today aggressive marketing and low fees and prices make these universities proactive in head-hunting for foreign students. Poland reported agreements and plans to invite Chinese students in large numbers.

In the case studies, it is often mentioned that good campus life conditions make international students more likely to contribute to the internationalization of the university environment. It would be interesting to see how an intercultural working environment contributes to a sustainable internationalized system. Without strong international and universal values, which have to be enhanced and supported by the university itself, how effective can the internationalization process be? When a university's strategy and mission include internationalization, one of the first steps is to create or to develop a unit in charge of international activities. In all the case studies, this correlation has been observed.

Activities related to stages 1 and 2 of internationalization

The difference between stage 1 and stage 2 of the internationalization process is not so much based on different sorts of indicators. That is to say, the activities or indicators are of the same nature but can vary depending on the point where the university stands in the internationalization process and the specific circumstances of the institutions concerned.

Foreign languages

One of the basic activities that leads to more internationalization is teaching foreign languages. The different foreign language course policies are significant. In countries that are isolated because of language constraints such as Finland, Poland, Moldova, and Sweden, there is a strong emphasis on teaching foreign languages. At stage 1 of internationalization, and in these cases, foreign languages are intensively taught and mandatory. For example, at the Academy of Hotel Management and the Catering Industry (WSHIG) in Poland, there are mandatory classes in two of three foreign languages: English, French, and German. Students get to choose a third from Spanish, Russian, and Italian. For those interested, a wide choice of optional classes is provided in Arabic, Greek, Chinese, Finnish, Japanese, Portuguese, Swedish, and Hungarian. This active policy must also be considered in the light of the WSHIG's specific mandate of being an Academy of Hotel Management and the Catering Industry. Its mission is thus to provide people with specific skills needed in an international working environment by definition (tourism). At HSE (Moscow), all students are required to study at least two foreign languages including English. The internationalization level increases when native speakers teach foreign languages (AESM, WSHIG, Poland).

Stage 2 is reached when regular programmes are taught in foreign languages. This is the case for most of the language-isolated countries studied – Sweden, Poland, and Finland – where parts of the regular programmes are taught in English. As English increasingly becomes used internationally for business and science, the ability to communicate well in English becomes more important. It is then necessary for higher education in a country to offer coursework in English not only to prepare their own citizens for global competition, but also to attract international students. In Moldova, because of the specificity of the country and its wish to be regionally attractive, the Moldovan universities provide regular programmes both in Russian and Romanian, and sometimes in English. The UK, Spain, and Russia are different since these countries have an expansionist language policy. The programme is naturally taught in English or Spanish or Russian. Nevertheless, Spanish courses for foreigners are established and well used by the international students in all Spanish universities with an internationalization strategy (University of Valencia, Technical University of Valencia, Miguel Hernandez University); this can be seen as a means of attracting foreign students.

Student and staff mobility

Before coming to the important dimension of partnerships within the internationalization process, let us comment on the student and staff flows according to stages 1 and 2 of the process. This falls directly into the priorities the EC has formulated within the Lisbon and Bologna processes and numerous communications by the EC. All the case study universities seem to use and take benefit from the European exchange and mobility programmes, including Erasmus, Socrates, and Tempus: 'Thanks to these programmes, the university has succeeded in making available study abroad opportunities to a large number of its teaching staff and its best students, many of whom later become instructors at the HSE themselves' (HSE, Moscow case study). On the one hand, European mobility programmes aim to enhance the cohesion of peripheral member states or develop a universalistic sense of humankind; on the other hand, the Lisbon Strategy has been tailored to the needs of globalization and has included a series of economic and political measures for 'enabling European higher education to make its full contribution to the Knowledge Economy and Society' (Jan Figel's speech at the EAC Conference, Brussels, 2005). Mobility programmes are thus used to boost the economy. But those are not the only means to create or intensify mobility between universities; bilateral agreements are also used to lay emphasis on mobility. Partnerships and agreements will be analysed below.

At stage 1, one can note that student mobility is much more important in terms of outgoing students than of incoming students. Universities at stage 1 of the internationalization process fail to attract foreign students. Nevertheless, they take benefit from sending their own students abroad mainly through well-developed student exchange programmes. But in this case, student exchange programmes appear to be quite unilateral, whereas they are normally based on the concept of reciprocity, bringing foreign students to a host country and sending domestic students to foreign universities for specific academic experience. The topic of unilateralism or reciprocity is worth further investigation, and a wide range of rationales such as a country's economic attractiveness, policies, and so on could explain why some host countries seem to fail in attracting foreign students. In the transition counties, the number of outgoing students seems to be more important than those incoming. This trend is deduced by observing that transition country university case studies strongly insist on the need and benefit of sending students abroad and prove that an important number of exchange programmes are signed. But when one looks at the number of incoming students, one can see that the rate is rather low. The social dimension of sending domestic students abroad requires that students come to terms with the cultural aspects of studying in a foreign country and the need to adapt to different personal, social, and economic living conditions. The social aspect of internationalization is linked to the first aim of the European Mobility Programme mentioned above: developing a universalistic sense of humankind.

At stage 2, it is seen that the trends are reversed. The number of incoming students is far more important than the outgoing ones. In Sweden, the trend is national: 'It is interesting to note that Lund University follows the national trend in having a much higher number of incoming students (1563) than those outgoing (911)' (Lund case study). In the UK, sending students abroad is considered an extra-curriculum experience. As the Director of the Nottingham International Office said:

> because the British are still very parochial about going out and certainly the heads of School are very cautious, they think that you can't get a proper degree in life if you are not watched over by the same people for the whole of the three years. So we are pushing both our postgraduates and undergraduates out with agreed partners and we have all sorts of exciting ideas for extending that. We think, and I think it is widely held, that employers believe that students who studied or lived abroad are probably a better prospect for them, so they are probably going to get better jobs and students are very employment driven. We think they probably get better degrees as well and students who went abroad say that their views of the subject have changed. (Nottingham case study)

The brain gain of attracting students from abroad is viewed as a bonus for the host country, whereas the associated brain drain for foreign countries is seen as a necessary side-effect of competition. In the framework of international competition, foreign graduates are seen as key to national or European trade relations, and as direct economic benefits (institutional incomes and net economic effect of foreign students). One might put forward the following hypothesis: once the university has seen the benefit from sending its students and staff abroad, as it enhances the general quality of the institution, it thus becomes more able to attract foreign students. For highly internationalized universities, their domestic students might consider that they will benefit from 'internationalization at home' that does not require any form of mobility. Another point is about competition to attract foreign students. In the UK, for example, non-EU students are a considerable source of university total income, since they pay higher fees than UK or European students. Institutions with an expansionist perspective develop strong policies on international recruitment and place less attention on sending their own students abroad; they understand higher education as a global marketplace with a benchmarking dimension.

At stage 1, staff exchange programmes are of great value to enhance an institution's quality and give academic staff the opportunity to receive continuing training, although this may be rather limited. The strategy of the HSE (Moscow) states that staff exchange programmes must be intensified: 'Expanding programs of academic mobility (increasing the number of study visits from 5–6 to 15–25 per department) . . .'. At stage 1, EU grants play an important role in attracting and upgrading academic staff that will contribute to the development of higher teaching quality. In fact, universities at stage 1 fail to attract foreign teachers or lecturers out of the exchange programme framework for various reasons, the most important being because of the low salaries on offer in Poland, Moldova, and Russia. Consequently, and so as to maximize the internationalization of the staff, another strategy implemented by low-income universities consists in calling for national teachers who have been trained abroad. HSE (Moscow) and Balti State University are good examples of this attempt to reverse the brain drain.

At stage 2, the level of incoming teachers is quite high, but it is rather difficult to determine whether it is a consequence of the inter-university partnerships that embody staff exchange programmes. What is obvious is the fact that universities at stage 2 have more resources to pay foreign teachers or lecturers well (Sweden, UK) and their reputation is an asset in attracting them. For outgoing teachers, there is no concrete information in the case studies of the competitive highly internationalized universities (Sweden, UK) that would help to define a trend except that teachers are recruited internationally (LSHTM, Nottingham, Lund, Jönköping), but no mention is made as to whether full-time staff engage in study tours or staff exchange programmes.

Curriculum internationalization

Partnerships
A widespread feature of internationalization is to integrate a university into a worldwide institution network and to create partnerships to facilitate cooperation. This is very common, and none of the universities studied is an exception to the rule. For example, the University of Valencia has 331 agreements with foreign institutions and belongs to four consortia; the Technical University of Valencia has numerous agreements with Argentina, Colombia, Mexico, Uruguay, Cuba, and others; Miguel Hernandez has signed international and bilateral agreements. Balti State University collaborates with Western Europe institutions through programmes, postgraduate studies, and by offering the necessary facilities (books and computers). But, the

number of agreements *per se* cannot be considered as a good indicator of the level of university internationalization. For example, at Lund University it is complained that there are 1012 agreements with 536 universities but too many of them are inactive or overlapping. Thus, it might be better to analyse the partnerships from the point of view of effectiveness. The effectiveness of inter-university partnerships leads to the implementation of different kinds of activities that can be related to stage 1 or 2 of the internationalization process. Partnerships are used as a means for curriculum and research internationalization.

Student and staff exchange programmes
One of the most common characteristics of partnerships is to create student or staff exchange programmes. The effect of these programmes on student and staff mobility has already been discussed. But speaking of the geographical exchange programme dimension, an interesting comment is raised in the AESM (Moldova) case study:

> Outstanding young people engaged in scientific activity have the possibility to continue their studies both at the Academy of Economic Studies and in the Romanian university centres, taking Masters or doctoral courses. In comparison with the cooperation with institutions from distant foreign countries, limited because of distance and different languages, the cooperation with Romania is possible practically for all the students and personnel of the Academy. (AESM case study)

This stresses the fact that partnerships can have a different geographical spread and be of a different nature because of national characteristics. A country's history, culture, and priorities shape the dimensions of relationships with other countries. In Moldova, it is understood that exchange programmes are more efficient when regionally established because of national priorities and culture, both understood as a key to internationalization.

Joint academic programmes, joint diplomas
When universities reach stage 2, student exchange programmes are developed into joint academic programmes. Joint academic programmes bring two universities together to offer dual or joint degrees to students. This kind of cooperation between two universities is no longer based only on course credit as it is the case at stage 1 with student exchange programmes; this can lead to the award of a degree in the name of the foreign university or jointly in the name of both partner universities. The case studies reveal a large range of joint programmes leading to a joint diploma. Examples include: HSE (Moscow) has a double degree programme of master's degree and doctorate in economics with Paris 1 and Paris 12, and with Erasmus University (Rotterdam) HSE students are given the opportunity of receiving a second diploma along with the Russian master's degree. The students who successfully pass the exams held by the External Board of Erasmus University are awarded the Diploma of Erasmus University. At the Technical

University of Valencia, the Mediterranean University of Science and Technology (MUST) has been established as a result of an agreement between the Rector of the Technical University and the President of the Ajman University of Science and Technology (AUST) and the former United Arab Emirates Minister of Education. The academic programmes offered by MUST are linked to those of the Technical University and AUST, and they are given in English. This example leads us to those cases where fully international schools have been established like the International Jönköping Business School (Sweden), or even the Siberian–American School of Management at the Baikal Institute (BIBIM, Russia), which provides two international programmes: the Russian–American programme and the Russian–Australian programme.

Let us analyse further the internationalization of the Russian–American programme that enables students to take a Bachelor of Management Degree and a Master of Management Degree from Irkutsk State University and a Bachelor in Management study from the University of Maryland, College Park (USA) without leaving Russia. This is like a branch campus arrangement between Maryland and the Irkutsk State University with a development assistance perspective to meet the 'needs in the administrative staff of Far East and Eastern Siberian regions' (BIBIM case study). This arrangement permits the students to receive three degrees/diplomas, including one from a foreign university that participates in designing the programme and delivers the diplomas without receiving the students on its campus. This can pose questions of quality. Could quality be compromised? How can one be sure that the Baikal Institute provides the same quality as Maryland does, considering that establishing such a programme sends strong signals to prospective students and their future employers? The case study mentions that the Russian–American programme has been certificated by the Commission on Higher Education of Central States Colleges (USA). It is said that the programme is taught using distance learning technologies, which implies communication with American tutors and students via the Internet.

Summer schools
Out of these partnerships, summer schools are also a part of the internationalization of a university, as we can see at the Cardenal Herrera University where, during the summer, external lecturers are invited to give different courses. The same arrangement is made at Pereslavl University. This can be used as an introductory experience to encourage students (both national and foreign) to undertake exchange terms. Summer programmes provide the opportunity for short-term mobility giving potential students and partners a taste of the institution. They are used as pre-sessional courses for intending students and they also provide exposure to international students to both academic and administrative staff. Summer programmes can be a first step for institutions that are embarking on the internationalization process.

Research internationalization

International research events: conferences, seminars, workshops
Partnerships can also bring scientific collaboration, thus internationalizing the research function of the university. Participating in international conferences is the first way to join the internationalization process. All the universities studied report that they participate in a range of international conferences, seminars, and workshops. This indicator could become relevant if a quantitative evaluation of the university's participation in international conferences is undertaken. Otherwise, this indicator is of little help since all the case study universities, even the least internationalized, participate in international research events. Inversely, organizing international conferences intuitively appears to be a more relevant indicator than participation when we consider that it is an activity that requires more resources and then demonstrates a will to invest in internationalization. Nearly all the case study universities claim that they organize international conferences. One must, therefore, consider these kinds of activity (participation in/organization of international events) as basic and traditional university activities of knowledge dissemination related to stage 1 of the internationalization process.

Joint research projects
At stage 1, universities are willing to foster collaborative research activities through joint research projects, and mainly through European projects that propose a cooperative framework of collaboration. This model of cooperation is based on universities' participation in European and international programmes and on bilateral relations with foreign partners. The University of Valencia, for example, mentions in its strategy that it is important to encourage the presence of its research groups in European programmes. The Poznan University of Economics participates in the main European programmes like Phare, ACE, and the 6th Framework Programme. Besides the European frameworks of collaboration, the universities of the transition countries are significantly involved in regional networks of scientific collaboration. The Alecu Russo University (Moldova) carries out joint research programmes with Ukrainian and Romanian universities. The Poznan Economics University focuses on Central and Eastern European market research. International-scale research programmes are mainly conducted through partnerships with US or Japanese institutions (HSE, Moscow, for example) but remain less developed.

Postgraduate exchange programmes, international researchers
At stage 2, the scientific collaboration between universities becomes more active in setting up postgraduate exchange programmes. For example, Alecu Russo University has postgraduate exchange programmes with Romanian universities. In the Spanish case studies, it is stressed that the number of foreign doctoral students who join their universities is constantly increasing. Some case studies relate that international researchers are hosted by

the institution. Whatever the form of cooperation (student exchange programme, joint research projects, postgraduate exchange programme), the geographical dimension remains a recurrent criterion of analysis. It is clear that in some cases the internationalization process is more of a regionalization process. It is, then, crucial to define whether or not the geographical scale matters in the evaluation of universities' internationalization.

Stage 3 of internationalization

Stage 3 is about identifying new trends or innovative practices in internationalization mainly linked to the growing export of education services, such as establishing a foreign campus or distance learning. These new developments pose challenges and involve greater entrepreneurial risks; very few case study universities are involved in this stage.

Foreign campuses

Opening a foreign campus is a particular form of institutional mobility that represents a direct foreign investment by universities (Nottingham, UK) or companies (JOKO Executive Education, Finland). The Nottingham case could be seen as an ideal role model for these extremely entrepreneurial international activities. Nottingham has developed its campuses in offshore locations: Malaysia and China. This kind of venture becomes possible when the regulatory framework of the host country allows foreign education providers to deliver higher education within their borders. However, the possible interference of the host country is seen in the Nottingham case study as an important risk. The Pro-Vice-Chancellor of Nottingham University told us that:

> China has moved to a new stage in its relationships with foreign educational institutions and recent legislation permits and encourages foreign institutions to establish campuses in order to modernise the HE system. In 2003 there was the signing of the foreign universities' law, which was also the trigger for going ahead. That law would make it possible for us to succeed in setting up our campus. The Chinese government will soon bend the laws to allow us to continue. There are legal rules (e.g. you may be required to have a specified number of library books for start up), but there are many other criteria which could not possibly be met in the start up phase in September (nine months after set up). In June 2005 the University expects to receive a licence to operate a foreign HEI in China; that will be the first ever foreign institution to operate and award foreign degrees in China. (Nottingham case study)

The idea of establishing offshore bases came about after the UK Government announced that it would no longer provide a subsidy for students from

outside the European Union and the University was among the first to realize that this provided an opportunity to market UK higher education as an
income-generation activity.

> This part of Nottingham's international strategy is based in part on the
> expectation that student recruitment into UK universities is unlikely
> to continue in the same way indefinitely into the future and that the
> most highly regarded global universities will be those that have made
> significant foreign commitments, (Nottingham case study)

> You cannot be so ambitious as we are without getting a high level of
> trust. In Malaysia it has been only in the fifth year that we have seen the
> research and development spin-off links coming along ... In the last
> year we got links with public universities there so that we can access
> public funding there (research funding and commercial and industrial
> funding). (Nottingham case study)

Opening campuses overseas could be driven by academic and business
reasons. It appears to be a win–win strategy that leads to beneficial outputs in
the receiving country's higher education sector, while involving lower campus set-up and running costs for the foreign partner. Furthermore, although
the students might not receive the same cultural and linguistic experiences
as with foreign study, it remains a good opportunity for both students and
national companies to have manpower trained by foreign institutions with a
global focus:

> The students receive a Nottingham degree and they can do a semester
> or a year at the other university campus. The curriculum is almost the
> same as in Nottingham. There are one or two minor changes for legal
> reasons and cultural differences. There are three categories of aca-
> demic staff: University of Nottingham academics there who have been
> seconded to the University of Nottingham in Malaysia; recruits from
> around the world to work in Malaysia; and local recruits. The teaching is
> all in English. (Nottingham case study).

Regarding the Chinese campus: 'All teaching is carried out in English
and the degrees awarded are University of Nottingham degrees. The
courses and teaching are subject to the same Quality Assurance processes as
courses and teaching in Nottingham' (Nottingham case study). Nottingham
insists that the same quality education is delivered in these campuses as in
England. Countries providing and receiving cross-border higher education
have a common interest in strengthening quality provision either to protect
their learners or to maintain the reputation of their higher education
abroad.

In some circumstances, risks and obstacles to export higher education
abroad might not come from the host country but from national regulations
and the cautiousness of the exporting country. At the HSE in Finland,

incorporation is seen as a useful way to operate abroad, avoiding the constraints exerted by the Finnish State:

> Internationalization is seen to be encumbered by the role of the university as an office of the state. The Helsinki School of Economics is leading up to operate also abroad but at the moment it is easier to realize through its JOKO Executive Education company. (HSE, Finland case study)

> I think that many ministries don't even understand why we should operate abroad. For example, if a foreign company wants to educate its middle or upper management in Asia or somewhere, I'm sure if you'd suggest to them that they could do it in Finland, they'd think you're joking. Of course we have to operate in the environment the companies do. Or we'll have to simply forget this fine-tuned education system of ours, or the idea that it actually has an international market. We should then stop saying that we're global and let the Americans or the British or the Australians take care of the global education market. If we don't have the right tools it won't work. And a government agency is not a suitable tool, this is obvious to everyone actually involved in this. (HSE, Finland case study)

> The executive education was incorporated in 1996 and the JOKO Executive Education was established. The Research Institute for Business Economy was annexed to the Helsinki School of Economics in 1996. In 1997 the research services were incorporated and the company has used the name LTT Research Ltd. since 1998. In 2000 an affiliated company of JOKO, Helsinki School of Economics Executive Education Pte Ltd., was established in Singapore and the company started in 2002 also in China. (HSE, Finland case study)

Distance learning

Many university leaders are sceptical but distance learning programmes appear to be more and more challenging as they are cross-national boundaries programmes with no physical movement of students or consumers. Distance learning leads us to consider that there are ways to internationalize higher education that do not necessitate mobility. A significant number of case study universities provide distance learning programmes. However, such programmes are often created to address distinct objectives. Distance learning can be seen as a new and innovative pedagogical channel for teaching a regular programme. In this case, the distance learning programme has no *ad hoc* form. For example, the HSE (Moscow) proposes to realize its business school's programmes in four distinct ways:

- as regular (daytime) study;

- as a night school;
- as personal-distance (modular) learning;
- as short-term programmes.

It is typical for HSE (Moscow) students to work and study at the same time. In particular, this concerns students from the former Soviet republics who have to earn money to pay for accommodation and living expenses in Moscow. These foreign students use Internet and electronic resources instead of being physically present at lectures and seminars. University managers at the HSE in Moscow encourage this style of study and accept passes in tests and examinations from e-students.

For the Baikal Institute, distance learning is an opportunity to save costs:

> The Institute cut down expenses sharply and turned to distance training on [the] American part of the programme. It also offers a complete degree through a distance training programme. Its main objective is to offer the modern educational-professional services to working managers. That is why the main features of the School of Business and Management are:
>
> - Minimal study while working due to modular-based programmes of internal training including Saturdays and Sundays.
> - Continuous education during [the] inter-modular period as a result of access to tutorial materials and tasks and active student–tutor and student–student interaction via the Internet. The equipment in classrooms and computer rooms is suitable.
> - Maximum applied character of all knowledge and skills thanks to using active methods of teaching such as training, business games, case studies, group projects etc. (BIBIM case study)

In this case, distance learning methods and the Internet are clearly seen as modern tools to attract a new category of students in employment who wish to improve their professional skills.

In Sweden, distance learning is understood as a tool for creating networks and connections and is used to promote a real community of practices:

> In terms of electronic learning and distance education, Sweden's universities are cooperating via a national Swedish Net University, exchanging information, know-how, and jointly providing a search platform of course offerings. The project offers 2600 courses, including 150 in English, from 35 universities and university colleges. Registration is with each individual provider; some require a physical attendance component; and as with regular courses in Sweden, no tuition is charged. To give some idea of relative activity in this field among Swedish cases, Umeå lists 124 such courses, Lund 93, KTH 41, Jönköping 16 courses. (Lambert et al., 2006)

At the LSHTM, the case is rather different, since distance learning programmes were undertaken, initially at least, solely to attract new customers and to generate new income at lower cost. It is often said that distance learning is more cost efficient than other traditional forms of education. The Internet enables a programme to reach a large number of students with relatively few teachers and no classroom or material costs. Nevertheless, the distance learning cost-efficiency assumption needs to be further investigated to be acceptable. The LSHTM distance learning programmes are directed to a new range of students, with specific and targeted content.

> With the help of a pump priming grant from the University of London Extra Mural Studies department the School created an innovative distance learning programme, mainly with the intention of generating a new source of income. This programme took its first students in 1999 and has grown enormously to become a fully integrated part of the School's academic strategy. The income from this programme amounted to €900,000 in 2004 or 2.4% of the School's total income. Students can study for a Postgraduate Diploma or MSc degree by distance learning in three subject areas: epidemiology (since 1998), infectious diseases (since 1998), and public health (since 1999). The distance learning programme continued to grow and by 2001 the number of students registered for the School's distance learning Masters programme was the same as those attending courses in person, each group numbering 799. There are currently 1,200 students registered in 120 countries (with funding from over 150 foreign agencies and governments). Developments are now underway for mixed mode study, so that students can elect to take a mixture of distance learning and London-based units.
> (LSHTM case study)

Conclusions

We have observed that international activities may lead to more entrepreneurialism but the reasons for this may be different. Although internationalization and entrepreneurialism can be closely linked, the correlation between the two concepts is ambivalent and multifaceted. The national context still persists over the supranational trends, but gradually globalization has taken its toll and affected the university management, in particular via international accreditation, courses and diplomas, exchange of students and their credits, and increasingly attracting overseas students from the transitional and developing countries (China, India, Russia, Kazakhstan).

In general, two approaches to internationalization can be discerned: one places internationalization activities in a framework of market competition, the other in the more traditional framework of networking and collaboration. In other words, there are two types of internationalization: that which is driven by financial incentives (the entrepreneurial model) and that by academic benefits or by more altruistic motives inspired by the belief in the intrinsic international nature of much scholarship. The case studies show that a competitive approach to the internationalization of higher education is emerging, and acknowledge the changing landscape. The trend towards more economically orientated rationales for internationalization is continuing. The UK case studies appear to be the leading model of this category. For the UK universities, foreign students, foreign campuses, and distance learning programmes are mainly a matter of income generation through recruiting fee-paying students while they may demonstrate other motives *post facto*. Their foreign activities are essentially different in motivation from, for example, the Swedish and Finnish universities, which are still guided by altruistic motives such as the intrinsic and traditional international nature of scholarship (no financial incentives for recruiting foreign students) but see the internationalization of education as being a key to raising their national profile. This model allows and encourages staff, student, and programme mobility through partnerships between institutions to create networks of excellence. Nevertheless, the two models develop an expansionist viewpoint and represent a top reference within the international higher education landscape. Internationalization is necessary to secure their position in the international landscape and to remain competitive whatever is the final objective. Universities are thus taking risks in developing international activities such as offshore campuses and distance learning programmes in the face of new challengers in the field.

The UK model of expanding international activities as a means of obtaining extra income for universities is increasingly gaining ground in Russia, Poland, and Moldova, which have great exposure to potential higher education markets in foreign countries. Nevertheless, quality education remains one of the main challenges for these universities. Internationalization is generally considered as a means to enhance the quality of the higher education sector and then indirectly to raise the national profile and attractiveness. International elements are introduced to contribute to the quality and the competitiveness of the national system or to the university itself by increasing efficiency in teaching as well as in research through shared efforts, mainly supported by western institutions, governments, and agencies. For instance, when looking at the source of funding, it is obvious that an important element is provided by foreign governments, or by the European Union. With the case studies of the transition countries, we progressively shift from the notion of internationalization motivated by economic or altruistic drivers to the notion of internationalization to assist in the development of countries' capacity. Indeed, in these universities, internationalization is considered more as a way to build or strengthen internal capacities, to find new ways to manage higher education, and to establish new practices in teaching or research. Twinning arrangements and partnerships with local providers (Russia, for example) are encouraged to facilitate knowledge transfer between foreign and local institutions, and thus to modernize and enrich the country. Encouraged by the Lisbon Strategy, these universities receive a benefit from internationalization or more accurately from European cooperation. Benefiting from international and pan-European trends and activities may be viewed as a sign of entrepreneurialism. These gains may create larger disparities between universities and within universities (i.e. winners and losers).

In conclusion, universities in countries that have a strong potential to work globally (the UK, Russia) have stronger motivations to enter into new and expanded international activities for financial reasons (income generation). In contrast, for the international activities of universities in Sweden, Finland, and Spain, financial motivations are not the main reasons at present. Poland and Moldova are mixed cases as a result of Poland's integration into the EU and Moldova's potential cooperation within the EU Bologna process, and as a consequence of the greater international exposure of their universities, they attract an increasing number of foreign students and the volume of international activities is growing rapidly together with the income it generates. While Sweden, Finland, Spain, and Poland have official regulations about the fees and other charges that foreign students should pay (or not pay), in the UK, Russia, and Moldova the number of foreign students and the levels at which fees are set are determined more by market forces and competition as well as by various forms of collaboration with foreign universities.

9

Impediments, inhibitors, and barriers to university entrepreneurialism

Bruce Henry Lambert

Entrepreneurialism and its impediments: an introductory discussion

This chapter addresses inhibitors, impediments, and barriers to university entrepreneurialism. The term 'entrepreneurial' means various things to different people. Our 27 case studies clearly detected diverse attitudes that some in academia narrowly believe entrepreneurialism only and always relates to revenue streams and managerialism, some consider it synonymous with being innovative, while others see entrepreneurialism itself as an impediment to their understanding of their scholarly interests.

Defining something as 'entrepreneurial' is a moving target bound in time and place. What is now termed an 'entrepreneurial activity' is temporal and relative; it can cease to be entrepreneurial after a period, or in a different environment might not be considered so at all. Relevance is a further fundamental problem: while some informants label entrepreneurial or innovative activities superfluous or irrelevant to the university's fundamental mission, others take pride in even arcane methods of revenue production if contributing to mission-critical funding. Finally, to focus on inhibitors is inherently difficult, as we seek to measure reasons that something does not take place or is an output in a lesser way.

Motivating university employees via university mission?

Entrepreneurialism in terms of outreach to society is often mentioned as a university mission along with teaching and research (Walshok, 1995; Cummings, 1998). Sweden's Higher Education Act of 1997 explicitly requires university interaction with society as a key task (Lambert et al., 2006). But while public engagement is a topic of growing importance among

European universities and around the world, its potential as a new funding source is a carefully studied component. Public engagement has important interactive elements that should open up new possibilities, but simple voluntarism, already noteworthy, is unlikely to generate much excitement.

University mission statements may mention fiscal responsibility, but it is uncommon to find mention of requirements for raising funds in most individual job descriptions. Yet many are confronted with fundraising needs. What are their motivations, and should they be encouraged by adjusting incentives and/or disincentives ('carrot and stick' combination)? With substantial incentives, people are motivated and find ways to bypass or overcome impediments, and they use a range of strategies. But motivation without direction complicates matters. Money is a handy proxy focus. Among our cases, notable positive outreach was achieved within Umeå University (Sweden) by the Faculty of Humanities, who diligently provide classes on ethics for the university's Medical Faculty. An encouragement to their eagerness is remuneration: Swedish state compensation per successful student year in humanities is €3597, but €12,577 in medicine – in other words, the same working hours taught in the medical faculty increases income by a factor of 3.5.

What some term 'impediments' are situational, and defined as impediments only in the light of minimal motivation, which in turn often reflects a lack of incentive. Motivation to change or experiment involves risk and exposure to unknown problems and uncertainties, from which many people shy away. The degree to which uncertainty is unwelcome varies substantially between individuals and between different cultures (Hofstede, 1980, 1986). The history of organizational change is rife with cases of failure as well as success. Market-orientated activities provide surrogate or proxy measurements of success via money, yet other measurements such as the Research Assessment Exercise (RAE) in the UK, or the Researcher Activity Index (IAIP) at the Technical University of Valencia in Spain, can provide useful performance feedback or metrics for comparison.

Quasi-market assumptions, intransigence, ill-health, and ignorance

Although the entrepreneurial university model is considered by some researchers/proponents as the default condition, such an assumption co-opts debate by assuming deliberate and reasoned non-participation. Thus Clark (2004a: 170) mentions that 'many universities will not attempt to transform themselves into a highly proactive form. They find one or another rationale for inertia . . .'. Yes, the condition of inertia may be real, but there need be no rationale. We could as well trumpet the benefits and need among faculty for physical fitness, prescribe jogging and marathon running for increased dynamism, and then impose the labels inertia or lethargy on the non-compliant and mock their lack of action. Among a wonderful array of useful endeavours, entrepreneurialism is arguably not fundamental to university operations, and a 'pay your way' system is not necessarily appropriate for each department or every scholar.

What constitutes a healthy university? Self-reliance is perhaps a highly desirable condition, but mechanisms have long existed for hands-off funding by external donors. 'Inertia' in matters entrepreneurial is not inertia in everything. Few academics have formal training in entrepreneurship, and many have no interest. Some worry about being engaged in a debate framed by accountants (explicitly mentioned in the case of Pereslavl), to be suddenly forced to justify their activities and to fund their campus existence. It is no surprise that many sense being bullied and avoid participation: the terms of discussion and a focus on fiscal responsibility have already been defined by others. Who would wish to justify being a parasite on society? The non-jogger, in a similar bind, may perhaps be cornered into belittling health.

It is costly to monitor and account for all functions and activities in a service-orientated university; many key areas are inadequately measured or have poorly developed metrics (such as value-added comparisons of teaching). Those areas attracting assessment might reasonably become more strongly emphasized, but this is internal reasoning, viable only under continuing assumptions of audit, penalty, or reward.

Few in universities are inert; people often are diligently working in areas of importance, but their work is being belittled as insufficient. This is an ideological as well as a practical problem. Actively entrepreneurial efforts may be deliberately unrecognized if individuals or work units are competing with the central administration. In many of our cases (Russia, Sweden, Poland), faculty are highly active externally for their own personal account; belated university efforts threaten to interfere. In Umeå (Sweden), many units had developed specialized entrepreneurial outreach and expertise – but this was undercut when the centre imposed an External Relations Office (ENS), a single large doorway to university activities. Not only do some now feel less well served, but they are also assessed for substantial overheads over which they have no control. University 'marketization' often leads to this complaint, as central services assess fees as a monopoly, with few controls and no competition. These are thus mere quasi-markets. Some have argued that universities are under the thumb of big industry (Sinclair, 1923), while others see higher education itself as a big industry that regularly exploits part-time faculty, teaching assistants, or administrative staff (Johnson and McCarthy, 2000; Lafer, 2003; Eveline, 2004).

Some of the most prolific academics are unskilled in marketing and negotiation. Slaughter and Leslie (1997: 224) quote an Australian pro-vice-chancellor: 'If these million-dollar-a-year staff ever realize how much they are worth to us, we are in a lot of trouble'. That Australian university is fortunate to have such valuable economic drivers among the faculty, but it is a problem if a university business plan is based upon continued ignorance. However, a similar lack of understanding as regards their substantial economic importance exists among many university subunits and universities themselves. Most are not truly bound geographically to their present location, and could migrate to a more favourable place. Corporations in other industries that employ large numbers of people and are key drivers of regional economies often negotiate benefits and concessions from local and regional governments; universities might do likewise. Most already operate tax-free as non-profit corporations, but further resources, such as land or buildings, might be negotiated. The foundation and continued operation of Jönköping University (Sweden) has been based on just such an active partnership that included free land and buildings for the university. It seems unreasonable that universities are asked to be businesslike until they begin assessing assorted fees and maximizing revenues. It is important to understand how (or if) the contractual formats and public service nature of universities differ necessarily from the operations of profit-maximizing businesses.

It is also of utmost importance to recognize that the university has multiple stakeholders, including alumni and existing students (among others); operations and reputation are held in trust by the overseers, faculty, and administration. The reputation of a fine university could be damaged through poorly conceived entrepreneurial activities. Alumni donations and other major internal resource flows can easily be disrupted. It is difficult to regain collegial respect or institutional balance once these are lost.

People and their ferment are needed to animate the university; administrative processes and buildings are important but secondary; where the university has no character, it is 'a hollow shell, a body without a soul, a mass of brick and stone held together by red tape' (Sinclair, 1923: 15).

Challenges for European universities

The Commission of the European Communities (2005) in *Mobilising the Brainpower of Europe* cited four major bottlenecks to European higher education: uniformity, insularity, over-regulation, and underfunding. Many of those interviewed in our case studies clearly agree that these are trying problems. The key challenges the Commission sees are achieving world-class quality, improving governance, and increasing and diversifying funding (CEC, 2005: 3). Van der Ploeg (2006) warns that in comparison with top universities in the United States, European universities now face substantive challenges to reform their funding models and generate more autonomy. Perhaps some of this can be achieved through building more independent and stable endowments. The Lisbon target to make the EU the most competitive and knowledge-based economy in the world by 2010 may have been more of a stimulus to higher education systems in the Far East and North America where it was seen as a call to challenge. Conversely, many key people in Europe still know little about such efforts, and the mobilization of energies and resources has been sporadic.

Fragmentation continues in Europe, in spite of Bologna, due in part to subsidiarity and national differences in recognizing that problems exist. Meanwhile, the idea of 'entrepreneurial universities' grows more interesting. Why not, if somehow universities can pay their own way, contribute to local and national development, and maintain excellent teaching and research? Finlay (2005: 73) states: 'One sometimes gets the impression when reading texts on the entrepreneurial university that there is an underlying political, sometimes even evangelical, subtext'. Certainly the vision of the entre-preneurial university, regional clusters, and the interaction of university research, industry, and government (the 'triple helix') makes a good story; it has generated interest, attracted funds, and become a minor industry in itself for researchers.

Inhibitors highlighted in the case studies

Many common challenges were repeatedly cited throughout the case studies. Entrepreneurship is inhibited by resource and logistic support limitations, while new investments in such areas are cited as promising levers for future successes. But universities are also developing talents in marketing spin: it can be difficult to determine chronic weak areas in the blizzard of forward-looking statements. Universities do admit lack of money is a weakness – they are candid in the hope of attracting funds, especially donations. The University of Buckingham (UK) is a case where a major endowment increase might clear up assorted bottlenecks; universities in Poland, Moldova, and Russia also complain of substantial underfunding in comparison with institutions elsewhere in Europe. Another widely troublesome area is with personnel rigidities. Many systems are unable to markedly adjust personnel costs, or (perhaps more troublesome) particular individuals in key positions, due to faculty tenure. Some systems (Sweden, Finland), in trying to guaran-tee openness and fairness in faculty hiring, created bureaucracies that are criticized as ungainly and sluggish. Most universities struggle with attracting truly top administrative and managerial staff, as corporate work is often bet-ter paid (specifically cited at Nottingham in the UK, Poznan in Poland, and Higher School of Economics in Moscow). The bureaucratic procedures at public universities put them at an additional disadvantage in being frustrat-ingly slow. The universities in Valencia reportedly suffer under considerable civil service rigidities. Many (perhaps all) universities resent ministry guid-ance or interference in their freedom of operations, particularly when the central ministry does not reasonably understand key factors, such as corporate-liaison needs (HSE, Finland) or regional challenges (BIBIM, Russia). Major accounting and assessment efforts are resented both for loss of control and for their required time and overhead costs (Pereslavl, Russia; Poland; UK). A further perceived need is to strengthen meaningful links between universities, local firms, and surrounding regions, but businesses and universities have different orientations and regularly misunderstand each other. On a positive note, many informants from our case study universities wish that there were better university incentives for entrepreneurship, which indicates an openness towards properly constructed change. More detailed summaries of inhibitors and impediments from all our case studies are attached in the addendum to this chapter.

Which inhibitors are most serious?

This question was the subject of an informal survey conducted among the multinational EUEREK Project group. Seventeen EUEREK researchers were asked the above question: each ranked what they believed were the top five inhibitors from a questionnaire that provided a total of 64 options (see below), plus a write-in alternative. A total of 84 answers was received, with 39 of the 64 options gaining one or more votes. By-far the most chosen answer (9 votes in total) was:

- Entrepreneurialism is not part of an academic's career assessment.

Only one other inhibitor received four votes as a major inhibitor to entrepreneurialism:

- Civil servant status within the university.

Other inhibitors chosen three or more times included:

- Personnel rigidities: seniority system and tenure and unions.
- Lack of financial autonomy: limitations and steering are imposed by the State.
- Entrepreneurialism not included within core goals.
- Few incentives for institution building and reform.
- Awkward governance precludes entrepreneurialism: need permission.
- There is no motivator, especially if work is now comfortable, with no demands for change.
- Organizational synergies, catalysts, and coalition building are still poorly developed.
- Conservatism.
- Traditional non-competitive mentality.
- University people are unwilling to share prerogatives with businesspeople or other outsiders.
- Selfishness precludes effective coalitions.
- The university and its people have a skills deficit in entrepreneurialism, economics, and management.

Most of these key inhibitors clearly relate to lack of motivation and incentives. But it is also clear that there is considerable uncertainty as to what the most important inhibitors might be (39 of 64 options were supported). These impediment options themselves were generated from EUEREK case study interviews (see addendum), combined with barriers gleaned from literature on higher education and organizational change and inductive reasoning. The potential impediments to university entrepreneurialism shown in Table 4 were included. Some of these impediments are logistical limitations, while others are unbridgeable limiting factors that preclude entrepreneurialism. Again, summary descriptions of the inhibitors mentioned in each of the 27 case studies are in the attached addendum.

Currie et al. (2003) conducted case studies at four universities (Avignon, France; Oslo, Norway; Twente, Netherlands; Boston College, USA) with over 150 respondents. The following key impediments to university entrepreneurialism were mentioned:

- 'once we enter into that game, we will become dependent on external finances' (Norway)
- 'threat to traditional university values' (France)
- 'risk of losing freedom and creativity' (France)
- 'professors are dependent on their students and have to give good grades for fear of being denounced as "incompetent" teachers' (France)
- 'some of the universities [will be] more expensive and some will subsequently be considered more important than others' (France)
- 'losing basic research and freedom to conduct curiosity-based research' (Norway)
- 'much of this [new, applied, funded] research is short-term and very conservative' (Norway)
- 'we spend so much time writing proposals, copying them, and trying to get money that we neglect our basic university duties' (Norway)
- 'For these new strategic programs from the Research Council, you need teams, and preferably they should come from all over the world. If you have a black, handicapped, Sami woman as your collaborator, you are more likely to get a grant' (Norway)
- If you want to study subjects that are not industry-related, then it is difficult to get money. And the projects are usually short-term' (Netherlands)
- 'You can become a slave to somebody else's ideas' (USA)
- 'potential for conflict of interest' (USA)
- 'teaching loses at the expense of research' (USA)

Currie et al. (2003: 65) summarize perceived *advantages* to entrepreneurialism as 'increasing financial stability, university autonomy, competition, staff productivity, and proximity between staff, students, the market, and outside world'. They cite an overarching need to maintain quality and equity (p. 54).

Siegel et al. (2003) looked at technology transfer, generating important data with regard to entrepreneurial impediments between university scientists and potential business partners. They surveyed key people active in technology management from three groups – academia, business, and Technology Transfer Office (TTO) facilitators – to learn of key impediments to successful technology transfer among potential stakeholders. The 55 people interviewed were based around five universities in Arizona and North Carolina, USA (Table 5).

Table 4 Potential impediments to university entrepreneurialism

Legal	The cooperation and ongoing permission of key people is expensive and troublesome
	Civil servant status within the university
	Entrepreneurialism not included within core goals
	Awkward governance precludes entrepreneurialism: need permission
	Personnel rigidities: seniority system and tenure and unions
	Academic freedom means people are pulling in different directions
	Lack of financial autonomy: limitations and steering are imposed by the State
	Tradition of micromanagement from above
	Tax rebate for academics and creative professionals (threatened?)
	High cost of salary overheads
	Existing programme rigidity
	National barriers to more international participation
	Legal barriers do not allow certain projects
	In contrast to North American universities, there are no fundraising expectations; no systems exist for contact with potential donors
	The university has a national or State character rather than pan-European or global
	Expansion brings difficulty because new staff cannot easily be severed
Measurement	Lack of measurable parameters and metrics
	Entrepreneurialism is a moving target
	Organizational synergies, catalysts, and coalition building are still poorly developed
	Few incentives for institution building and reform
	Entrepreneurialism is not part of an academic's career assessment
	Unclear incentive system, especially with teaching
	Focus on technological research, but not enough on expanding other forms of knowledge
	Career ladder rigidity (the need to gain the habilitation)
	Research Assessment Exercise (RAE) stifles risk; rewards publishing in high-impact journals
Mental	Too little contact and interaction with the wider world; ivory tower syndrome
	Bureaucratic sclerosis: over-reliance on standard operating procedures
	Groupthink
	Conservatism
	Scholars must protect the dignity of their work against the encroachment of market
	Rivalry often stifles collegiality
	Universities must protect their 'brand' in the interests of a range of stakeholders
	Are we trying to build intellectual capacity or to build intellectuals?
	There is fear of being debased by mercantilism
	Society does not expect universities to be entrepreneurial

(Continued overleaf)

Table 4 Continued

	There is no motivator, especially if work is now comfortable, with no demands for change
	Many people still believe the State will care for all: 'Don't worry, be happy!'
	Lack of practical emphasis
	Traditional non-competitive mentality
	Reputation: staid, 'red', etc.
	Some people celebrate failure; eager to crow that scholars are not so smart
	Youth and imagination may be more likely to generate new and entrepreneurial ideas; they may be at the university, but are disregarded
	Universities and society require counterproductive shows of deference
	Scholars often work with incrementalism and measuring reliability, which contrasts with entrepreneurial uncertainty in the face of multiple variables
	University people are unwilling to share prerogatives with business people or other outsiders; selfishness precludes effective coalitions
Resources	Need for a system of 'training the trainers'
	Lack of good models: no best practice
	Universities are too loosely coupled: difficult to generate enthusiasms
	Students may have a voice, but their presence is short term and the learning curve high, so they are ineffectual; initiatives and reform cannot be ushered through to completion by students
	Entrepreneurialism may detract from a scholar's main mission
	The university and its people have a skills deficit in entrepreneurialism, economics, and management
	Lack of personal incentives, especially compared with making an independent business
	Entrepreneurialism may mean more work without more pay
	Limited English abilities are a barrier to international outreach and collaboration
	Administrative staff is spread unevenly
	Over-reliance on tenuous or variable income streams
	Siting limitations (physical plant insufficiencies)
	Lack of money
	Too many people expect a benefit: corruption
	Capable people already have an overflow of work, and are pressed to the limit
	Time limitations: too much to do already
	Opportunities may be lost in the long time required for consensus-building
	In terms of human resources, university management is too homogeneous
	We cannot even do well what we should do: where is our inspirational teaching?

Table 5 Stakeholder perceptions of barriers to university–industry technology transfer

Barriers	Type of stakeholder		
	(1) Managers/ entrepreneurs	*(2) Technology Transfer Office (TTO) directors/ administrators*	*(3) University scientists*
Lack of understanding regarding university, corporate or scientific norms and environments	90.0	93.3	75.0
Insufficient rewards for university researchers	31.6	60.0	70.0
Bureaucracy and inflexibility of university administrators	80.0	66.0	70.0
Insufficient resources devoted to technology transfer by universities	31.6	53.3	20.0
Poor marketing/technical/ negotiation skills of Technology Transfer Offices	55.0	13.3	25.0
University too aggressive in exercising intellectual property rights	80.0	13.3	25.0
Faculty members/ administrators have unrealistic expectations regarding the value of their technologies	25.0	40.0	10.0
Public domain mentality of universities	40.0	8.3	5.0
Number of interviews	20	15	20

Note: Values in columns (1)–(3) are percentages of respondents who identified an item as a barrier to technology transfer.

The same respondents suggested the following potential countermeasures (Siegel *et al.* 2003: 122):

Suggested university-based improvements:

- Universities need to improve their understanding of the needs of their true 'customers', i.e., firms that can potentially commercialize their technologies
- Adopt a more flexible stance in negotiating technology-transfer agreements and streamline UITT (university–industry technology transfer) policies and procedures

- Hire licensing officers and TTO (Technology Transfer Office) managers with more business experience
- Switch to incentive compensation in the TTO
- Hire managers/research administrators with a strategic vision, who can serve as effective boundary spanners (tie to boundary spanning literature)
- Devote additional resources to the TTO and patenting
- Increase the rewards for faculty participation in UITT by valuing patents and licenses in promotion and tenure decisions and allowing faculty members to keep a larger share of licensing revenue (as opposed to their department or university)
- Recognize the value of personal relationships and social networks, involving scientists, graduate students, and alumni

Suggested firm-based improvements to the UITT process:

- Be proactive in their efforts to bridge the cultural gap with academia
- Hire technology managers with university experience
- Explore alternative means for tapping into UITT social networks

Clearly, there are substantial gaps in vision and resources, suboptimal skill sets, and basic misunderstandings of motives and entrepreneurial promotional requirements.

Classifying inhibitors and impediments to entrepreneurialism

No doubt additional inhibitors exist, as well as alternative ways to group them. Groupings might focus on the level from which the inhibitor is generated, or where it impinges. Subsets might be resource orientated, or perhaps grouping needs or requirements that are unfulfilled.

Where does the inhibitor intrude or impinge? (*or,* where is the problem generated?)
 Universal // National // University-level // Faculty or departmental level // Individual
Needs or requirements (resource dependence):
 permissions // resources // ideas // etc.
What kind of limitation?
 legal // measurement // mental // resource

Some problems apply widely throughout the higher education industry, other concerns are specific and local. Proper inhibitor definition is a prerequisite to developing stimulant measures, practical policy, and organizational redesign.

Universities as a platform for pluralistic competition

Shattock (2003) explicitly addressed university inhibitions to becoming entrepreneurial, analysing shortcomings and developing key concepts. Building on Clark (1998) and after considering five UK cases, Shattock (2003) defined four intrinsic levels or classes of university inhibitors: the State; culture and tradition; diffusion of authority from where it is needed; and lack of an effective 'strengthened steering core' (pp. 154–5). The first inhibitor, the State, is depicted in its most extreme as represented by tramlines from which there is no deviation. The State was often cited as an impediment in our case studies as well, although the focus of complaints varied considerably (unsurprising, given that we were analysing such a variety of institutions in seven different nations). Some limitations were legalistic, other such State/university frictions might be classed as culture and tradition, with reliance on standard operating procedures. Shattock's latter two inhibitors are organizational: the 'strengthened steering core' representing an alternative both to over-personalized leadership (Clark, 2004a: 83) and to highly fragmented governance. These inhibitors are helpful, but perhaps are too solidly focused on operational difficulties and on barriers to policy implementation. We cannot presume entrepreneurial sparks are being stifled, or an entrepreneurial vision has failed; we must also determine if there is an entrepreneurial impetus or vision, and if not, why not.

Over the past millennia, scholars have largely broken away from State and Church controls. University autonomy in many parts of the world means that no central authority can simply force the university to operate as it dictates. Such autonomy has been hard won, with decision-making often devolved to faculty or departmental level and substantial individual independence. Developing a 'strengthened steering core' puts governance once more in the hands of a few. It speeds decision-making, but implementation may lag if people not consulted do not cooperate with policies they find disagreeable.

Due to lack of guidelines, best practice, and entrepreneurial tradition in universities, it is no surprise that many universities are not 'taking advantage of the entrepreneurial climate that has been stimulated by increased market forces and institutional competition' (Shattock, 2003: 146). Our cases turned up fundamental operational and legal anomalies. For example, when a private programme in Poland (WSHIG) competes successfully with highly subsidized State programmes nearby, its survival and growth in some sense undercuts the argument of the others for entitlement to State subsidies. Revenue generation for tax-subsidized organizations, or for non-profits, is also cause for resentment and friction when they offer services that compete with private sector businesses. The Technical University of Valencia has been sued three times by local business associations for unfair competition.

Proponents of New Public Management (NPM) have approached efficiency reforms as if they were an inevitable or natural process – yet they are not; university entrepreneurialism is a policy choice. Not all in the university accept that they are facing an economic imperative. Criticism of market encroachment into university decision-making is ancient, yet proponents of commercial exchange continue to challenge alternative models of collegiality and the ivory tower. Certainly not many faculty were hired specifically for fundraising or their revenue-generating abilities. Certainly a loss of academic voluntarism would change many calculations. It also is not difficult to imagine ways in which monetary 'donations' might corrupt the processes of university admissions and assessment. Society benefits from faculty impartiality and disinterested evaluation, though others perhaps could take up such roles. Part of the problem is that business would like to 'cherry pick' only certain profitable components of the university and its data. How will other key functions be provided? Simply to criticize business as self-interested misses this more important point.

In the United States, the economic imperative of NPM is being imposed on institutions such as museums and prisons as well as on universities. The same mechanism has partially hollowed out the US military: private firms now recruit manpower ('mercenaries') for the administration of Iraq, circumventing normal checks-and-balances. Slaughter and Leslie (1997: 4) explain that professionals were known for serving the interests of clients and community, and did not seek to maximize profits; but this can be hard to understand for those who have never experienced such a thing. More understandable perhaps is the costliness of oversight: the military, academia, and other professions, which have developed over a long period, benefit from public trust. Radically changing such systems undermines trust and imposes new auditing costs. Academic, legal, medical, and other professionals still exist, and while they do, it might be useful to ask what might demean their profession; after marketization, those are areas of moral hazard where corporate interests dedicated to maximizing shareholder value are likely to cut corners.

Envisioning an entrepreneurial faculty

'Marketization' sounds great until it is realized that those with resources can shut out others. Those without funds, regardless of other merits, may be denied access to the university. (Low faculty salary is a parallel problem, where only those with means can afford to take certain jobs; the better qualified who are reliant on salary must go elsewhere.) A hybrid system is perhaps more politically palatable. One dimension is an unrealized (pent-up) demand for entrance to top universities. Suppose, for example, Cambridge University were to offer special admission to large donors (I do not believe that such a system presently exists at Cambridge). The normally high admissions standards might be relaxed for those paying €150,000 tuition per year (more than 25 times normal EU student rates); an incentive could be offered to faculty introducing such students (5%). An admission-by-donation system might be justified in that substantial resources are thus provided for the use of all students. Yet as the system becomes widely known, it might damage the value of both existing and future degrees. Alumni interests might be hurt, without countervailing benefits.

Simple purchase of degrees and qualifications undercuts the present market; and untested validation is also unreasonable. But if non-students could anonymously sit exams, it is likely that some might be properly prepared and pass. Is that unreasonable? Are we ready to forgo the apprenticeship of requiring years of student registration for such efficiencies (and additional revenues)?

Researcher ethics are also under scrutiny. One highly active, sometimes contentious, collaboration is with industry-sponsored pharmaceutical trials: university researchers conduct trials under agreed parameters, with the pharmaceutical company retaining control of intellectual property and publication rights. Trials with adverse results are sometimes never published; later successful trials can result in drugs being cleared for use that have hidden health risks. Another key difficulty is when university researchers (and other medical doctors) receive compensation from industry, often as consultants, but fail to divulge such personal interests; in any case, it would be difficult to distinguish unbiased medical information from advocacy.

Entrepreneurialism is often unrecognized and poorly charted. As mentioned already, many academics, in addition to their primary affiliation, cultivate multiple income streams from various sources. This has functional benefits for their university work: grounding theory with practice, building links to a wider community that might be useful for research, and helping to assist students with postgraduate recruitment. A university that tightens its rules and seeks to curtail such outside activities risks losing key people, those people most skilled in cultivating practical mutual arrangements outside a narrow academic department.

To what extent is shared energy in a mobilized university community important, common, or sustainable? Stringfellow (1975) bemoans a loss of university autonomy and self-directed vision:

> Appropriately for technocracy, the university, more and more, has the facade of a fortress, and the ambience of a factory, and the internal surveillance of a medium security prison. It is said that the students study more, but that comfort is small if what there is to learn is radically diminished and dehumanized. What, in fact, we behold in the university is a principality bereft of autonomy and integrity, and, instead, consigned to a vassal status, subservient to other powers – the political and commercial and military and intelligence institutions prominent among them.

Goodall (1999: 466) recognized his university lacked community when searching for a place 'during or after work where I could . . . share in the unfolding narrative drama of persons, ideas, and work that mattered to me'. Instead, he found 'an organized silence, a professional level of personal loneliness accompanied by an aching, endemic lack of meaningful talk'. Universities that fail to generate a shared community or joint outreach/ entrepreneurial activities may become mired in conditions such as these:

> In the end, I, like so many of my colleagues, just did – and do – the work of the State. Our work is, with the help of increasingly competitive recruitment strategies and accompanying grade inflation, to process increasingly ill-prepared students with higher levels of personal self-esteem through a system designed to reward the obedient, the cheerful, the well dressed, and the strategic, as well as those who are overly confident. I, perhaps like you, enter into a tacit exchange agreement with the State, wherein we help students acquire a language of cultural niceties peppered with strategies for landing jobs in exchange for paychecks that do not keep pace with inflation and a dwindling sense of respect for our increasingly limited authority. If we are obedient and lucky, eventually we get tenure and promotion and are vested in a mediocre retirement plan. (Goodall, 1999: 468)

Sykes (1988) discussed the expansion of private interests among academic faculties, and specified that this was typically self-interest, rather than departmental or institutional private interest. He also criticized the small percentage of university budgets earmarked for instruction, and the emerging dangers of proprietary secrecy (Sykes, 1988: 233).

Universities can be bureaucratic, large, and unwieldy, though some organizational forms are more agile and open to adjustment than others. Yet university conservatism is also an impediment to change. Universities are regularly criticized (not least by their own more political students) for being too unresponsive a part of the social power structure.

The self-reliant university?

There is a great amount of freedom within the universities we studied. Faculty and students can pursue self-determined intellectual challenges. But for those who would draw a salary or obtain a degree, there are requirements and obligations. Universities are far from being autonomous; they must be (and have been) responsive to the wider society and assorted stakeholders such as industry or other paymasters. Separate components of influence – the State, the Church, external funders – may shift considerably in importance; yet relative reshuffling might leave the sum substantially constant. In the research we did not seek to measure or hypothesize about what professors would do if given more unstructured time or less-restricted resources. Perhaps not much would change.

Universities over the centuries have had to adjust to changing expectations, and varying levels of self-reliance. Church and State have often become involved in university affairs. Those now seeking better working conditions or more resources enjoy luxury already compared with more arbitrary past periods, when the Church exacted grim punishment for heresy or the State harshly repressed assorted political crimes and transgressions.

Universities operate under a grant or licence from national authorities. Many higher education systems impose fundamental rigidities upon their nation's universities such that to be 'businesslike' or entrepreneurial is severely constrained. In Sweden, for instance, the number of places at each university by subject of study is fixed after negotiations with the State (ongoing programmes can generally change only by modest increments); and it is not possible to charge tuition to students. Thus, two major pillars of a university's potential business operations are constrained: supply is artificially limited, and revenues from such activities are fundamentally non-adjustable for both undergraduate and postgraduate education. Many systems, including Sweden, also limit university autonomy in the making of personnel decisions, especially with severance but also with hiring faculty. If a business were restricted in how much it could sell, at what price, and with what staff, it would at least gain sympathy if its performance was not stellar.

National university systems are sometimes classified as characteristic of codified models. Simply, the Humboldtian ideal has humanistic liberalism blossoming in an atmosphere of freedom for research, while the Napoleonic model positions education as a servant to the State. The Central and Eastern European model has been an elite education focused on vocational output in service to the State, which developed during socialist central planning; a further Nordic model is of mass access to free higher education that also de-emphasizes educational competition as a screening mechanism. In looking at inhibitors, however, these classifications may be of little practical use. Modern universities are, in fact, highly heterogeneous, perhaps increasingly so, and not 'black box' unitary actors (Allison, 1971), although national characteristics exist. The larger contrast is in terms of a creative class (loosely modelled on Florida, 2002), or perhaps an intelligentsia, a subset of people who seek to blossom in their university and the academy – in undefined ways – as distinct from a larger group who pursue functional, instrumental, or utilitarian training paths. Most universities offer opportunities for both of these groups.

Certainly there is much conformity among professors – and this is not surprising. Training processes for scholarly achievement demand conformity in mastering a complex catechism, requiring decades of often tedious effort from early childhood. Part of this dynamic involves imagination, and a measure of self-confidence. Fromm (1942) posited that most people 'escape from freedom', avoiding isolated aloneness by looking to outside authority, and ceding control, with a self-directed illusion maintained in actual submissive circumstances.

University faculty members are predominantly trained to be researchers, often in narrow subfields (for example, Elizabethan romance literature or modified Newtonian dynamics). Instead of seeking to redefine faculty job requirements away from teaching and research, many universities simply offer opportunities and incentives for parallel administrative or entrepreneurial activities. Otherwise, being forced into managerial activities is often resented. This is understandable: institutional administration differs greatly from most research areas (which in the wider terms can seem narrow and perhaps expendable); colleagues from business and economics can often dominate administrative and entrepreneurial activities as a result of being relatively more familiar with those skills and perspectives. Finally, we found evidence in many faculties of parallel approaches to academic professionalism: many sought to maintain their jobs in research, largely avoiding administrative entanglements; operating in conditions that others might label denial of managerial realities. Summarily rejecting proposed processes with the argument that 'it's not my job' seems to mitigate against entrepreneurship and change; reasoned unwillingness may be shorthand for a lack of perceived benefit or an expectation of unwelcome costs.

Some people migrate away from university work and academia due to relatively poor compensation. Institutional development in the wider private sector typically offers management both salary and equity, but few university posts can offer equity (share ownership) incentives. As universities become more businesslike in terms of operations, what some consider attractive elements of university ambience may diminish, such as collegiality, job security, and a comparatively less frenzied pace. This would appear to mitigate against choosing a university career. However, Bonner (2006: 62) notes cases where industrial researchers migrate to academia in search of more control over choice of research area. Universities can conduct research in domains that offer insufficient prospects for direct commercial return to industry, but where great impact is nonetheless possible. One example is work with Third World health problems, amply illustrated in the UK case study on the London School of Hygiene and Tropical Medicine.

There is a demonstration effect (Audretsch and Stephan, 1996), both positive and negative, where contact with successful or wealthy colleagues or classmates can generate new-found hungers and motivation. But in similar circumstances, others may be overwhelmed with envy (Page, 2003) or become injudicious in narrowly seeking more.

Knowledge (or lack of it) is a further variable factor. When change occurs rapidly, best practices are uncertain. In a competitive field, there are a growing number of substantial disincentives to sharing insight, knowledge, and techniques with competing individuals or institutions.

Even when motivation is high, progress and success are not assured. It may be difficult or impossible to overcome university personnel rigidities, legal constraints, financial barriers, or time limitations. A further chronic organizational anomaly among universities is that most top leaders and managers have inappropriate education. University top officials and academic faculty often are completely untrained in management and institutional development (this is counter-intuitive, as university leaders thus belittle the formal training offered by university systems). Staff-level university administrators more appropriately trained in functional fields seldom have sufficient leverage to guide the organization by themselves. Many organizations none-theless muddle through; others thrive. The internal processes of some organizations allow new or reformed operations to take root without full-scale confrontation or the need for wide consensus. The varied interests of multiple stakeholders may or may not be reconciled.

Competitiveness

Recharged competitiveness is a fundamental component to entrepreneurialism. Shattock (2003: 156) seems an unabashed proponent of such competitiveness:

> Entrepreneurial universities compete vigorously in the national and international academic markets for excellent staff, for students and for major grants, and they are ruthless at analysing their failures; they will not be satisfied with a modest performance which can be dressed up to look as if it meets the targets set by the State because they will want to succeed in every forum in which they compete.

This florid competitive vigour contrasts starkly with the scepticism found by Currie et al. (2003), where competition is seen as leading to heightened internal friction and external rivalries. Informants from the University of Avignon (France) worried that differential fees might lead to an explicit ranking of universities, while the worry was raised from the University of Oslo (Norway) that rating universities is not Scandinavian, but 'a very Anglo-American way of thinking' (Currie et al., 2003: 71). Norwegian informants also voiced hope for competition, however, where an applied dimension might put knowledge to better use than as 'small pieces in the so-called international journals that no one reads' (p. 72). Another senior Norwegian academic criticized Norway's small research budgets and poor competitive output:

> Norwegians think they are best in everything. I don't think they have [an idea]. For instance, if you compare Norway with Switzerland, which is about the size of Norway, about 2.8 percent of their gross national product goes into research and development. Switzerland has 20 Nobel prizes in physics, chemistry, and medicine. So, I don't think this govern-ment understands what competition is. (Currie et al., 2003: 73)

A reported increased use of university ranking lists or league tables (Roberts, 2007) is unsurprising. Given the rising costs of higher education, consumers are interested to know what they are buying with their time and money, and wish for good value. While some in universities scoff at such lists as unsubstantiated and biased, reflecting the cultivation of universities as brands, others trumpet cases of success. Rankings and reviews are approximations including an assortment of measurements; they are at best comparative surrogate indicators for quality and progress. As rankings grow in importance, entrepreneurialism and experimentation could be inhibited if such activities might harm a university's relative ranking. Certainly many universities around the world are paying increased attention to reputation management, but still 'most universities do not significantly differentiate themselves' (Shattock, 2003: 147). In any event for those that score poorly, there is no relegation – those at the bottom are not forced to close.

Community

Some in academia feel responsible to a wider community of scholars, but others do not. There are no generally recognized central offices representing academia or the scientific community. Some scholars have a strong sense of wider professional service, others volunteer within their narrow discipline, whereas to some all outreach is self-promotion. Harvard University Dean Theda Skocpol (2006) spoke of the faculty community at Harvard as 'individual super-stars' behaving 'like perpetual, market-maximizing free agents'. She quotes a predecessor, David Riesman, as describing the faculty as 'polar bears on separate icebergs'. A recent shared sense of crisis (in regard to their controversial former president) brought the Harvard community together in new functional arrangements – might there be hope for a stronger sense of community within the wider domain of academia? If so, this could become a catalyst for substantial change in universities.

Ortega (1930/1946) visualized a greater university of both scale and impact. His conception ultimately sees University replacing Church as the new First EState (my terminology), to act as a 'spiritual power' guiding society:

> in our times, the ancient 'spiritual powers' have disappeared: the Church because it has abandoned the present (whereas the life of the people is ever a decidedly current affair); and the State because with the triumph of democracy it has given up governing the life of the people, to be governed instead by their opinion. (Ortega, 1930/1946: 76)

Ortega saw universities, and also journalists/the press, as positioned to nourish, to guide, and when necessary to criticize. Though himself a journalist and publisher, the press is described as concentrating on the low, sensational, notorious, and under the influence of money. Ortega (1930/1946: 77) believed the university should strongly intervene in 'the great themes of the day' in matters cultural, professional, and scientific. Universities, with the basic mission to instil culture (p. 46), should also be assertive, as an uplifting principle, in providing checks and balances on business and politics, and not fear addressing management of that which matters greatly to most people, human life.

Further discussion

Universities around the world are being buffeted by change. Some challenges are financial, some are technical, and others deal with vision or positioning. The immediacy of challenge is felt differently in different circles. Some universities, departments, and individuals are operating without much sense of fiscal pressure, perhaps sheltered from market rigours thanks to stable and secure financing. But many more have had their budgets cut, and somehow must respond or creatively adapt. But the possible range of flexibility may be so highly constrained that little or nothing is done.

What actually is the process of entrepreneurialism? Can it be distilled to imagination and, then, advocacy/promotion? If so, and the process needs key personnel as catalysts, we are perhaps looking in wholly the wrong place. Academics and administrators should not be relied upon for solutions to these problems (we would not expect the College of Cardinals to best demonstrate how to party). In the process of their long training, some academics simply add to their skills set. Many others learn to see the world differently, but not always with more imagination. Some effectively lose their abilities to argue with passion, and without footnotes. Why not invite a mix of other people into the universities to help tackle such challenges?

To benefit best from innovation and first mover advantages, society must seek out and somehow cultivate the unorthodox and highly entrepreneurial. Some universities (examples include Umeå and KTH in Sweden, Twente in the Netherlands, and many dozens more throughout the world) have developed successful programmes promoting faculty innovation and spin-off business incubators. But the best place to look for highly imaginative people is likely not to be among faculty at traditional universities. In contrast to centuries ago, many more independent routes exist that are attractive to such people: alternatives in the arts or other avant-garde environments. Highly creative people also might be found in greater numbers among venture businesses or social entrepreneurs rather than within universities. Such outside people can be usefully introduced into a faculty to act as catalysts for innovation, leaving further development to technicians and students.

Risk and reward

Should we expect that academics or university administrators with an entrepreneurial bent can reasonably evaluate opportunity? As already mentioned, university people typically are not trained or well equipped to handle risk. What in fact are university-based entrepreneurs risking? In extreme cases, they risk public funds, public trust, and the potential devaluation of their university's degrees. Their jobs, however, might be secure. These are the type of people who might accept least-cost construction bids with minimal due diligence from shady operators, and are then surprised when their project markedly deteriorates in the first five years. If such people worked in the private sector, they would probably be fired; in centuries past, they might have been shot or lynched. In a modern university, such a person may simply be reassigned, perhaps to their former research post.

Where universities are disconnected from any need to provide demand-driven services, there must be other incentives. In some cases, there is reluctance (or explicit laws) that forbid universities from providing certain services; university outreach has been challenged in Spain as unfair competition by unsubsidized businesses. Another example from among our cases is where the Universities of Lapland, Plymouth, and elsewhere claim that their region is almost exclusively made up of small and medium size firms, with few potential paying customers for the university's services. But a major impediment is rigidity in those universities' service models: potential customers are being asked to pay in advance, prior to receiving any benefit. An innovative approach might instead be where the university seeks to assist individuals or firms, and is later compensated with shares or equity. This allows looking at the market in a different way, and such local regions might actually offer exceptional opportunities and first-mover advantages for university-based services.

Ownership

University personnel often claim that their hands are tied unreasonably; they have no lack of reasons why something cannot be done. But they complain in the midst of substantial subsidies, while constructing barriers-to-entry against those they have determined are interloping outsiders.

Some of the conditions imposed on university researchers under the rubric of 'market-driven universities' are extremely unreasonable. For example, grant applications require disclosure of key research ideas with detailed research plans. This grants process is highly competitive and often involves substantial funds, but the researcher is required to divulge both prior ideas and their creative development without guarantees of confidentiality. The researcher has no way to protect a research idea, which can easily be purloined and copied by others. Ideas are often valuable; they are carefully protected as key assets by industry, but are bandied about in a cavalier fashion in the academic world.

Entrepreneurial businesses and private sector organizations typically have a clear organizational hierarchy that defines responsibility and provides individual incentive for those driving change or championing a new venture. Universities may fail to assign adequate 'ownership' (and sufficient incentives) for a new venture, especially if it is outside of normal academic operations. The likelihood of success may diminish, perhaps greatly, if responsibility and incentives are diffused over many people. A corollary to this is the flow of decision making. Committee-led operations and group decision-making are cumbersome procedures that require much time. Groups would seem to have the potential to generate more ideas and objections than a single individual, but incentives and motivation are needed if organized sclerosis is to be overcome. These management variations, and how they relate to vision and integrity, are likely to affect project timeline, costs, and success. Managing and motivating university faculty is a considerable challenge, and university institution-building is a substantial and important job. Yet there are generally no stock options available for university leaders, nor do they enjoy the deluxe benefits available to top corporate administrators in the private sector. Ultimately, many of the best managers and administrators consider migration, and some leave for the corporate sector.

Managers at traditional universities need to work backwards with reform – many rigidities preclude or inhibit change. For example, many full-time faculty jobs cannot be scaled back or eliminated even when course enrolments have declined. Faculty jobs often are 'protected' – there may be few incentives (and assorted disincentives) to attracting more students. When the university must maintain programmes or courses for which there is little or no demand, such rigidities can promote poor service-mindedness.

Indeed, a provocative statement in Shattock (2003: 156) casts considerable doubt on the entrepreneurial potential of the average university:

> To be successful as an entrepreneurial university academic staff of high quality are required; there is little evidence that entrepreneurial activity flourishes on a sustainable basis in second or third tier institutions. Being entrepreneurial means first, being entrepreneurial in academic matters not in finance; financial success follows academic success, and reinforces it, but cannot create it.

The idea that 'academic staff of high quality are required' is unsupported by specific example. Though I am tempted to agree that quality is important, perhaps critically important, the staff need not narrowly be academic people, they might also be practitioners, at least in some departments. For example, perhaps the most well-known and even iconic department at Loughborough University, their School of Sport and Exercise Sciences, is more practical than classically academic. The Juilliard School (New York City, USA) is highly regarded for undergraduate and graduate training in music, dance, and drama; Berklee College of Music (Boston, USA) is also extremely highly regarded. The future may in fact be bright for niche or 'boutique' universities that focus on narrow areas, do their work well, and attract substantial funding and support. An extension to the argument above is that functions or departments that detract from institutional excellence may come under increased pressure from other segments of the institution.

Veblen (1918) and Sinclair (1923) were early critics of the interrelationship between universities and business in the United States. Sinclair presented micro case studies of what he determined was a subservience of universities to the business world. He also criticized the universities as being largely a waste of student time, 'dreary' and 'uninteresting' (Veblen, 1918: 9). Students, ultimately, were being trained as workers to obey and to behave. Such warnings ring true today, even amidst new teaching tools and entrepreneurial programmes. We should not lose sight of the fact that the university community often fails to offer a fascinating feast for the mind; students instead often find the fare inedible and poorly prepared, only obtainable in meagre amounts.

In Europe in particular, many universities and higher education traditions developed from Church sponsorship and a strong monastic tradition. In America, according to Vidich (1994), even those universities with strong links to churches have from the start been strongly utilitarian, orientated to train clerically educated social leaders. 'It is not that disinterested scholarship has been perverted by the values of businessmen but that learning in the United States has never been disinterested' (Vidich, 1994: 647).

Ortega (1930/1946: 74) believed the 'institutionalizing of intellect is the originality of the European compared with other races, other lands, and other ages'. Writing in 1930, he envisioned *the* university, in the sense of a wider community of scholars. *Universitas* as in academy now seems under dismantlement by proprietary institutionalism, fragmentation of the professoriate, assertion of intellectual property rights. The important critical function of universities as a platform for detached objective expertise is being lost to individual analysts marketing themselves. The present impetus is rather that universities withdraw into minor subcontracting or logistical roles.

New entrants in the higher education market often now trade on the accumulated reputation and achievements of universities, styling their corporate names and qualifications as similar to (or equivalent to) universities. Such organizations may or may not need to undergo vigorous validation by national governments or other outside accreditation bodies, and some are able to operate successfully with little oversight. This type of change is also occurring elsewhere in society; for example, banking is an industry greatly changed by the electronic age. The old 'bricks and mortar' business model with large prominent bank buildings has given way to electronic banking, networked automated teller machines, and the possibility that migrant customers can use cashpoints at any of dozens of new competitor firms. The world has changed for banking, and it is changing for universities. There may be new opportunities, such as with distance learning, marketing to newly mobile students, and intellectual property licensing. But there are also dangerous pitfalls in a struggle to maintain quality and efficiency without cutting corners. Competition can lead to a dangerous 'rush to the bottom'. The new UK 'fast-track' two-year bachelor's degree (see, for example, the University of Buckingham case) risks heavy criticism from countries such as the United States and Japan, where the typical undergraduate programme requires four years; will this cast aspersions on all UK degrees? Perhaps the wider system is threatened when some universities allow credit (or degrees) for passing certain tests, or where life experiences accumulate credit. Universities lack a true international governing body, so there are few rigid limitations. The higher education industry already enjoys huge fund flows; good new ideas promise realignments and other first-mover advantages. This means there is certain to be experimentation, which sometimes will raise objections. All universities can be hurt by bad publicity. But in a competitive market, those who move too slowly miss key opportunities. Such are the entrepreneurial risks to universities now.

Conclusions

There is much potential in the universities, but it is a substantial challenge to develop and extricate unrealized wealth. University institutions and the scholars within are resistant to change; seeking to force conformity can easily be counterproductive. To some extent autonomy is a key factor in innovation and growth. For the scholar, an outward-looking attitude should not distract too much from the creative process of research, teaching, and other necessary focal work.

Universities are changing. New incentives and better comparative measurement of key functions and operations are now motivating those in universities, driving both entrepreneurial innovation and new forms of community interaction. Regardless, surely many scholars will continue feeling they lack sufficient time, that they are misunderstood by those outside their guild, and that their contributions are insufficiently recognized.

Entrepreneurship may be unrecognized except in comparison with elsewhere. Change, and tolerance for it, becomes commonplace; a continued introduction of novel programmes over time can become unremarkable. Both the changes and their effects can be transformative.

It is wise to bear in mind the key impediment highlighted by Shattock (2003: 157), that entrepreneurial universities 'are not necessarily comfortable institutions to work in'. University people who prefer a comfortable workplace may try to thwart change. Yet the demands of environmental change, especially shrinking entitlement funds, ultimately may require entrepreneurial response(s). Many in universities now feel pressured to alter their workways. This is not unjust; and is likely quite useful – pressure makes diamonds!

Addendum: inhibitors to entrepreneurialism mentioned in the case studies

Some inhibitors to entrepreneurial action were cited explicitly within the case studies (as were aspects that promoted entrepreneurialism and change). These are summarized below.

Umeå University	Sweden
Explicitly cited inhibiting factors	*Explicitly cited nurturing factors*
• the university's past reputation for political radicalism is perhaps a deterrent to those interested in business and commercialization	• lengthy effort to attract and develop a valued university into the region
• no possibility to charge direct tuition; student numbers and compensation rates per student are key rigidities constrained ultimately by the State	• income from external commissioned courses is twice the national average
• leadership continuity is poor: after three years, deans and prefects revert to being normal faculty	• a need for action is natural in light of the geographic isolation
• Swedish language is still widely used, though English may be more appropriate to the university's international positioning	• lack of funds is a motivator to find more external funding
• many from the medical faculty work also externally, including with small businesses, but the wider faculty is not encouraged to do this	• university board no longer run by teachers but by external appointments (always including students); now more open to society
• full four-year funding must be arranged before each doctoral student admission; this is a bottleneck	• a newer dynamic university, with some mistrust of the older establishment
• each unit pays for the central External Relations Office (ENS); there seems to be no limit on its costs, and such development expertise in each faculty is now under-utilized, even discouraged	• the university developed a centralized professional External Relations Office (ENS)
• external funds often do not cover continuing costs, such as machinery maintenance, which then must be drawn from the basic budget	• positive spillovers from foreign students
• some satellite campuses are in small northern settlements with minimal local talent	• risks are very small
• difficult to develop selectivity and competitiveness due to central government rigidities in student and faculty recruitment	• more open markets for faculty services fuels responsiveness
• salary scales are rigid, individual incentives for entrepreneurship are poor (such success is not considered an academic merit), and envy of rewards among peers is problematic	
• geographic isolation requires action; physical distance from the capital and from corporate decision makers is an inhibitor	
• too much comfort; little entrepreneurial hunger; too few success stories	
• business and industry often bypass the university, unaware of what can be offered	

Royal Institute of Technology (KTH)

Explicitly cited inhibiting factors

- subject-based organizational structures can be unduly rigid, permitting narrow thinking
- more diversity is needed but hiring rigidities, limited childcare, and other limits make a relatively poor working environment
- university support services for innovation need further development
- Swedish academics own their intellectual property; perhaps a hindrance to development

Explicitly cited nurturing factors

- multidisciplinary meta-centres are being developed to stimulate new project directions
- diversity is expanding

University of Lund

Explicitly cited inhibiting factors

- huge, comprehensive, ungainly organization
- applied efforts are considered of a lower status than basic research; simple money making is considered 'ugly'
- academics only recently are engaging in two-way dialogue with industry; previously it was one way: merely going out to teach society
- 'a culture resting on old traditions with a focus on academic excellence has its own incentives and rewards, not always with the same goals as those that characterize enterprise'. Several respondents mentioned this, though it may unreasonably equate entrepreneurialism solely with commercialism
- time is limited; academics are 'swamped' with too many activities already
- large external projects and patents are not appropriately valued as academic merits

Explicitly cited nurturing factors

- central steering core allows more sense of 'pulling together' as well as actual progress

Jönköping University	Sweden
Explicitly cited inhibiting factors	*Explicitly cited nurturing factors*
• Rector has much personal responsibility and little job security; lacks the full range of private sector remuneration and financial incentives	• large number of partner universities (210) around the world helps circulate new ideas and best-practice operational development
• struggle with newer university positioning and identity (including the name? Jönköping has non-standard characters internationally, and is often mispronounced; properly: 'Yunshepping')	• close links with the local region, which also acts as a landlord; freedom from the rigidities of the nationwide firm handling rents for Sweden's academic premises
• uncommon governance system (four corporations under the umbrella university foundation) can be unwieldy; sometimes unclear or conflicting goals, while synergies can mean ceding control to the central administration	
• still bound to Swedish State rules on tuition limits and student numbers, though a private foundation	
• entrepreneurial mindset in Sweden is considered to be limited; too complacent in believing that the State will ultimately provide	

Higher School of Economics, Moscow (HSE, Russia)	Russia
Explicitly cited inhibiting factors	*Explicitly cited nurturing factors*
• still rather new organization with substantial successes but also some who are in opposition; near to being evicted in September 1998 when government changed. Some might consider such uncertainties a disincentive to stay and work for institutional development – perhaps the private sector is more predictable and rewarding of good work	• relatively high compensation and clear incentives for mid-level faculty and top people
• early staffing bottlenecks seem to have been largely overcome through group training, but perhaps this has engendered more 'groupthink' than found elsewhere; also, the most capable people migrate into business and away from academia	• uncertainty has been used to fuel speed of growth; to slow down invited potential collapse
• friction with outside work competing with the institution, though activity elsewhere may bring ideas and techniques back to the organization	

- classrooms, student housing, and facilities for sport are insufficient, even below standard, which causes problems for attracting and retaining the best students possible and precludes attracting fee-paying diverse foreign students with useful experiences
- path to success unclear particularly in Russia
- Ministry of Education future path, regulation, and funding unclear
- professional standards are still developing nationally
- (big) business demands have been urgent and are fundamentally short term in nature (unsupportive of experimentation)
- initiatives such as new departments that cannot be successful leaders in their disciplines may slow overall progress and tarnish the overall reputation
- need for internationally able faculty
- the institution is little involved with smaller outside contracts due to individual faculty handling such activities on a private (personal) basis; this is also a bottleneck to internal information flows
- efforts to impose more centralized management have caused estrangement
- prior failure (Higher School of Journalism) may lead to caution that stifles new entrepreneurial initiatives
- links to government can be both a benefit and a constraint
- some rigidity in thinking as to the proper role and status of a business school
- compensation and incentives are still inadequate at the lower end and for entry-level staff; this still necessitates multiple outside jobs ('lecture tour')
- in an active, unsettled market that is full of novelty, it is difficult to clearly distil which factors lead to success or failure

Baikal Institute of Business and International Management of Irkutsk University (BIBIM)	Russia
Explicitly cited inhibiting factors	*Explicitly cited nurturing factors*
- need for more flexible professors with foreign language abilities, practical experience, and interest in collaboration	- close protective relationship with the larger Irkutsk State University, though independent

- some State licensing is still in a comparative state of change/unsettled
- great distance from Moscow may lead to underestimating the region
- the whole system is in such a state of flux that many may have unreasonable expectations; 'More than half of the graduates have a job different from their studies' – is this so strange? Also – they have jobs!
- very high demand on resources (classrooms and equipment) is unhelpful
- serious problems with monitoring accounts and drawing out basic funds
- links to local industry are often not to the advantage of the university
- considerable uncertainty over whether the organization will survive long
- difficult to conduct effective branding

University of Pereslavl

Explicitly cited inhibiting factors

- former 'professional deployment' kept the region stocked with high-level human capital; now many of the best people are leaving the region for better opportunities elsewhere, while few good people come to replace them
- serious shortage of well-qualified teachers; poor pay; low motivation
- accountants are a law among themselves, with an expanding cohort and substantial leverage in all areas of university affairs
- fragmentation of functions; no effective 'rules of the game'
- radical restructuring seen as possible (foreign buyout, etc.)
- substantial liquidity crisis is likely to dampen risk-taking behaviour

Moldova State University (MSU)

Explicitly cited inhibiting factors

- expressed need for promotion of innovative technologies for pedagogical development, also better training methodology
- unclear how Center Prometheus links to market needs

- innovative flexibility with time: night or weekend studies
- building links to Japan
- 'Baikal' regional managers training

Russia

Explicitly cited nurturing factors

- close links with local industry
- good atmosphere of creativity

Moldova

Explicitly cited nurturing factors

- promising activities in the Center Prometheus

Alecu Russo State University of Balti (BSU)

Moldova	
Explicitly cited nurturing factors	*Explicitly cited inhibiting factors*
• regular salaries are low, but supplements and incentives have been made available to pay teachers	• the US State Department supplies outside funding that the university has no accounting for; is it clear how long the funding will continue? • regional universities may be disadvantaged in national competitions for financial support; are there measures for good representation in the capital? • prejudice remains from Soviet times over the term 'entrepreneurialism'

Academy of Economic Studies of Moldova (AESM)

Moldova	
Explicitly cited nurturing factors	*Explicitly cited inhibiting factors*
• strong alumni network • dynamic growth; good reputation	• local businesses have yet to become interested in university operations • knowledge of modern management is still relatively poor in the country • prejudice remains from Soviet times over the term 'entrepreneurialism'

Trade Cooperative University of Moldova (TCUM)

Moldova	
Explicitly cited nurturing factors	*Explicitly cited inhibiting factors*
• strong niche links in the cooperative movement and with consumer cooperation	• is the cooperative movement progressive in terms of mercantilism, perhaps with special skills, or perhaps anti-commercial? • can the cooperative movement and the State continue to fund this effort, or must the proportion of fee-paying students (and fees paid) rise greatly?

University of Tampere

Explicitly cited inhibiting factors

- focus areas for the university are diffused
- what seems cutting-edge may simply be local testing of innovation coming from elsewhere (low value-added)
- recent external membership on university board begun, but limited to a single person from whom little is expected; Consultative Committee between university and key local persons exists, but has yet to become dynamic
- cross-departmental cooperation is difficult
- departmental leadership is done begrudgingly; university leadership is constrained; the centre has limited levers for providing direction
- resource-sapping projects may be accepted for limited marginal benefits
- highly risk averse, with limited vision
- many more applicants than are accepted; the university thus has no driving need to develop its marketing; images of 'the red university' persist
- State control and traditions are so strong that only 'mental entrepreneurialism' is possible – that is, 'without compensation'
- administrative rigidities; researchers also feel entitled to do or not to do what they want

Finland

Explicitly cited nurturing factors

- Tampere has much surrounding industry, both traditional and in newer services
- excellent experience in attracting donated professorships
- change is only possible to implement slowly, but that may be good for institutional survival, being ultimately safe and stable

University of Lapland (ULA)

Explicitly cited inhibiting factors

- northern region is often considered bleak and desolate; the university is seen as an arm of regional policy more than a novel energy of its own
- administrative rigidities smother and stifle initiative
- professional managers are needed
- external funding is pursued even where there is little added value or promised positive spillover effects
- project-based personnel groups may be underfunded by their projects
- the region has few potential paying customers for external services (using present compensation formats)

Finland

Explicitly cited nurturing factors

- most northern EU university, with a pioneering mentality and exotic image
- network faculty in economics and tourism is a novel effort to bridge disciplines and distance
- the university effectively markets the surrounding 'frontier environment'
- Province College has been set up to support local development
- explicit focus on the idea that only change is

Helsinki School of Economics (HSE, Finland)

Explicitly cited inhibiting factors

- researchers are not as driven to change, or as excited, as management
- consensus-based change is gradual and slow
- the State and ministries constrain the range of possible action – almost like a 'command economy': 'the planning machinery of the State defines how many students are educated, in which fields, who trains them, with what resources and regulations' – it is mostly pre-planned
- the civil servants in the ministries are ignorant of the true needs of companies (for example, conducting executive training of Finnish corporate personnel to be posted abroad may best be done in Asia)
- the international education market is difficult to robustly enter due to central government rigidities; relatively low pay is a barrier to attracting top researchers or teachers, and many instead migrate away
- demands are recognized that cannot be met because they fall outside the focal areas determined by powers outside the university
- grant applications require disclosure and claim to be a competition, but the researcher has no way to protect a research idea – many can be easily purloined and copied by others
- internal (affiliate) corporate development is of unclear legality
- any financial surplus might be taken by the Ministry of Finance
- many believe that policy makers should not affect the work of researchers
- tenured professors are difficult or impossible to replace, and retain much authority, so change is very slow

Finland

Explicitly cited nurturing factors

- cross-cutting phenomenon-based research starting to be stressed (multi-disciplinary)
- explicit efforts to bridge teaching, research, and outreach
- innovative programme educating 1400 Korean businesspersons with the Executive MBA is building an important network and bridge likely to be useful in the future, as is outreach to China and Singapore
- substantial internal corporate development that can pay top salaries for top teachers
- good success with corporate partnership and donor programmes
- some believe that universities should only change slowly, being instead stable institutions

Technical University of Valencia (UPV)

Explicitly cited inhibiting factors

- Rector-appointed General Manager, the sole professionally trained manager on the management team, has considerable expert power and perhaps veto leverage
- civil servant (permanent) status for long-term faculty and staff may be unwieldy and rigid; those who have yet to achieve such status may be constrained and wary of experimentation
- former Rector was unusual and held office for 18 years; seemingly 'a hard act to follow' for the subsequent management team as the university is without any new strategic plan
- efforts by the university to stimulate outreach have been interpreted as reflecting more interest in business than in academics; low university overheads for outside contracts (10%) may be unsustainable, yet raising them substantially might also stifle further outreach activities
- much independence, but internal conditions are such that much inertia reigns
- internal doubts that some institutes are proper research units; personal leverage may have created institutions without content
- the 30% retained by researchers is reportedly poor compared with what might be gained in the private sector
- local businesses, generally SMEs, often do not know much about what UPV can offer (they learn from their contacts abroad); institutional marketing may thus be insufficient
- internal circulation of information is often poor
- there seems to be no clear consensus on what is the proper role of university outreach (UPV has been sued by three local professional organizations for unfair competition)
- there is reported interference between teachers and their private consulting; they 'never teach everything they know to students'. Whether or not this is so, the criticism shows a perhaps costly internal lack of trust
- collegial decision-making requires bargaining that is costly in time and resources
- some claim clearer objectives, guidelines, and procedures would encourage entrepreneurialism
- teaching is too theoretical, out-of-touch, and should be better attuned to the labour market

Spain

Explicitly cited nurturing factors

- if well constructed, the Researcher Activity Index (IAIP) will provide incentives for entrepreneurialism and innovation; if not, the IAIP is itself an impediment
- various levels of incentives for excellence and outreach from both the university and the regional government

University Jaume I of Castellon

Explicitly cited inhibiting factors

- complex and unwieldy bureaucracy for hiring to permanent positions; rules set by national government (not the institution); some able people choose other career paths to avoid the bureaucracy at the university
- development plans have a ragged schedule of implementation; business-like controls and imposition of change on subunits is very difficult
- 'people are turning into professional risk managers, treasurers, computer program promoters, etc.' and away from their original job type
- there is a worry that research results may pass to a monopolistic secretive company, instead of going to all who might need the new technology (this shows perhaps a misunderstanding of market forces, risk, and promotion)
- legal limits to being a part of companies is an impediment
- very good project managers are needed (and are difficult to attract)
- risk is proscribed; people do not wish to take on new responsibilities
- non-technical research and innovation is undervalued and often overlooked

Spain

Explicitly cited nurturing factors

- New Technology Education Centre (CENT) has a history of pioneering innovation
- strongly worded '*Decalogue*' encourages institutional dynamism
- exceptional Innovation Incentive Programme

Cardenal Herrera University (UCH)

Explicitly cited inhibiting factors

- no Office for the Transfer of Research Results (OTRI) set up yet; external research projects and research contracts still very modest in scale
- such a private university is reportedly disadvantaged when competing for national funding, but there are many international possibilities that perhaps have not been adequately investigated
- a religious dimension to most entrepreneurial activities is mentioned, but what this entails is unspecified; the religious connection may be a positive point, or it may be a liability in comparison to secular organizations
- bureaucracy is a major impediment; more unit-level independence would reportedly help, with professional management

Spain

Explicitly cited nurturing factors

- extensive outreach links with regional businesses through UCH work experience placements
- emphasis on quality and individual attention might set a good foundation for innovation and entrepreneurialism

University of Alicante (UAL)

Explicitly cited inhibiting factors

- the civil servant status is an obstacle to entrepreneurship and flexibility
- seed money for new projects is difficult to garner
- the work placement system could reportedly benefit from more freedom
- the 'contracted doctor' system is a new form of permanent job status, but it is still small in scale; it is unclear how it differs from civil servant status – it might be an attractive innovation, but it might be the start of a new academic underclass; does it threaten existing staff in any way?

Spain

Explicitly cited nurturing factors

- the Employment Initiatives Office (GIPE) builds liaison with area businesses, and through placement and assistance builds both goodwill and communications channels to the surrounding region
- liaison is also developed through shared research facilities (via SICAI)
- innovative projects with Asia open a novel window that may provide new opportunities for the university
- numerous satellite campuses can spread the university presence if managed successfully

Miguel Hernandez University (UMH)

Explicitly cited inhibiting factors

- more imagination is needed to reward entrepreneurs with more than simply financial benefits
- too much paperwork and administrative rigidity

Spain

Explicitly cited nurturing factors

- PESCA (Quality Strategic Plan) thus far very positively implemented
- the University Career Service seems very proactive and successful
- Technology Working Breakfast initiative brings together businesspeople and researchers
- PAREDIT overcomes some of the inefficiencies of properly deploying bureaucratic resources

University of Valencia (UV)

Explicitly cited inhibiting factors

- inertia and 'generation gap' stifle entrepreneurship
- problems defining what is proper for university activities; seeking to avoid 'unfair competition' with the private sector
- societal intolerance of failure (includes unspecified 'punishment') leads to risk-averse behaviour
- Incompatibilities Law limits lecturers and other civil servants from certain types of participation, rewards, etc., and also limits time that can be spent on external activities
- poor liaison between the university and surrounding society; there is basic disconnect between the classroom and the outside practical world
- civil servant status and job security might promote abuse of such things as sick leave (which is mentioned as a problem)

Spain

Explicitly cited nurturing factors

- OTRI (Office for the Transfer of Research Results) working to develop entrepreneurial links and networks

Academy of Hotel Management and Catering Industry (WSHIG)

Explicitly cited inhibiting factors

- differential between the full- and part-time programmes (for example, with the lower language requirement in the latter) likely to be harmful to institutional reputation (dilutes the brand)
- owner and founder has attracted substantial loyalty (or at least long service) among faculty and staff, but it is unclear if he is effective in drawing out ideas and innovation from them in the present top-down (rather than collegial) arrangement
- a large proportion of professors are elderly, themselves educated during the period of Communist central planning; how well can they train students in hospitality and service orientation?

Poland

Explicitly cited nurturing factors

- effort to instil combination of theoretical knowledge and practical skills links strongly to 'employability' – attractive to students and a growing network of surrounding businesses
- foreign and domestic training, and on-site Beverly Hills Movie Restaurant, build a special brand and *esprit de corps*
- affiliated high school is a good link for continuity and student intake

- new programmes offered at public institutions (AMU, PUE, etc.) compete successfully for students with WSHiG but have a fundamentally different, subsidized cost base
- national limitations on granting higher degrees, and long years between application and permission, puts private institutions at a considerable disadvantage compared with public institutions; an associated uncertainty also makes attracting top faculty difficult

Poznan University of Economics (PUE)

Explicitly cited inhibiting factors

- national government regulates which institutions can grant the MA and postgraduate degrees; long years between application and permission puts private institutions at a considerable disadvantage compared with public institutions; this uncertainty also makes attracting top faculty difficult (but once granted the ability to offer such degrees, such institutions enjoy a barrier to entry against new competitors)
- reliance on teaching services for income is very high; is there a chance to generate an endowment to stabilize financing, and allow more risk taking?
- some innovation with the title of 'full professor' but still the career system is rigid; central government now limits holding on multiple jobs by professors – perhaps good, but why can't market define what is best?
- generally, the State is still greatly involved in regulating the higher education industry, imposing numerous rigidities not seen elsewhere; top academics with the option to migrate outside the country at substantially better compensation and work terms may be tempted to do so

Poland

Explicitly cited nurturing factors

- well-recognized institutional reputation; this is helpful in recruitment; plans to double exchange student numbers within four years, and better internationalize the faculty (bringing in new ideas and strategies)
- successful MBA programme draws in excellent revenues; builds a strong network likely to be of use in future
- consulting office of the PUE Foundation links the university with surrounding industry
- tax advantages for knowledge professionals is a subsidy that may help keep clever people in the universities, even though academic salaries are low

Adam Mickiewicz University (AMU)

Explicitly cited inhibiting factors

- ungainly collegial decision-making requires much expenditure of time and energy in all levels of the organization
- national subsidies for research take little note of social sciences and humanities
- national standards for salaries do not allow much institutional flexibility or special incentives for excellence
- part-time studies receive the same diploma – are the students required to do the same work? The cachet of State-funded full-time students contrasts with privately funded part-time students; the latter are less able at admission, but what about upon graduation? Is there a need for better quality control?
- evening and weekend teaching is a good source of additional income for faculty, but is also tough; the need to emphasize teaching income has taken time and energy away from research
- external activities by universities (for example, publishing) are being severely curtailed; VAT imposed on R&D (draws resources elsewhere)
- proportion of fee-paying students is fixed by central government, which sets a ceiling both on revenues and potential outreach through that route
- no central campuses; offices and facilities are scattered throughout the city of Poznan, limiting potentially useful interaction
- a fear of institutional entrepreneurialism is noted: faculty worries that new rules may require more or different work, which may cut into their own overall incomes

Poland

Explicitly cited nurturing factors

- strong collegial tradition in contrast to managerialism
- perhaps Polish academics have needed to be entrepreneurial to survive: pressure makes diamonds!
- AMU Foundation provides offices and logistic support for new ventures
- satellite divisions likely to help secure a strong regional presence and commitment into the future

University of Plymouth	United Kingdom
Explicitly cited inhibiting factors	*Explicitly cited nurturing factors*

University of Plymouth	United Kingdom
• surrounding geographical area is economically depressed, with relatively high unemployment, low skills base, and low productivity (this might be seen as an opportunity by visionary university leadership) • as yet immature liaison between the universities and the South West Regional Development Agency; the interactive mechanisms and agenda for excellent regional cooperation have yet to be achieved; various and diverse parallel initiatives among multiple actors is likely wasteful and frustrating • branding of the region and its strengths seems to be confused; links to the sea and to tourism are only partly developed • the university is relatively weak in its research agenda and output; though having four Centres of Excellence in Teaching and Learning, and coping with/driving change relatively well. Compared with more prestigious universities, the University of Plymouth is not nationally considered cutting edge; this may depress the quality of recruitment (students, staff, and faculty) • doubt was expressed in the case study on Plymouth's entrepreneurialism as the level of risk in their multiple projects was low; if risk averse from lack of ambition or vision, then certainly an impediment – but if low-risk paths bring ample or substantial reward, risk taking may be constrained • is the university hampered by conflicting institutional visions of elite vs. regional vocational development? What is the peer group of this university, and what is its reputation there? • large-scale and unwieldy structure impedes effective management; communications among units, and throughout the university, is ragged • time strictures and general resistance to change impede progress	• the University of Plymouth Colleges: an innovative local network for widening participation that serves to funnel students information and ideas from throughout the region; also Channel Island University Consortium • Peninsula Medical School: forces contact and collaboration with University of Exeter (otherwise a rival) • award-winning Widening Access to Education initiative draws attention to innovative activities • successful with various gateway initiatives for training and partnership • Enterprise in Higher Education programmes are well subscribed

University of Buckingham

Explicitly cited inhibiting factors

- scale is likely too small; difficulties with recruitment abroad as multiple larger British university rivals have magnified their outreach; substantial shrinkage in enrolment gives the impression of a university in trouble – which further impedes recruitment of top students or faculty
- Bologna standards may negatively impact flagship two-year bachelor (honours) degree; extended 'stretch' year (to three years) possibility may only dilute the impact of prior marketing and sow confusion
- unmentioned was the potential for generating endowment through loyal and grateful alumni: perhaps not yet adequately developed (much could be done if given €70 million additional endowment); the unique strengths and human network of the university are as yet inadequately tapped

United Kingdom

Explicitly cited nurturing factors

- Buckingham's personal small-group teaching is a good environment for nurturing students, exchange of ideas and development of novelty (compared with many typical large lecture formats)
- both success (Buckingham Angels) and failure (History of Art Department) are likely to have been valuable lessons for management

University of Nottingham

Explicitly cited inhibiting factors

- grand action to begin operations in Malaysia and China, along with new domestic initiatives, might give the impression that entrepreneurialism and innovation mainly stem from the centre; rather, ideas and initiative from the disparate units, and from individuals, are also essential
- base salaries are classed as ungenerous, management of university staff is seen as notoriously difficult, and academic jobs fundamentally generate no economic equity; if doing cutting-edge businesslike activities, why not instead work in business, where the bureaucratic frustrations are probably less and the economic rewards are greater? ('we are akin perhaps to a firm of solicitors with 1400 partners' – yet solicitors are paid much better!)
- new Veterinary School ideally should have strong demand, but rural location of studies is quoted as a deterrent; perhaps distance from London and more exciting cosmopolitanism is an inhibitor generally to recruitment and retention of students and faculty

United Kingdom

Explicitly cited nurturing factors

- strong, cutting-edge operations with many market-orientated activities
- risk/reward recognized via €4 million pump-priming fund set up for research commercialization; professional PR (public relations) hiring
- active steps to consolidate departments and minimize inter-departmental competition for students (68 departments and > 31 schools); interdisciplinary focus allows quicker initiative and dynamic new 'stories' on promising R&D paths

- while in many senses the university is highly entrepreneurial, there is mention still of resentment and rigidity with regard to entrepreneurial projects; time limitations are a bottleneck to effectively driving change; the Research Assessment Exercise is quoted as a primary aim, when in fact it is merely a surrogate measurement of excellence

- there seems to be recognition that some projects will not work, but are they given long enough to blossom? For example, the e-university collapse, and the Thailand campus effort both have been largely abandoned, but were they given sufficient chance? The vice-chancellor 'made it clear that a major entrepreneurial venture of this kind (Malaysia campus) is not achieved without a considerable amount of hard work, sustained commitment, and willingness to bear some risk'. But is the time frame clear? Is it a strategy that first mover advantages must be realized within three to five years, for example?

London School of Hygiene and Tropical Medicine (LSHTM)

Explicitly cited inhibiting factors

- compensated outreach has been de-emphasized; consultancy is shrinking; this may limit wider outside interaction and cross-fertilization

- 'For most academics here, entrepreneurialism is seen as "hard capitalism" and they tend to shy away from that'; this statement displays a limited and rather grim view of entrepreneurialism (rather than, for example, innovation driving change in a desired direction)

- 'risk' has a different meaning for medical fieldworkers developing countermeasures to disease, including risk of death

- central London location has very limited space; land and facilities elsewhere have been sold; no information on the university's arguments considering the need to be sited in the present location

- the Research Assessment Exercise is considered superficial point-scoring (with focus on high-impact journals rather than, for example, on saving lives); the case implies a strong anti-authoritarian undercurrent – which could be (but does not seem to be) harnessed for entrepreneurial operations and redesigned operations

- explicitly recognize that not all innovation works out, but remain upbeat: 'we need to position ourselves so that once every five to ten years we can make €20m (from IP exploitation)'

- strong recognition of marketization and a changing, more competitive environment in UK academia

- broke new ground with the appointment of a Chinese professor (nuclear physicist Yang Fujia) as University Chancellor, no doubt bringing much attention in China to the university

United Kingdom

Explicitly cited nurturing factors

- clearly defined and focused activist mission 'to contribute to the improvement of health worldwide', with focus on behaviour and vectors rather than basic science; almost a missionary zeal to 'help the health in the worldwide community without financial gain' (that has attracted good quality academics distrustful of marketization and 'hard capitalism')

- wide outreach (distance education includes students from 120 countries)

- intellectual property protection has been instituted, albeit almost defensively (much is licensed in the Third World at low cost)

- hiring of a press officer shows a recognition of need to better interact with surrounding institutions and public

10

The dilemmas of the changing university

Risto Rinne and Jenni Koivula

The university world generally and in Europe faced an irreversible change of paradigm at the end of 1980s. The change had common roots with more general changes in the entire social context and in the atmosphere and ideologies of economic, social, and educational policy. The timescale has varied between different countries and different higher education models with different traditions. For example the Anglo-Saxon countries have been forerunners in this respect, whereas in the Nordic countries major changes only began taking place in the 1990s. The trend included state budget cuts, pressures for efficiency, conditional contracting, and the introduction of evaluation systems, managerialism, and an emphasis on the values of an enterprise culture. After the wave of these reforms, globalization and then Europeanization have been the most important factors in creating pressures on higher education. In this chapter, we consider the consequences of these pressures in different higher education models. The trend that began in the 1980s has continued but there are also new aspects. In many countries, universities have been harnessed to increase national competitiveness and their tasks have increased. A changing environment and increasing demands have also caused fundamental changes within universities. Market orientation together with entrepreneurial behaviour is the mode of operation that increasingly defines universities' activities today.

Global competition and pressures on universities

The economic and political changes that have accompanied globalization have been shown to put pressure on national competitiveness, and consequently on higher education policy. Neo-liberalism, increased competition promoted by globalization, the privatization of the economy, and the weakening of the public sector and of the status of the nation-state has modified the relationships between various actors and has created challenges for established modes of action (see Currie, 2003). The liberalization of trade in higher education services is also under discussion and evokes uncertainty as to whether it will take place under the GATS process.

In Europe, fierce competition with the United States and Asian countries for global supremacy has generated a defensive reaction. A well-known goal set for the EU in Lisbon in 2000 was 'to become the most competitive and dynamic knowledge-based economy in the world, capable of sustainable economic growth with more and better jobs and greater social cohesion'. This sentence is also used to rationalize the current activity of the EU in the area of education in general and higher education in particular. In the communication entitled *The role of the universities in the Europe of knowledge* (CEC, 2003a), the role of universities is seen as highly significant in the development of the know-how society, economic competitiveness, and social cohesion. Universities should become more flexible by utilizing the expanding possibilities offered by the service market.

In addition to the EU, the OECD, World Trade Organization, World Bank, and UNESCO have a strong influence on trends in education. Globalization and the activities of these supranational organizations have created a whole new vocabulary for education that is now used throughout the world. The changes in higher education cannot be understood any longer as national educational changes. They are part of global transformations and trends. However, the existing structure of each national higher education system still, historically and culturally, determines any possible future modifications (Clark, 1983), which means that countries with different higher education systems and cultures naturally respond differently to changes and demands in the environment.

The differing higher education models

Many scholars have presented various groupings of different higher education models. The groupings vary according to the viewpoints and issues under consideration. Probably the most used historical classification at the European level separates the Humboldtian (German), the Napoleonic (French), and the Anglo-Saxon (British/Newmanian) models (e.g. Husén, 1996). Kivinen and Rinne (1996) elaborated this classification by connecting the Anglo-Saxon model to the American model, unifying the Humboldtian and the Napoleonic models to the Western European (or Continental) model, and making the Nordic model a separate model (see also Rinne, 2004; Fägerlind and Strömqvist, 2004). From a European perspective one can, in addition, identify a Central and an Eastern European (transitional) model. In these models, state regulation, university governance, competition, and funding bases have had different forms. In this chapter, we classify the countries included in our comparative study under the Anglo-Saxon (UK), the Napoleonic (Spain), the Nordic (Sweden and Finland), and the transitional (Poland, Russia, and Moldova) models.

The *Anglo-Saxon model* can be described as a large-scale, market-driven, diversified, and hierarchical system where competition between institutions is general. This has been most characteristic of the university system in the United States, but in the 1980s the UK system faced a tremendous change from the situation that had obtained since the Second World War and adopted features of the US model. For example, fees for overseas students were introduced at the beginning of the 1980s and differential fees for home postgraduates in the late 1980s. Later, in 2000, fees were also introduced for home undergraduates. Legal and financial autonomy is what distinguishes the Anglo-Saxon universities from the European ones. The UK system is quite a different system from those of other European countries; it is based on a quasi-market where higher education institutions sell their services to the State and consumers, and where a regular research assessment system has strong consequences for the university funding.

The *Continental model* includes the distinct and different *Humboldtian* and *Napoleonic* models. The most important principles of the Humboldtian model are freedom of research and teaching; their inseparability and the priority of *Bildung* over professional training. The academic freedom of university professors is greater than in the Anglo-Saxon model. In the Napoleonic model, the societal relationship of universities is close and higher education institutions have the important task of training state civil servants. In the EUEREK Project, Germany and France, historically significant exemplars of Humboldtian and Napoleonic models, were not represented but the Spanish model can be seen as an example of the Napoleonic model. In the traditional Spanish model, state regulation was rigid, the system was formally homogeneous, study programmes were identical, and universities had a strong professional orientation.

In the *Nordic model*, the higher education sector has followed the wider educational and state policy, and has been surrendered almost entirely into the hands of the State. Universities have been almost entirely publicly funded. The institutions have been, at least formally, homogeneous and equal, and there has been no educational market. A centralized administration and state management have guaranteed limited competition. An important principle has been to keep degree level education free of charge, in the spirit of the Nordic welfare state model.

In the *Central and Eastern European/transition country model*, until the 1980s the function of higher education was mostly the training of a highly qualified workforce. The system was a quite elitist, labour market-led, polytechnic system. Higher education institutions were strongly controlled by the State and the system was centralized and ideological. Private universities did not exist. Poland, Russia, and Moldova fit into this category, although there are many differences between the higher education systems in these countries.

The changing role of the mass university towards the 'third mission'

One reason for the changed role of the university is the massification of higher education. The transition from elite to mass and to a universal system (Trow, 1974) has made the university more central in society and has entailed the creation of new types of higher education institutions, the diversification of study programmes, and the growth of research activities. The first wave of 'enrolment exploitation' occurred between the 1950s and 1970s. The second wave began in the 1990s. According to Trow, a universal system is reached when more than 35% of each generation enters higher education. This was reached two decades ago in the United States and in a few other countries; it is now also more common within European countries. The transition countries probably faced the largest massification of higher education in the 1990s as a consequence of the loosened regulation of higher education and the emergence of the private sector. Poland is a good example of this: since 1990, there has been an almost 400% rise in enrolments and the participation rate grew from 13% in 1990 to almost 50% in 2004.

As mentioned above, the role of universities is currently seen as highly significant in the development of economic competitiveness. In the academic world, the growth in the economic significance of knowledge, society's firmer hold on the production of knowledge, the utilization of academic work in industry and the service economy, and the shift from national and international research systems to international and global research networks have led to crucial changes (Jacob and Hellström, 2000: 1; Nowotny et al., 2001: 82). These changes have affected the place and the role of the university as well as the functions and structures of the university system. Etzkowitz et al. (2000a) envision the development of closer cooperation between universities, the business world, and the State (the so-called triple helix model) in a knowledge-based economy where the potential of the universities as a part of an innovative system is exploited. Such cooperation and the growing significance of knowledge are also seen as explanations for the birth of the entrepreneurial paradigm in universities.

Besides other definitions, 'the entrepreneurial university' can be seen to be more responsive to social and economic demands than the traditional university. In the so-called knowledge society, universities are expected to adapt faster than before to maintain their leading role in contributing to societal progress. The third mission has in some countries been added to the law on higher education (for example, in Sweden in 1996 and in Finland in 2005) and it has meant increased demands for universities. Interaction with society, innovation, knowledge transfer, and the exploitation of scientific research have been emphasized in national policies to create well-being and economic competitiveness. Universities are supposed to have a central role and responsibility in the knowledge production system through being actively engaged in entrepreneurial activities.

In the UK, for example, the government increasingly emphasizes knowledge transfer from universities as a means of making the country more economically competitive and to create well-being. In the University of Nottingham, 'exploiting the commercial use of cutting-edge ideas has been high on the agenda in 2003–04, following the Lambert Report calling for higher education to develop closer ties with business' (Nottingham case study). In Spain, universities today provide more and more different kinds of services: they have developed incentive programmes for research, innovation, and knowledge transfer, and the curricula and teaching style have been modified to meet the needs of society. All in all, the trend is to integrate universities in the local and national society.

> For example, the so-called 'third mission' of the university is becoming more and more important; its strategy is becoming more oriented towards society in a very general sense of the word, as a point of contact with research and higher education, lifelong training is becoming more important, cultivating relations with businesses is becoming an issue, etc. In addition, the European situation is becoming more important and requires fresh efforts to modernize and internationalize the university. (University of Valencia case study)

In the Nordic countries, the third mission has had an especially significant impact on the operation and target setting of universities: 'The external environment has become more important for strategies and activities' (Lund case study). The expectations of universities are enormous.

> Nowadays, or already for a while now, universities have been seen as institutions that have all the answers. People feel that universities should have been the source of all things good and beautiful. So the outside world has strong expectations for universities. (Lapland case study)

In the transition countries, there are parallel trends to those in the Western European countries, although the difference in contexts means that there are different reasons for responding to the demands of society. In Moldova, a current trend is to promote entrepreneurial activities, technology transfer, and the role of the universities in an innovative system. Many trends can be considered consequential on changes in political and economic circumstances. In Moldova, the training of students is intended to synchronize with the needs of the national economy and to move to more practical student training. In Russia, the rapid rise in the number of departments of economics, management, and law has meant that the previous exact science and engineering orientation has been reversed in favour of a business orientation that reflects adaptation to the emerging market-orientated economy.

Internationalization has also increased national competitiveness. Nation-states should be able to attract a labour force and professional workers from all over the world and this is best realized by attracting the people at an early stage, as students. Universities are thus encouraged to internationalize their activities. At the European level, there is a concern about the integration of

Europe. The building up of the European Higher Education Area (EHEA) and the European Research Area (ERA) are good examples of these new aspirations. The Bologna process has led to important transformations to the degree structures and study programmes in every country except the UK. The Spanish university system is increasingly integrated with Europe. The Poznan University of Economics 'has changed its curricula, adapting them to European educational standards in all major fields of training and specializations' (PUE case study). Universities in the transition countries are trying to meet European standards and to create links with Europe and worldwide. In every country, the number of foreign degree students has increased as a consequence of internationalization. Universities create English language degree programmes to attract foreign students who, in some cases, pay higher tuition fees than internal students. In the UK, one reason for the increased numbers of foreign students is that these students represent an increased income stream. In many Nordic universities, the university mission states that one of the future goals is 'to be more international', 'internationally leading' or a 'globally categorized' university. The proportion of foreign students and faculty is still quite low in many Nordic universities, although it has been rising. For example, the Royal Institute of Technology (KTH) in Sweden states that it intends to raise the proportion of international faculty, which at the present time is about 11%, whereas in the world's top universities the proportion may be 50%.

From state control to market discipline?

In all the EUEREK countries, the official tendency has been towards increasing the autonomy of universities away from the State. In the UK, the ideological change regarding the role of the State took place in the 1980s and the other countries have been following this route. In the 1990s, this was most visible in the transition countries: the curriculum had been de-ideologized and universities had more autonomy regarding their study programmes. In Poland, universities gained more autonomy and the new higher education law in 1990 gave the universities the chance to begin to respond to the new social, political, and economic conditions. In Spain, the University Reform Act in 1983 was the first legislation to begin to emancipate higher education from the control of the State and the University Act in 2001 gave universities and autonomous regions further independence.

Although the policy rhetoric has been to increase autonomy, and in some ways universities have acquired more freedom, conditional contracting and increasing demands for quality assessment and accountability have restricted autonomy. For example, in Finland the interviewees in the case study universities said that state steering had not loosened. In the Nordic countries, the autonomy of universities has increased in some ways, but new forms of accountability, evaluation, and quality assurance systems constrain autonomy:

Now of course there's also the fact that funding can be used more freely. But the framework, quite tight not to mention, does still exist. So I don't know whether autonomy has really increased. Sometimes it even seems like it has decreased. (HSE, Finland case study)

The increase in autonomy is relative, because universities have been 'responsibilized' (Neave, 2000: 17). According to Trow (1996: 311–12), this is simply an alternative to confidence, and in fact means a reduction in university autonomy. Managing by results gives centralized management a lower profile, but the hierarchy that separates those being evaluated and those undertaking the evaluation is very clear. In a fast moving competitive society, universities are expected to act more efficiently and instead of putting trust in their performance, governments seek to control the results. Output control and efficiency are the main principles of New Public Management policies. The UK was one of the first countries to adopt them: in the competitive environment that emerged when the regulated quasi-market was created, management needed to be geared towards performance: 'Universities have had to streamline decision-making processes, be more alert to income earning possibilities and be prepared to take some risks' (Williams and Kitaev, 2005).

One interviewee pointed out that it could be that market discipline is what nowadays restricts university autonomy: 'Some kind of lash of capitalism has emerged instead of the lash of the State' (Lapland case study). One reason for this type of view is that the mechanisms and sources of universities' income are changing. The proportion of state funding has fallen in many European countries for different political reasons, but mainly because the role of the State has quite radically been changed and market forces have been given a larger role.

Within the countries involved in the EUEREK Project, the dependence of the universities on non-state funding has increased most markedly in Moldova; in Poland and Finland, it has increased from between 10% and 45%. In contrast, the change in the UK was negative or close to zero between 1994 and 2004. This is not to say that change in the UK has been non-existent: the major change in the UK took place before the 1980s. In Moldova and Russia, the increased external funding consists mainly of student fees. For example, at the Moldova State University (MSU) the budget in 1994 was composed entirely of state financial resources but in 2004 state funding constituted only 17.5% of the university's budget. The rest of the budget, more than 80%, consisted of student fees. In the transition countries, the public universities have also begun to take in fee-paying students, so nowadays both public and private sectors rely heavily on student fees. This may in some cases lead to a situation where 'the main goal of the Institute is to maintain the inflow of the students who can pay tuition fees' (BIBIM case study). In the UK and Poland, the universities' reliance on student fees has also increased. Even in the Nordic countries, where free education has been a historically respected principle, the governments have investigated the possibility of charging fees to non-EU and non-EEA students. The latest agenda of the Finnish Government is the possibility that individual master's programmes should be given permission to charge fees to students from outside the European Union. Fees for overseas students are also under discussion in Sweden. An increase in non-state funding would probably make it possible for institutions to widen and diversify their activities. From the Moldavian case studies, one could sum up the impacts of increased non-state funding as:

> Organization (reorganization) of new chairs and faculties; introduction of new study programmes and courses; reinforcement of the laboratory and material base of the universities, creation of publishing and sport centres, procurement of computers and other equipment; employment of more teaching staff; and introducing of MSc degree courses. (Gaugash and Tiron, 2006)

However, the increase in non-state funding may have also unexpected and undesirable consequences. The increase in external funding for research has impacted on the working culture of universities in many ways. At Jönköping University, for example, 'the recruiting system is changing; a strong merit is now attached to active participation in and leading of externally financed research projects' (Jönköping case study). Instead of long-term, patient work, research is nowadays mainly conducted in short-term projects. Public funding is allocated through competition: researchers spend a greater part of their time searching for grants, and competition is fierce. The availability of project funding may even lead to 'project greediness' whereby people accept projects wherever these are available, thus reducing the time devoted to the basic work of the university (Lapland case study). Some interviewees thought that competition was too demanding in terms of the resources that those single grants subsequently provide. Because of the competitive atmosphere, 'many feel that researcher autonomy and intellectual potential are threatened' (Umeå case study). External funding may also impose limits on research if the funders regulate it strictly. In any case, competition for funding dominates universities' operations:

> I mean we have to focus on activities for which funding is available. This has changed the way we conduct our activities in a way that nowadays it is extremely important to try and influence the funding preferences of the Academy of Finland and Tekes. This has spawned a totally new mode of operations. (Lapland case study)

New Public Management and project management

The central challenges for the modern university stem from its increased range of functions, massification, shortage of public funding, and rapid changes in its operational environment. These challenges require universities to reform themselves in many areas of their activities. Universities must be increasingly active and proactive and must take the initiative in responding to external change, but they should also try to reshape the internal dynamic of universities in the areas of teaching, research, funding, administration, organization, and leadership (Tirronen, 2005).

Many changes in higher education institutions are often regarded as being a question of size: expanded universities with expanded tasks need, for example, new forms of governance to improve management. The role of leaders in universities has changed. Leadership is much more demanding because of the various planning tasks and the search for funding now imposed on universities. The question is whether universities have sufficient leadership expertise and know-how. In Spain, for example, a need for more professional university governance has been identified: 'The administrative management has also become more complex' (Alicante case study). The increased complexity of university governance and the more demanding roles of leaders are evidenced in the trend to appoint new kinds of vice-rectors, as in Finland, in Spain (vice-rector for communication, quality, and image), and Moldova (vice-rector for quality assurance and a vice-rector responsible for European integration and international relations): 'Vice-rectorates have been created recently to respond to specific needs such as the Vice-rectorate for Communication, Quality and Image. The reason why it was created: to carry out studies which assess these needs' (UCH case study).

In the Nordic countries as in Spain, there is a trend towards New Public Management and a change from collegial to more hierarchical managerial systems and corporatist formats to give university administration greater flexibility. In Finland, the entrepreneurial role of universities has changed their administrative strategies; the strategies are increasingly aimed at integrating academic, commercial, and bureaucratic cultures, and decreasing the gap between universities and society, and between universities and the business world (Kutinlahti, 2005: 159). In Finland, it has been decided that the higher education system and the system of university governance should be restructured. The first move is to build up two large 'university consortia of innovativeness and excellence' by merging five universities. In Sweden, at Lund University, interviewees' statements indicated that some quite fundamental changes in the way the university is governed have taken place.

> Before, departments were more or less independent, governed by a department board and director, *prefekt*, elected by the colleagues, but now the directors are mostly appointed from above. There is also stronger steering from the faculty leadership level. (Lund case study)

A more responsive attitude to the needs of society and the need to adapt to the changing environment may also require a reform of organizational structures:

> The first step was to create an internal organizational structure that would enable the university to meet the challenges of increasing

stringency in core funding from the HEFCE and to respond positively to the opportunities being created in the national higher education system. (Nottingham case study)

Merging units into larger entities may be an attempt to achieve managerial efficiency. In Lund University, mergers and other types of restructuring have been commonplace in an attempt to achieve greater efficiency, to share administrative and other infrastructure costs, to achieve synergies, and to reach 'critical mass'. This ideology has been quite strong. Often the reason for restructuring is simply the evolution of scientific fields. Old disciplinary departments are not seen to be functional and it has been decided to create groupings that are more appropriate (for example, in the University of Plymouth and the University of Tampere). New universities have also undergone changes that are typical for growing institutions (Lapland, Tampere, and Jaume I of Castellon case studies).

In addition to reorganization, the interaction between universities and the private sector, which has increased contract research and the expectation of immediately applicable research results, has given rise to various new types of units in universities. Units mentioned in the case studies included, for example, interdisciplinary research centres outside traditional academic structures (i.e. faculties, schools, and departments), technology and science parks, incubators, intermediary public–private structures, consultancy offices, and external relations units. As one interviewee stated, 'the idea at the bottom of these changes has been that the university could better react to the demands of the environment' (Tampere case study). New tasks also demand supporting activities and structures: offices for managing research contracts, research or entrepreneurship support programmes, mechanisms to promote the creation of spin-offs, programmes to promote cooperation, and different research, innovation, and transfer offices. Project working, an approach that is becoming more common, also means that there is a need for new categories of staff to manage the projects:

> There are a surprising lot of these project-related titles, project designers, project secretaries and such. So maybe this is how this development has steered development towards a more project-based way, I guess there could be more research-related titles and jobs. (Lapland case study)

The problems of real life do not fit within the strict boundaries of scientific disciplines. Some universities like Lund University and the Helsinki School of Economics (HSE, Finland) have created new programmes as thematic areas rather than programmes that are based on traditional disciplines to respond to social and business needs. Some programmes respond to regional needs: the University of Lapland has started several multidisciplinary master's programmes and other tailored programmes that have been directed to the needs of the region. There is also an increased number of short course programmes and programmes tailored to certain student groups and the needs of the local business community: 'We've developed distance education, it has low entry barriers. We have an outreach campus and work with the regions to develop courses where there are needs. This is part of the region's strategic plan' (Umeå case study).

This raises the question of whether the teaching function of the university is becoming less important in the face of these other and new tasks. Research is, of course, the other fundamental function of the university, but in many universities research has become a higher priority than teaching (Slaughter and Leslie, 1997; Dill, 2003). As the modern trend is to sell services to society (Amaral and Magalhães, 2002: 9), it may be easier to commercialize research than teaching. For example, all Finnish universities have lately stressed the research task and most Finnish universities wish to be seen as 'research universities'. On the other hand, they note that it is not their intention to abandon students. In Jönköping University in Sweden, professors and researchers are given more time for their research as an 'incentive' when they succeed in securing external grants. There are examples of anxiety among some academics that the basic tasks of the university are forgotten in other countries: 'The academics emphasized that the UPV is more interested in obtaining money via contracts with businesses than in academic research and that this has a negative effect on the quality of teaching' (UPV case study). A contradictory trend can be found in Poland, where an interest in research is declining because teaching is the activity that guarantees funding.

Higher education models today

Similar changes and trends have taken place in all the countries studied. However, the foundations of each higher education model are strong and they influence the adoption of new principles. The trend towards marketization and entrepreneurialism means that the Anglo-Saxon model is diffusing into the other higher education models. In Europe, the UK has been leading this development because of the major changes that took place there in the 1980s. But the market model has also deepened there during the last ten years. As one interviewee noted, 'the environment of HE has been shifting quite dramatically towards a more commercial model' (Nottingham case study).

Entrepreneurialism in the UK means for the most part income generation. The relationship between the universities and the State changed in the late 1980s when 'a regulated quasi-market' was created. At the end of the 1980s and the beginning of the 1990s, the State encouraged higher education institutions to generate funding from non-state sources. One of the income-generating strategies has been to attract fee-paying students, especially full-cost fee-paying foreign students. The universities have also established partner campuses abroad. So in the UK, the main reasons for change have been market competition and responses to external pressures. Commercial pressures have forced universities to be entrepreneurial. The universities are operating in both a research and a student market that is of a very competitive nature and in which the universities need to succeed if they are to survive:

> We have grown considerably in the last five years, not simply in student numbers but also in the knowledge and the innovative approaches that we take. 2000 was great, but had we not moved forward we would have gone backwards; there is no such thing as standing still because the market is moving so quickly and new and very good players are coming in. It has never been more competitive than it is now. (Nottingham case study)

Competition has also increased in the other countries but they do not have similar education markets to the UK. In the Nordic countries, states are trying to increase competitiveness between universities by reducing funding and establishing massive assessment procedures to guarantee the quality of the universities and to make them work more efficiently. The expectations placed on universities are enormous. The state core funding per student has decreased and universities increasingly have to compete for public funding. The management-by-results system, the efforts to shorten study times, and the new results-based salary system reflect the desire for effectiveness. The domination of a top-down effectiveness-based approach is seen by many as damaging and the resistance to market-orientated changes is strong in many institutions. In Finland, free education is still an important principle and it has been noted that the introduction of fees for non-EEA/non-EU students by the government is not an easy task. As mentioned above, there is now a government proposal that it could be possible for individual master's programmes to charge fees to students from outside the European Union. In the Nordic countries, the influence of the State on universities is still significant and it puts limits and conditions on universities. The market model and entrepreneurialism are being applied without guaranteeing a financial safety net, and this is seen as a serious problem by universities. Thus the competition that exists between universities is state-led, not market-led. However, the whole operational environment and social context of the public sector, as well as the cultural and the political climate, has changed. This is evident in a response by one interviewee. When asked about the factors that have influenced change, the answer given was 'government working through market forces' (Umeå case study).

In Spain, the progress has been surprisingly similar to that in Finland and Sweden. The share of private funding for higher education has increased and the Anglo-Saxon model has filtered into the Spanish higher education system since the late 1980s. State influence is also still strong in Spain and it is mainly legislative changes that have caused changes in university governance. Other important drivers are the increasing external pressures and entrepreneurial attitudes that are emerging in some universities. Changes in the European higher education framework were also mentioned as drivers of change in Spanish case universities: 'After the University Organization Law (LOU) came into force in 2001, some teaching aspects had to be changed and new plans were implemented. In addition, the university had to tailor its supply to cater for market demands' (Jaume I of Castellon case study). The third mission of the universities has been promoted very strongly in Spain. All the universities studied have, for example, created new agencies for knowledge transfer, innovation, and research and also incentive programmes for these activities. Universities have started to provide new services for the wider society.

In the transition countries, the political changes of the last fifteen years have meant significant transformations in the education systems. For example, in Poland,

> the sudden passage from the more or less elite higher education system of pre-1989 communist times to mass higher education with a strong and dynamic private sector has transformed the situation beyond all recognition. The transition has resulted in a new set of values and changes in position, tasks, and roles for academe in society. (Kwiek, 2005a)

In Moldova and Russia, universities have gained more autonomy to make decisions about their study programmes. In these countries, universities are adapting to the emerging market-oriented economy and synchronizing education with the needs of the national economy. The role of the State in the education system is under discussion. Uncertainty about the role of the State is reflected in university funding: state funding has collapsed. At the same time, the demand for higher education has increased, but the public sector has been unwilling and incapable of responding to the demand, resulting in the emergence and very fast growth of the private sector. At present, there are 315 private higher education institutions in Poland, whereas immediately after the collapse of communism the private sector was almost non-existent. About 30% of the student body goes to private sector institutions, an almost entirely teaching sector. Competition between higher education institutions and the public and private sectors has increased, especially for fee-paying students.

In Poland and in several transition countries, there are strong tensions between the Humboldtian (German) model and the pending Anglo-Saxon model. In Poland, the Anglo-Saxon model has been introduced through the private sector (Kwiek, 2005b). Polish higher education has faced many changes but some of the trends evident in Western Europe have not yet reached Poland: the AMU case study states that, 'as opposed to global (and especially Anglo-Saxon) trends of managerialism in running public universities, AMU has been ruled by the traditional spirit of collegiality rather than by any forms of corporatization' (Kwiek, 2005a). Also, the debates on internationalization, globalization, competitiveness, and universities as engines for economic growth are still marginal.

When classifying the varying historical university models, the overriding question is what is the direction of change? Are the national higher education systems going in the direction of homogenization or diversification and what is the weight of their historical origin and tradition in this process? From this research, we can come to the conclusion that the models are surviving but are breaking their boundaries at the same time. There is no doubt that in the last ten years the models have moved closer to each other but that they still clearly differ. We can also divide the EUEREK countries into three groups. The UK has moved to a quasi-market system because of market competition and the need for universities to try to respond to external pressures. In Sweden, Spain, and Finland, state influence is still strong and it is mainly the State that is pushing universities towards market-orientated behaviour. In the transition countries, the tendency towards a stronger market orientation of the university system stems mainly from the need for universities to adapt to a market economy and its needs, as well as to the unclear role of the State and the increasing demand for higher education (see Figure 3).

The new university culture and academics

Reviewing the case study universities it is hard to see them as single entities and decide whether they are entrepreneurial or not. Instead, we see that a transformation is going on and in every university one can find at least some entrepreneurial individuals or units. The culture in the higher education institutions is changing. It is moving towards an entrepreneurial culture even in those systems that have had strong state control. In these systems also, the State's attitude has changed profoundly. The universities are strongly

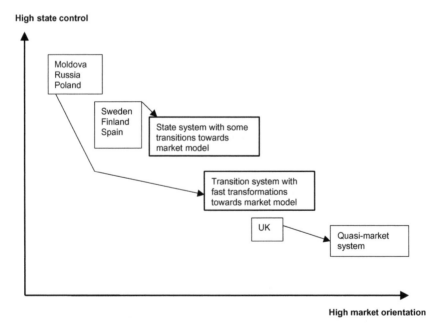

Figure 3 University systems moving from state control to market orientation in EUEREK countries

encouraged to play according to market rules, seek external funding, and adopt a new culture. The 'competition principle' has penetrated the whole educational field. Continents or economic areas are competing for world domination, states are competing in their wish to be competitive, and finally universities and academics are forced to compete against each other to support the competitiveness of states and continents:

> Most of our interview persons say that there has been a marked shift toward encouraging and supporting entrepreneurial activities at the university, and point out some units and also some individuals that could be labelled as particularly entrepreneurial. The many mechanisms created by the university, supporting entrepreneurship and innovation, are an indication of an ongoing transformation process. However, a culture resting on old traditions with a focus on academic excellence has its own incentives and rewards, not always with the same goals as those that characterize enterprises. It is a question of mind-set, according to several interviewees. Some have it, but most do not. (Lund case study)

It may take generations to change people's attitudes in bottom-heavy organizations like universities. But the case studies show that most academics now appear to accept the need to collaborate with external partners and to generate extra resources as an entrepreneur, and that universities are increasingly driven by funding requirements:

> Nottingham is now more focused on expansion and getting money in, but I guess that has come from the fact that things changed in the last ten years . . . Certainly six to eight years ago I was conscious of a lot of colleagues thinking that, what this University is doing, that it is driven more and more by money and less and less by what universities traditionally did. But now we have probably gone through that and everybody is quite used to the way that universities have to operate. (Nottingham case study)

> The main change in the UPV in recent years has been the change of attitude and mentality. Nowadays, earning extra money as an entrepreneur is seen as positive in the academic community. This is a fundamental change to promote entrepreneurial behaviour. (UPV case study)

In many universities, there is still resistance to the commercialization of knowledge and other aspects of marketing and entrepreneurialism, which are seen to conflict with academic values. In all the Finnish universities, traditional academic values were emphasized; in four of the Spanish universities, it was stated that academic motivation is more important than economic motivation when considering the functions of the university. New ways of action and collaboration with the business world are acceptable as long as they occur on terms appropriate to the research and to a university environment:

> But because I feel I have been educated now through this business

fellow scheme, and my colleague next door has also done it, I think that accepting money from industry or elsewhere is perfectly acceptable, as long as you do it on your terms. I would not like to do contract research, but we can do it under our terms and conditions, and if it is a means to an end to the extent where our research is progressing further because of collaboration with industry. (LSHTM case study)

In at least two Finnish universities, some interviewees thought that change in itself is not intrinsically valuable, so it is partly good that people in universities – the places of critical thinking – should be critical towards changes that are taking place:

> We do have some structures, but they're very flexible. And the legislation doesn't really pose any limits anymore. The limitations are actually posed by the traditions and by people's attitudes. But you also have to bear in mind that change shouldn't be an intrinsic value either. I think it's good that we have some of these things that slow down the changes. I think this is very suitable for the university institution. (Tampere case study)

Is the innermost nature of the university changing?

Neave (1985) and van Vught (1990) specified five trends in governments' higher education policies: budget cuts, pressures for efficiency, managerialism, conditional contracting, and the introduction of evaluation systems. These trends have continued and deepened. But there are also new aspects because of global competition and internationalization – the phenomena of the 1990s and the new millennium. Universities are expected to support national innovation systems and to increase competitiveness at both national and EU level. Because of this universities have also had to assume new tasks. One significant transformation in several countries is adapting their different degree structures to the 3-5-8 structure. The harmonization of degrees will probably facilitate the development of the Europe-wide higher education market.

Universities in most European countries have faced state budget cuts since the 1980s for various political reasons. Recently, states have been withdrawing further from their role as funders of universities. Universities have become responsible for seeking their own funding to carry on their activities. New funding sources include research contracts, consulting and other kinds of services, student fees (especially from foreign students), establishing campuses abroad, distance learning programmes, and so on. This development has led to increasing market competition between universities. At the same time as state budgets have shrunk, universities are supposed to produce better results with less funding. Competition between institutions is a strong incentive to make universities act more effectively. Efficiency has also certainly risen because of massification and the consequential fall in state funding per student. Demand for higher education is high and there have already been signs of oversupply of higher education in recent years. University education has faced inflation, the unemployment of graduates has to some extent increased, and employees are often claimed to be over-educated for the needs of the labour market.

In the 1980s, strategic management was introduced into universities as a part of a trend towards managerialism. This seems to be a part of the wider New Public Management movement. The values of the enterprise culture were emphasized. Today, the general trend in every country and university model is an increased emphasis on professional management. The changing environment, increased tasks and working methods will challenge the management skills of academics. Managerialism has meant a concentration on the achievement of pre-stated objectives and the monitoring of results. The model of conditional contracting means an ongoing process of negotiation between universities and the state and that funding is tied to specific objectives and results. The introduction of transparent evaluation systems is a natural consequence of this kind of model. In many countries, universities have received, step by step, more autonomy, but assessment, accountability, and market competition are strong restrictions on their freedoms.

In the face of these new challenges, there is a fear that the university sector might start to resemble any corporate sector and that universities will start to play the role of a shopping mall, a degree mill, or a patent factory run on the basis of quarterly economic statements. There is great concern about the fate of creativity, independence, criticality, long-term perspective, and moral consciousness (see Rinne and Koivula, 2005). The modern university will need to achieve various goals that may be in conflict with each other. The transformation of the university into the motor of economic development will severely affect its values and culture. Shouldn't there also be sailors who would cast anchor and be aware of the history? It is worth reminding ourselves that universities are almost unique in that they still do not operate as part of the market sector. Universities have a long history that cannot suddenly be overridden by the external objectives of competitiveness. Despite fundamental changes in the environment over the course of centuries, the university, with its long traditions, is one of those institutions that have preserved their basic characteristics and status in society. Two other institutions of similar vintage are the Church and the State (Fuller, 2005):

> There's a certain shared consciousness in universities about the nature of universities, about what their traditions and history are. Sometimes this is even beneficial. If it wouldn't be, we wouldn't have any of these old universities. Companies aren't that old, for example Nokia is just 140 years old, but the University of Helsinki is much older. The fact that universities are this old and there's still demand for them indicates the fact that they do have a good reputation and they fulfil a certain function within society. And this function isn't tied just to the current situation in Finland. (HSE, Finland case study)

11

Entrepreneurialism and the knowledge economy in Europe: some conclusions

Michael Shattock

The decade of 1994 to 2004, over which our data were collected, saw very substantial change in most European higher education systems. It is dangerously simplistic to see these changes as all pointing in the same direction, towards greater institutional autonomy and marketization, because each national system has confronted – and continues to confront – these issues in its own way and within its own economic, organizational, and constitutional framework (as described in the national country studies that were part of the project and which are available at: http://www.euerek.info/Public_Documents/Country). It is clear, however, that a new agenda for higher education is emerging, but more rapidly in some countries than in others and that the pace of change can vary between systems of higher education, between institutions of the same type, and even within institutions themselves. An individual system's propensity to change can also be viewed from different perspectives by scholars from different countries. What is clear is that we have not found a European Higher Education Area marching to a single drumbeat, but a variety of national systems and universities moving in the same general direction but certainly not necessarily towards precisely the same structural goals. In Chapter 10, Rinne and Koivula note that a move towards greater entrepreneurialism is general and, with the financial and other pressures that universities have to contend with, 'unstoppable' but that it also excites considerable opposition in some countries. They also point up the argument that a good part of the change involves the sacrifice of what, to someone brought up in the Anglo-Saxon tradition, would be seen as the tyranny of state control for the more inherently risky tyranny of the market.

The foregoing chapters have tried to assess and highlight how these changes have been addressed under a number of headings, reviewing the institutional drivers and mechanisms, as well as the inhibitions and impediments to entrepreneurialism. Each chapter has been written separately by scholars drawing on the same data but their contributions are nuanced, as one might expect, by differing interpretations of such a complex set of cross-national studies and by their own national perspectives. However, there was remarkable unanimity with respect to the overall research findings and conclusions that follow.

Although national systems are moving at different speeds, certain common features can be identified. Of the two dominant European models, the Humboldtian and the Napoleonic (the third model, the Anglo-Saxon, being generally regarded until recently as divergent), one could argue that the former has proved to be more flexible, if our case studies of Sweden and Finland are to be believed, whereas in (Napoleonic) Spain, although the Valencian university system has moved a long way, the retention of civil service status and a national reward system that recognizes publication to the exclusion of other research outcomes (research contracts with industry, etc.) has limited the extent to which institutional autonomy and greater involvement with society and the economy can be achieved. In the transition countries (where Humboldtian characteristics were sometimes retained below the surface of communist regimes), the old rigid state higher education systems have been put under enormous pressure; in Poland and in Russia, one result has been an extraordinary growth in private sector higher education and in those countries and in Moldova the policy of charging fees to a significant proportion of students in the state universities has enabled the university systems to survive the extreme economic downturns of the 1990s. But in all these countries, the adoption of this policy has left a legacy to be overcome. In Russia, it would seem, resources are beginning to flow back into the university system and, as our case studies demonstrate, there have been innovative steps to re-energize state universities; in Poland, the introduction of reforms that restrict the number of institutions at which an academic can teach should, over time, bring more order into the system, and Poland's integration into Europe is already bringing about change. But it remains the case that in all three countries teaching requirements take precedence over research and this has consequences for the development of entrepreneurial or third mission activities. Research and technology transfer are limited both by the absence of investment in research and by the lack of the necessary economic 'pull' factors that incentivize academics to undertake industrially supported research or establish spin-out companies; third mission activities in teaching, for example, to address regional deficiencies, are constrained by the financial imperatives of a teaching-dominated budget.

It is common to see the third (and sometimes fringe) European model, that of the UK (and particularly England), as being at the forefront of realizing the benefits of institutional autonomy and in exploiting the introduction of greater marketization and institutional competition. The benefits can perhaps be seen in the Research Assessment Exercise (RAE) in driving a greater concentration of research in universities, in the full-fee recruitment of international students and the international marketization that has accompanied it, and the free market that exists in fee charging and recruitment of UK and EU postgraduate students. (The introduction of variable fees and income contingent loans in 2006, except in Scotland, falls outside the period of our research.) Nevertheless, it is easy to exaggerate the extent to which the Anglo-Saxon model now differs from those in the rest of Europe: state steering is very strong, reinforced by formula-funding mechanisms, and it is important to recognize that undergraduate UK numbers, which bring with them nearly 80% of the core state recurrent monies, are tightly controlled by the Funding Councils, institution by institution, with the possibilities of 'claw back' of grant for under-recruitment and penalties for over-recruitment. The English universities in the study have, nevertheless, moved earlier and further in the direction of the market, institutional competition, and entrepreneurial behaviour than those of the other countries studied, except perhaps Russia. This has partly been because financial stringency and New Public Management approaches came to the UK nearly a decade before most other European countries and partly because the long established financial autonomy of universities in the UK enabled many of them to come to terms with the exploitation of financial independence much sooner. As a consequence, UK universities attract a greater share of their income from non-state sources than universities in other EU countries, but because the process had begun in the 1980s the actual share had more or less peaked by 1994. The next step towards marketization – the introduction of variable fees for home and EU undergraduate students – only took place in 2006 and its impact is insufficient yet to form a view of what its long-term effects may be.

These national trends have directly shaped the movement towards greater entrepreneurialism in the state-funded universities included in our case studies, and have indirectly also shaped the development of the private universities. Thus, in Poland the continued low salaries in the state universities fuelled the growth of private universities where the bulk of the teaching was provided by academics from state universities holding parallel posts. In Russia, and to a much lesser extent in Spain, the creation of private universities represents a 'break-out' from a dominant state university system. Similarly in the UK, the University of Buckingham was a 'breakout' from the highly homogeneous public university system of the 1970s, but in the 1980s and 1990s Buckingham was adversely affected by the willingness of the state to fund a continuing expansion of home students over the period in the polytechnics and the new universities and it is only in 2006 with the introduction of variable fees for home students that a more level playing field is being provided for between the large public and the very small private sector of higher education in the UK.

To attempt to synthesize over such a disparate set of institutions and national systems carries with it obvious dangers of oversimplification but we do believe that our research has thrown up a set of conclusions that have general applicability:

- European universities are more entrepreneurial than is often thought judged by their performance in diversifying their funding bases, exploiting their research in the wider world, extending their teaching to new markets, and in regional engagement. In financial terms, while the UK seemed to have reached a particular level of proportionate reliance on non-core income by 1994, which has not changed since, the other systems have moved rapidly in the last decade and, if international student fee-charging systems were introduced, some would be very comparable with the UK position.

- The decade reviewed has seen enormous advances in universities' commitment to knowledge transfer, and universities have recognized that this must be institutionalized through research and technology transfer offices or special units for educational outreach. These offices exercise an important role within institutions. Nevertheless, it remains the case that for the successful realization of research findings, commercially or in other ways, society must exercise a 'pull' factor. Universities that have no industrial hinterland or small populations in their regions are going to find industrial partners hard to track down. Universities that do not have access to venture capital funds cannot be expected to generate numbers of spin-out companies. If there are no likely users of patents and licences, the intellectual property to be derived from research is of little value.

- National and international policy makers need to recognize the importance of diversity of institutional mission: the expectations of achievement from old, urban-based comprehensive universities will necessarily be different from those of newer universities established in economically disadvantaged regions, albeit some of these institutions have demonstrated that they can develop areas of strength of international significance. Specialist institutions can be enormously effective in concentrating efforts across a narrow range of disciplines; international competition among them can often be a driver for more entrepreneurial, innovative, and risk-taking approaches.

- Entrepreneurialism in research grows out of fundamental research; it is therefore natural that large concentrations of research expertise (mostly found in urban comprehensive or specialist institutions), if supported by appropriate knowledge transfer machinery, will usually produce the most commercial and other outcomes. But, however effective the knowledge transfer machinery may be, research-based entrepreneurialism, like research, is bottom up not top down in its motivation. Less research-intensive universities can develop nodes of research if they have a flexible regulatory climate that encourages 'academic intrapreneurs' and gives them sufficient autonomy in a research centre or institute to develop their ideas.

- Entrepreneurialism is not confined to research and some of the most entrepreneurial activities we have identified have been in teaching (Nottingham and WSHIG). Such entrepreneurialism is generated by a vision or an idea as much as it is by the expectation of increased resources. However, entrepreneurialism in teaching is often also found in regional universities that have devised new ways to address the needs of disadvantaged communities. The contribution of entrepreneurialism to the knowledge society through the transmission of education to students financed on a non-core-funding basis should be accorded equal importance to that of research.

- Public universities have demonstrated that public funding, when appropriate incentives are included in funding systems, can generate a much greater willingness to engage in entrepreneurial extensions to their academic mission than an absolute reliance on private income in the private universities. The mixed-economy university in Europe seems better suited to stimulating entrepreneurialism that is linked to creativity and innovation than purely privately financed institutions. Public money can be seen, in the right conditions, to lubricate and underpin income-generating entrepreneurial activity. But all public universities in Europe are operating in conditions of financial stringency because funding has not kept pace with massification. If research-led entrepreneurialism is to realize the economic benefits that the EU Commission is demanding, adequate public funding is necessary.

- Full institutional autonomy is a necessary condition for universities to be entrepreneurial. Where autonomy is restricted, entrepreneurialism is restricted. But full autonomy does not guarantee that universities will become entrepreneurial. The most entrepreneurial institutions in our data set (Nottingham, London School of Hygiene and Tropical Medicine, Jönköping, Pereslavl, and WSHIG) do not conform to any discernible pattern of entrepreneurialism. Institutional entrepreneurialism takes many different forms, as the case studies of these five institutions amply demonstrate.

- Universities become entrepreneurial for a variety of different reasons – dynamic leadership, financial shocks to the system, a sense of regional isolation, a response to local economic pressures, or the leverage exercised by certain kinds of funding systems. But it remains the case that the bottom-up drive of individual 'academic intrapreneurs' also represents a key factor in motivating institutional entrepreneurialism. An institution may not be entrepreneurial overall but may have distinctive entrepreneurial enterprises within it. Some universities (for example, the Technical University of Valencia) encourage entrepreneurial satellite ventures even though they have a non-entrepreneurial, traditional core. Removing inhibiting regulation at institutional level and giving greater autonomy within institutions are primary steps towards generating greater entrepreneurialism in universities as a whole.

- Institutional governance that incorporates a 'lay' element – that is, involves at the level of the governing body a significant (usually a majority) membership drawn from the external community – makes an important contribution to the development of entrepreneurialism. Traditional governance structures, such as in Spain or Finland, which rely on collegiality alone, can inhibit entrepreneurialism and can impede innovation.

- A key factor in developing entrepreneurialism in universities is flexibility in the management of human resources. Universities whose recruitment processes and staffing structures are linked to their state civil service are significantly inhibited from incentivizing staff in terms of innovation and academic performance or from penalizing staff who do not perform; universities need to manage their own human resource issues in line with their own strategic objectives without the impediments of civil service rules or permanent tenure.

- The case studies reveal a number of examples of flexible human resource management practice that have encouraged entrepreneurialism: permitting staff to 'buy' research time out of research grants and contracts (Lund), permitting staff to earn additional salary from research grants and contracts (the International Business School, Jönköping, the Technical University of Valencia), flexible performance-based (including third mission) academic promotion procedures (Nottingham), providing bridging support for successful researchers supported by 'soft' money to give them continuity between research grants (LSHTM), offering productivity incentives (Spain), and encouraging staff to undertake external consultancies. Individually, these schemes may not transfer easily from one national setting to another, but cumulatively they paint a picture that more flexible, incentivized reward systems can act as a stimulus to academic entrepreneurialism.

- Entrepreneurialism does not flourish in heavily bureaucratic environments, which discourage opportunism and encourage conformity. Universities therefore need to create organizational cultures that motivate staff (not necessarily for financial reward) to pursue innovative entrepreneurial, or simply extra-core, activities utilizing and drawing on their own academic and professional expertise. Entrepreneurialism in a university setting is about generating activities, perhaps in response to identifiable and particular market needs, which extend a university's traditional boundaries, rather than being simply a matter of generating non-state income.

- A reliance on state funding systems or on fees only can limit universities to a restricted range of core activities. Entrepreneurialism widens the contribution they can make to the knowledge society and the knowledge economy and can drive new ideas and organizational change. Entrepreneurialism is growing in European universities but there remain in some institutions and in some systems inhibitions and impediments that prevent all universities from realizing their potential contribution to the Europe of Knowledge.

We believe that these conclusions have a broad application for the formulation of higher education policy in Europe and for the reforms of national systems. We do not believe that they point to the homogenization of higher education but rather to the release of initiative and to the freeing up of universities to play the part which the EU Commission's Lisbon Strategy (CEC, 2005) is calling for. One of the striking points to emerge from our case studies is the complexity and variety of the European higher education scene and the extent to which national perceptions, institutional histories, location, and differentiation of mission resist easy categorization or central direction. In spite of the Bologna process, we are a long way from having a 'European system' in the sense that one can say, with all its avowed decentralization, that there is a 'US system'. There is, however, plenty of evidence from our case studies that changes are taking place and that universities are breaking away from their traditional structures, but there is also evidence that individual 'intrapreneurs' are being held back by over-regulation and that the human resource aspects of institutional management are given insufficient attention. The case studies demonstrate that entrepreneurialism comes in many different forms as 'intrapreneurs' and institutions pioneer new categories of activities that can change the traditional shapes of universities. If these new activities are to take off and embed themselves, we need less bureaucratic caution, less control and direction from governments, and the creation of a climate that is much more conducive to individual and corporate innovation.

All this points to new forms of management in universities, not the pejoratively described 'new managerialism', but participative management that motivates the academic community not only to continue to commit itself to the fundamental tasks of research and teaching but also to look outward, to be prepared to take risks – reputational and financial – and to engage in the broader range of activities that being entrepreneurial demands. At the heart of this lies the question of creating organizational cultures that are motivational rather than regulatory, that are competitive but respect academic values, and that are entrepreneurial, in the sense in which we have defined it, where the generation of activities which extend a university's traditional boundaries is encouraged and incentivized.

Entrepreneurialism in higher education makes a much broader contribution to the knowledge economy than is encompassed in the establishment of notional targets for R&D expenditure because it unleashes a range of activities that can have a dynamic impact on more widely differentiated elements of society than the economy narrowly defined. The commitment of Lund and Nottingham, for example, to research must be balanced against the activities of Umeå and Plymouth in the education services they offer to economically disadvantaged regions or LSHTM's distance learning programme to the Third World. Entrepreneurialism cannot of its nature be planned and it represents therefore an incalculable contribution to the knowledge economy but, because its activities depend on individual or institutional initiative and are often unstructured, divergent, or the product of particular circumstances, it fuels social and economic innovation in a way that the more standard components of the knowledge economy cannot do.

Appendix 1: A statistical overview

Gareth Williams

The main EUEREK statistical data came from 24 universities from six countries, as shown in Table 6. Some data were also received for three Russian higher education institutions and these are shown in some of the tables. Two of the 24 universities, one in Spain and one in Poland, enrolled over 50,000 students; five others had more than 25,000 and five had fewer than 5000 students. Table 7 shows that three universities experienced a decline in student numbers over the decade 1994–2004, two small private institutions in England and Spain, and the University of Valencia, which appears to have compensated for its loss of local students by increasing its foreign student recruitment very considerably. All the others had grown in size; in eight cases the student numbers more than doubled. Foreign student numbers increased especially rapidly in Finland, the UK, and Spain, and postgraduate numbers grew especially rapidly in at least one of the universities in all the countries.

Table 8, together with Figures 4 and 5, show that income sources vary considerably between countries and between universities. At one extreme, three institutions, all of them private, receive over 90% of their income in the form of student fees. At the other end of the spectrum, the universities of Finland and Sweden receive virtually no income from fees (Table 9). The London School of Hygiene and Tropical Medicine obtains nearly two-thirds of its income from research, while none of the institutions in Moldova and only one each in Poland and Russia receive more than 10% of their income from research. Third mission also varies, ranging from over a quarter of the income of two of the Russian institutions and one English university to less than 5% in six institutions. It should be noted, however, that third mission is not a well-defined concept and these figures must be treated as indicative rather than precise measures.

Staff numbers have risen broadly in line with student numbers but again there are substantial differences between countries and institutions (Table 10). Of those for which figures are available, nine institutions (two in England, one in Finland, three in Moldova, one in Poland, one in Spain, and one in Sweden) have experienced a deterioration in student/staff ratios over the period – that is, there were more students per teacher in 2004 than previously. However, in another nine (two in England, two in Finland, one in Poland, three in Spain, and one in Sweden) the ratios have improved.

Figure 6 tests the hypothesis that there is an association between student/staff ratios and the proportion of income from sources other than core government income. It shows that broadly a 19% improvement in student/staff ratios is associated with a 100% increase in the proportion of income from non-core government sources. As with all correlations, it is not possible to determine causation from this association: it could be that a favourable student/staff ratio enables staff to have more time to undertake research and third mission work. Alternatively, it may be that that success in earning third stream income may enable universities to employ more academic staff (Table 11).

This brief statistical review is indicative of the differences between the case study institutions and highlights the very great diversity of higher education institutions in Europe. Generalizations from international comparisons are difficult, but the figures do confirm a general trend by European universities towards diversification of their missions.

Table 6 Income and student numbers in case study institutions

	Total income, 2004 (€)	Total student numbers, 2004	Percent change in student numbers, 1994–2004
Finland			
HSE	35.9	4,343	16.4
Lapland	39.3	4,434	104.7
Tampere	127.0	15,394	23.6
Moldova			
AESM	–	14,218	188.9
BSU	–	–	–
MSU	6.8	22,910	259.9
TCUM	–	2,728	637.3
Poland			
AMU	82.2	53,760	–
PUE	98.0	13,704	31.2
WSHIG	2.2	1,500	–
Spain			
UAL	150.0	26,491	−5.3
UCH	–	6,748	–
Jaume I of Castellon	82.3	13,394	69.7
UMH	84.5	11,549	–
UPV	244.0	36,551	9.7
UV	256.1	52,661	−17.7
Sweden			
Jönköping	60.8	8,098	32.6
KTH	291.4	14,195	47.3
Lund	514.1	30,520	13.1
Umeå	300.3	19,286	36.3
UK			
Buckingham	9.5	684	−30.1
LSHTM	56.7	2,701	86.7
Nottingham	441.2	30,105	198.1
Plymouth	128.7	29,384	56.9

Table 7 Changes in student numbers in case study institutions, 1994–2004

	1994			1999			2004			Percent change, 1994–2004		
	Total	Foreign	Postgraduate	Total	Foreign	Postgraduate	Total	Foreign	Postgraduate	Total	Foreign	Postgraduate
Finland												
HSE	3,730	9	470	3,787	46	384	4,343	106	407	16	1,078	–13
Lapland	2,166	2	206	3,404	22	271	4,434	66	205	105	3,200	0
Tampere	12,451	189	1,359	14,178	262	1,702	15,394	319	1,880	24	69	38
Moldova												
AESM	4,921	39		7,996	111		14,218	141	264	72	185	–
BSU	3,481	51		5,101	25		8,478	22		144	43	–
MSU	6,365		118	12,022		279	22,910	300	793	160	8*	184
TCUM	370			1,172			2,728			637	–	–
Poland												
AMU	10,447	72	1,543	39,529	76	29,956	53,760	94	32,386	36*	–	8*
PUE				15,261		7,195	13,704		8,471	31	31	449
WSHIG							1,500			–	–	–
Spain												
UAL	27,982	5	1,410	28,554		1,474	26,491	835	1,783	–5	–	26
UCH							6,748	49	94	–	–	–
Jaume I of Castellon	7,891		312	12,377	18	386	12,507		413	58	880	32
UMH			440	5,307	8	510	11,549	26	514	117*	225*	0*
UPV	33,319			37,424		1,265	36,551	2,214	1,860	10	–	310
UV	64,011	108	2,900	62,704	337	3,181	52,661	357	2,848	–18	231	–2
Sweden												
Jönköping	3,482			4,990	256	196	8,098	696	295	133	271*	50*
KTH	9,634			11,553	580	3,128	14,195	901	3,096	47	55*	–1*
Lund	26,996			25,265	968	4,601	30,520	1,563	4,840	13	61*	52*
Umeå	14,147			16,623	270	1,776	19,286	414	1,969	36	53*	11*
UK												
Buckingham	978	497	117	696	445	118	684	495	103	–30	0	–12
LSHTM	1,447	240	219	1,487	143	237	2,701	1,420	321	87	492	47
Nottingham	10,100	1,313	1,800	22,235	3,335	3,897	30,105	4,817	6,086	198	267	228
Plymouth	18,723	363	2,211	24,028	566	2,949	29,384	1,119	5,093	57	208	130

Table 8 Profile of income sources in case study institutions, 2004

	Core government		Other		
	Education/teaching %	Research %	Research %	Fees %	Third mission, etc. %
Finland	64		23	0	13
HSE	66		12	0	22
Lapland	78		8	0	14
Tampere	66		22	0	12
Moldova*					
AESM	10	0	0	77	13
ARSUB	26	3	0.1	70.7	0.2
MSU	13	4	0	83	0
TCUM	0	0	0	100	0
Poland	52	9	2	31	6
(Public)	62	11	3	19	6
(Private)	0.3	0.4	0.3	96	3
AMU	62	9	1	18	10
PUE	44	5	1	41	9
WHSIG	0	0	0	94	6
Russia*					
BIBIM Irkutsk	14	1	62	33	
HSE	22	12	21	17	28
Pereslavl	72	17			11
Spain*					
Alicante	70		14		16
Hernandez	85		3		12
Herrera	0		1		99
Jaume I of Castellon	74		13		13
UPV	70		9		21
U V	73		9		18
Sweden	65	16	0	19	
Jönköping	65	7	10	2	16
KTH	55	32	9	4	
Lund	32	30	26	5	7
Umeå	68	18	0	14	
UK	30	8	16	25	21
Buckingham	0	0	11	70	19
LSHTM	18	26	37	13	6
Nottingham	21	13	15	28	23
Plymouth	54	3	5	27	11

* National figures not available.

Table 9 Percentage of non-core income compared with total income in case study institutions, 1994–2004

	1994				1999				2004				Total growth		Annual growth rate	
	Fees (%)	Research (%)	Other (%)	Total (%)	Fees (%)	Research (%)	Other (%)	Total (%)	Fees (%)	Research (%)	Other (%)	Total (%)	Fees (%)	Other (%)	Fees (%)	Other (%)
Finland																
HSE	0			29	0	6	23	29	0	10	22	34	–	10.3		1.6
Lapland	0			20	0	12	19	31	0	8	14	22	–	10.0		1.0
Tampere	0			24	0	16	17	33	0	22	12	34	–	41.7		3.5
Moldova																
AESM	23		9	32	79	0	9	88	77	0	13	90	234.8	44.4	12.8	3.7
BSU					80	0	0	80	71	0	0	71	–11.3	–	–2.4	–
MSU					78	0	0	78	83	0	0	83	6.4	–	1.3	–
TCUM																
Poland																
AMU	10	2	18	20	16	6	18	24	18	1	28	29	80.0	61.1	6.1	4.5
PUE	25	1	14	40	40	1	13	54	41	1	9	51	64.0	–28.6	5.1	–4.3
WSHIG	100			100	99	0	1	100	94	0	6	100	–6.0	500.0	–0.6	43.1
Russia																
BIBIM Irkutsk	4.4	0.1	87	91	16	1	73	100	63	1	21	84	1320.5	–75.5	30.4	–13.1
Pereslavl				11	93		7	99	79		21	100	–14.8	219.7	–3.9	33.7
HSE				52	20	19	34	72	17	21	36	75	–11.8	8.4	–6.1	4.1
Spain																
UAL																
UCH**									99	1		100	–	–	–	–

Jaume I of Castellon																
UMH																
UPV																
UV																
Sweden																
Jönköping*						6	19	25		10	14	28	–	12.0	–	2.3
KTH										31	7	45	–	–	–	–
Lund***												38	–	–	–	–
Umeå												32	–	–	–	–
UK																
Buckingham	94	4	2	100	72	9	19	100	70	11	19	100	–25.5	400.	–2.9	17.5
LSHTM	13	51	10	74	15	48	13	76	13	63	7	73	0.0	14.8	0.0	1.4
Nottingham	23	20	23	66	24	21	23	68	28	15	22	65	21.7	–14.0	2.0	–1.5
Plymouth	43	7	12	62	26	13	9	42	27	5	11	43	–37.2	–15.8	–4.5	–1.7

* 1999–2004, ** 2000–2004, *** 2002–2004.

Table 10 Changes in staff numbers in case study institutions, 1994–2004

	1994		1999		2004		Percent change	
	Academic	Other	Academic	Other	Academic	Other	Academic	Other
Finland								
HSE	175	193	190	200	260	219	49	13
Lapland	168	213	243	351	281	325	67	53
Tampere	730	906	871	921	1,158	995	59	10
Moldova								
AESM					641	43		
BSU	255	446	337	439	327	701	45	57
MSU	609		897		1,618		166	
TCUM	147	35	176	44	202	47	37	34
Poland								
AMU†			2,201	1,960	2,538	1,908	15*	–3*
PUE†	451	464	546	555	612	564	36	22
WSHIG†	19	18	33	28	46	45	142	150
Spain								
UAL	1,102	487	1,430	484	1,870	1,108	70	128
UCH								
Jaume I of Castellon			789	298	844	435	7*	46*
UMH‡			563	258	963	399	71*	55*
UPV			2,057	908	2,577	1,476	25*	63*
UV	2,640	1,490	3,028	1,553	3,466	1,683	31	13
Sweden								
Jönköping	111	75	304	324	657	656	491	874
Lund	3,539	2,037	3,507	1,788	3,744	2,247	6	10
UK								
Buckingham	107	138	87	110	84	112	–21	–19
LSHTM	169	242	305	260	398	315	136	30
Nottingham	1,414		1,793	360	2,380	1,436	70	299*
Plymouth	724		989		970		34	

Notes:
* 1999–2004 only.
† Data drawn from 1995 not 1994.
‡ Data drawn from 2003 not 2004.

Table 11 Student/academic staff ratios in case study institutions, 1994–2004

	1994		1999		2004	
	Academic	*Other*	*Academic*	*Other*	*Academic*	*Other*
Finland						
HSE	21.3	19.3	19.9	18.9	16.7	19.8
Lapland	12.9	10.2	14.0	9.7	15.8	13.6
Tampere	17.1	13.7	16.3	15.4	13.3	15.5
Moldova						
AESM					22.2	330.7
BSU	13.7	7.8	15.1	11.6	25.9	12.1
MSU	10.5		13.4		14.2	N.A.
TCUM	2.5	10.6	6.7	26.6	13.5	58.0
Poland						
AMU			18.0	20.2	21.2	28.2
PUE	23.2	22.5	28.0	27.5	22.4	24.3
WSHIG	0.0	0.0	0.0	0.0	32.6	33.3
Spain						
UAL	25.4	57.5	20.0	59.0	14.2	23.9
UCH						
Jaume I of Castellon			15.7	41.5	14.8	28.8
UMH			9.4	20.6	12.0	28.9
UPV			18.2	41.2	14.2	24.8
Sweden						
Jönköping	25.7	38.0	16.4	15.4	12.3	12.3
Lund	7.6	13.3	7.2	23.2	8.2	12.9
UK						
Buckingham	9.1	7.1	8.0	6.3	8.1	6.1
LSHTM	8.6	6.0	4.9	5.7	6.8	8.6
Nottingham	7.1		12.4	61.8	12.6	21.0
Plymouth	25.9		24.3		30.3	

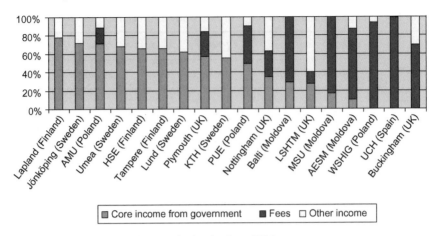

Figure 4 Main sources of income by institution, 2004

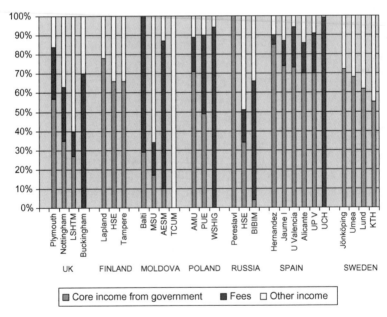

Figure 5 Main sources of income by country and institution, 2004

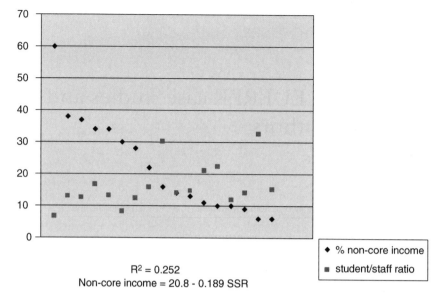

R² = 0.252
Non-core income = 20.8 - 0.189 SSR

◆ % non-core income
■ student/staff ratio

Figure 6 Student/staff ratios and percent non-core income

Appendix 2: EUEREK case studies and case study authors

EUEREK case studies

Twenty-seven universities from Finland, Moldova, Poland, Russia, Spain, Sweden, and the United Kingdom, all publicly available at: www.euerek.info

Finland
Helsinki School of Economics (HSE, Finland)
University of Lapland (ULA)
University of Tampere (UTA)

Moldova
Balti State University (BSU)
Academy of Economic Studies of Moldova (AESM)
Moldova State University (MSU)
Trade Cooperative University of Moldova (TCUM)

Poland
Adam Mickiewicz University in Poznan (AMU)
Academy of Hotel Management and Catering Industry in Poznan (WSHIG)
Poznan University of Economics (PUE)

Russia
Baikal Institute of Business and International Management of Irkutsk University (BIBIM)
Higher School of Economics, Moscow (HSE, Russia)
Institute of Programming Systems of the Russian Academy of Sciences, University of Pereslavl (PSI RAS)

Spain
Cardenal Herrera University (UCH)

Miguel Hernandez University (UMH)
Technical University of Valencia (UPV)
University of Alicante (UAL)
University Jaume I of Castellon
University of Valencia (UV)

Sweden
Lund University
Jönköping University
Umeå University
Royal Institute of Technology (KTH)

United Kingdom
London School of Hygiene and Tropical Medicine (LSHTM)
University of Buckingham
University of Nottingham
University of Plymouth

Case study authors

Finland
Finnish National Report: Jenni Koivula
Higher education in Finland
Helsinki School of Economics: Jenni Koivula
Case study of the Helsinki School of Economics, Finland
University of Lapland: Jenni Koivula
Case study of the University of Lapland, Finland
University of Tampere: Jenni Koivula
Case study of the University of Tampere, Finland

Moldova
Moldova Case Studies: General Analysis: Petru Gaugash and Stefan Tiron
Overall analysis of Moldova case studies

Poland
Academy of Hotel Management: Marek Kwiek
A case of study of the Academy of Hotel Managment and Catering Industry
(Poznan, Poland)
Poznan University (UAM – AMU): Marek Kwiek
A case study of Poznan University (Uniwersytet im. Adama Mickiewicza w
Poznaniu – Adam Mickiewicz University), Poznan, Poland
Poznan University of Economics: Marek Kwiek
A case study of Poznan University of Economics (Akademia Ekonomiczna w
Poznaniu), Poznan, Poland

Russia
Higher School of Economics, Russia: S Filonovich
Study of Higher School of Economics, Moscow, Russia
University of Pereslavl: S Filonovich
Case study of University of Pereslavl, Yaroslavl

Spain
Report on Valencian Universities: Valencia Team
Report prepared for an OECD Committee as part of the OECD project
   Supporting the Contribution of HEIs to Regional Development
Cardenal Herrera University: Valencia Team
Report on the Cardenal Herrera University
Miguel Hernandez University: Valencia Team
Report on the Miguel Hernandez University of Elche
Technical University of Valencia: Valencia Team
Report on the UPV
University Jaume I of Castellon: Valencia Team
Report on the University Jaume I of Castellon
University of Alicante: Valencia Team
Report on the University of Alicante
Universidad Politecnica de Valencia, Spain

Sweden
Swedish Higher Education Policies: B.H. Lambert, A. Sandgren, and G. Stromquist
Swedish Higher Education, Research & Innovation Policies: Universities as
   Engines of Economic Growth
Jönköping University: A. Sandgren, B.H. Lambert, and G. Stromquist
Report on Jönköping University
KTH (Royal Institute of Technology): B.H. Lambert, A. Sandgren, and G.
   Stromquist
Report on KTH
Lund University: G. Stromquist, B.H. Lambert, and A. Sandgren
Report on Lund University
Umeå University: B.H. Lambert, A. Sandgren, and G. Stromquist
Report on Umeå University

United Kingdom
UK Policy Review: Gareth Williams
London School of Hygiene and Tropical Medicine: Michael Shattock and Rosa
   Becker
Case study of the London School of Hygiene and Tropical Medicine, UK
The University of Buckingham, UK: Michael Shattock and Rosa Becker
Case study of the University of Buckingham
The University of Nottingham, UK: Gareth Williams and Rosa Becker
Case study of the University of Nottingham, UK
The University of Plymouth, UK: Paul Temple and Rosa Becker
Case study of the University of Plymouth, UK

Bibliography

Allison, G.T. (1971) *Essence of Decision*. Boston, MA: Little, Brown.

Amaral, A. and Magalhães, A. (2002) The emergent role of external stakeholders in European higher education governance, in A. Amaral, G.A. Jones, and B. Karseth (eds.) *Governing Higher Education: National Perspectives on Institutional Governance*. Dordrecht: Kluwer Academic.

Audretsch, D.B. (2002) *Entrepreneurship: A Survey of the Literature*. Brussels: Commission of the European Communities.

Audretsch, D.B. and Erdem, D.K. (2004) Determinants of scientist entrepreneurship: an integrative research agenda, in S.A. Alvarez, R. Agarwal, and O. Sorenson (eds.) *Handbook of Entrepreneurship Research: Interdisciplinary Perspectives*. New York: Springer.

Audretsch, D.B. and Stephan, P.S. (1996) Company–scientist locational links: the case of biotechnology, *American Economic Review*, 86(3): 641–52.

Bargh, C., Scott, P., and Smith, D. (1996) *Governing Universities: Changing the Culture?* Buckingham: Society for Research into Higher Education and Open University Press.

Barnett, R. (2000) *Realizing the University in an Age of Supercomplexity*. Buckingham: Society for Research into Higher Education and Open University Press.

Barnett, R. (2003) *Beyond All Reason: Living with Ideology in the University*. Buckingham: Society for Research into Higher Education and Open University Press.

Barnett, R. (2005) Convergence in higher education: the strange case of 'entrepreneurialism', *Higher Education Management and Policy*, 17(3): 43–58.

Barnett, R. and Coate, K. (2005) *Engaging the Curriculum in Higher Education*. Maidenhead: Society for Research into Higher Education and Open University Press.

Birch, D.L. (1979) *The Job Generation Process*. Cambridge, MA: MIT Press.

Bok, D. (2003) *Universities in the Marketplace: The Commercialization of Higher Education*. Princeton, NJ: Princeton University Press.

Bonner, J. (2006) Reaping rich rewards, *New Scientist*, 30 September, pp. 62–3.

Braun, D. and Merrien, F.-X. (eds.) (1999) *Towards a New Model of Governance for Universities? A Comparative View*. London: Jessica Kingsley.

Bryan, L.L. and Joyce, C.I. (2007) *Mobilising Minds*. London: McGraw-Hill.

Clark, B. (1983) *The Higher Education System: Academic Organization in Cross National Perspective*. Berkeley, CA: University of California Press.

Clark, B. (1998) *Creating Entrepreneurial Universities: Organizational Pathways of Transformation.* New York: Pergamon Press.

Clark, B. (2001) The entrepreneurial university: new foundations for collegiality, autonomy, and achievement, *Higher Education Management*, 13(2): 9–24.

Clark, B. (2004a) *Sustaining Change in Universities: Continuities in Case Studies and Concepts.* Maidenhead: Open University Press

Clark, B. (2004b) Delineating the character of the entrepreneurial university, *Higher Education Policy*, 17: 355–70.

Clark, B. (2005) The character of the entrepreneurial university, *International Higher Education*, Winter, p. 38.

Commission of the European Communities (CEC) (2003a) *The role of the universities in the Europe of knowledge.* Communication from the Commission, COM 2003/58. Brussels: CEC.

Commission of the European Communities (CEC) (2003b) *Entrepreneurship in Europe.* Brussels: CEC.

Commission of the European Communities (CEC) (2005) *Mobilising the brain power of Europe: enabling universities to make their full contribution to the Lisbon Strategy.* Communication from the Commission, COM 2005/152. Brussels: CEC.

Commission of the European Communities (CEC) (2006a) *Delivering on the modernization agenda for universities: education, research and innovation.* Communication from the Commission, COM 2006/208. Brussels: CEC.

Commission of the European Communities (CEC) (2006b) *Europe needs modernised universities.* Communication from the Commission, COM 2006/208 (http://europa.eu/rapid/pressreleasesaction.do?reference=IP/06/592).

Cummings, W.K. (1998) *The Service University in Comparative Perspective* (Special Issue of *Higher Education*). Amsterdam: Kluwer Academic.

Currie, J. (2003) Australian universities as enterprise universities: transformed players on a global stage, in G. Breton and M. Lambert (eds.) *Universities and Globalization: Private Linkages, Public Trust.* Paris and Quebec: UNESCO Publishing, Université Laval and Economica.

Currie, J., Deangelis, R., De Boer, H., Huisman, J., and Lacotte, C. (2003) *Globalizing Practices and University Responses: European and Anglo-American Differences.* Westport, CT: Praeger.

Dahrendorf, R. (2000) *Universities after Communism.* Hamburg: Edition Korber-Stiftung.

Darvas, P. (1997) Institutional innovations in higher education in Central Europe, *Tertiary Education and Management*, 3: 119–32.

Department for Education and Skills (2003) *The Future of Higher Education.* CM 5735. London: HMSO.

Dill, D.D. (2003) Allowing the market to rule: the case of the United States, *Higher Education Quarterly*, 57(2): 136–57.

Drucker, P.F. (1985) *Innovation and Entrepreneurship: Practice and Principles.* London: Pan Books.

Etzkowitz, H. (2002) *MIT and the Rise of Entrepreneurial Science.* London: Routledge.

Etzkowitz, H. and Leydesdorff, L. (1998) The endless transition: a triple helix of university–industry–government relations, *Minerva*, 36: 203–8.

Etzkowitz, H., Schuler, E., and Gulbrandsen, M. (2000a) The evolution of the entrepreneurial university, in M. Jacob and T. Hellstrom (eds.) *The Future of Knowledge Production in the Academy.* Buckingham: Society for Research into Higher Education and Open University Press.

Etzkowitz, H., Webster, A., Gebhardt, C., and Cantisano Terra, B.R. (2000b) The future of the university and the university of the future: evolution of ivory tower to entrepreneurial paradigm, *Research Policy*, 29(2): 313–30.

Eveline, J. (2004) *Ivory Basement Leadership: Power and Invisibility in the Changing University*. Crawley, WA: University of Western Australia Press.

Fägerlind, I. and Strömqvist, G. (2004) Adapting the Nordic model to the future, in I. Fägerlind and G. Strömqvist (eds.) *Reforming Higher Education in the Nordic Countries: Studies of Change in Denmark, Finland, Iceland, Norway and Sweden*. New Trends in Higher Education. Paris: International Institute for Educational Planning.

Figel, J. (2005) 'Higher education: universities must deliver their full potential to contribute to the Lisbon strategy', Europa Press Release, Brussels, 20 April.

Finlay, I. (2005) The idea of the 'entrepreneurial' university', in G. Hayward (ed.) *Expanding Higher Education: Issues and Challenges* (SKOPE Monograph 8; Spring 2005). Oxford: Centre on Skills, Knowledge and Organizational Performance.

Florida, R. (2002) *The Rise of the Creative Class: And how it's Transforming Work, Leisure, Community and Everyday Life*. New York: Basic Books.

Fromm, E. (1942) *The Fear of Freedom*. London: Routledge & Kegan Paul. (First published in 1941 as *Escape from Freedom*. New York: Holt, Rinehart & Winston.)

Fuller, S. (2005) What makes universities unique? Updating the ideal for an entrepreneurial age, *Higher Education Management and Policy*, 17(3): 27–49.

Gaugash, P. and Tiron, S. (2006) *Moldova case studies brief analysis* (http://www.euerek.info/PublicDocuments/Country).

Gayle, J.C., Tewarie, B., and White, A.Q. (2003) *Governance in the Twenty-First Century University: Approaches to Effective Leadership and Strategic Management*. San Francisco, CA: Jossey-Bass.

Gibbons, M., Limoges, C., Nowotny, H., Schwartzman, S., Scott, P., and Trow, M. (1994) *The New Production of Knowledge: The Dynamics of Science and Research in Contemporary Societies*. Thousand Oaks, CA: Sage.

Goodall, H.L. (1999) Casing the academy for community, *Communication Theory*, 4: 465–94.

Gueno, A. (1998) The internationalization of European universities: a return to medieval roots, *Minerva*, 36(3): 253–70.

GUS (1990–2006) *Higher Education Institutions and Their Finances*. Warsaw: GUS (Central Statistical Office; in Polish).

Hattie, J. and Marsh, H.W. (1996) The relationship between research and teaching: a meta-analysis, *Review of Educational Research*, 66: 507–42.

Haug, G. and Kirstein, J. (1999) *Trends I: Trends in learning structures in higher education*. Brussels: European Universities Association (http://www.eua.be/eua/en/publications.jspx).

Hofstede, G. (1980) *Culture's Consequences: International Differences in Work-Related Values*. Beverly Hills, CA: Sage Publications.

Hofstede, G. (1986) Cultural differences in teaching and learning, *International Journal of Intercultural Relations*, 10: 301–20.

Husén, T. (1996) The idea of the university: changing roles, current crisis and future challenges, in Z. Morsy and P.G. Altbach (eds.) *Higher Education in an International Perspective: Critical Issues*. New York: Garland Publishing.

Jacob, M. and Hellström, T. (2000) Introduction, in M. Jacob and T. Hellström (eds.) *The Future of Knowledge Production in the Academy*. Buckingham: Society for Research into Higher Education and Open University Press.

Jansen, D. (ed.) (2007) *New Forms of Governance in Research Organizations: Disciplinary Approaches, Interfaces, and Integration.* Dordrecht: Springer.

Jarzabkowski, P. (2002) Centralised or decentralised? Strategic implications of resource allocation models, *Higher Education Quarterly*, 56(1): 5–32.

Johnson, B. and McCarthy, T. (2000) Casual labor and the future of the academy, *Thought and Action: The NEA Higher Education Journal*, Summer, pp. 107–20.

Kantor, R.M. (1983) *The Change Masters: Corporate Entrepreneurs at Work.* London: Unwin Paperbacks.

Kezar, A.J. (2005) Consequences of radical change in governance: a grounded theory approach, *Journal of Higher Education*, 76(6): 634–68.

Kirby, D.A. (2003) *Entrepreneurship.* Maidenhead: McGraw-Hill Education.

Kitagawa, F. (2005) Entrepreneurial universities and the development of regional societies: a spatial view of the Europe of knowledge, *Higher Education Management and Policy*, 17(3): 65–92.

Kivinen, O. and Rinne, R. (1996) Changing higher education policy: three western models, in Z. Morsy and P.G. Altbach (eds.) *Higher Education in International Perspective: Critical Issues.* New York: Garland Publishing.

Knight, J. (1997) Internationalisation of higher education: a conceptual framework, in J. Knight and H. de Wit (eds.) *Internationalisation of Higher Education in Asia Pacific Countries.* Amsterdam: European Association for International Education.

Knight, J. (2005) *Internationalisation of Higher Education: New Directions, New Challenges,* 2005 IAU Global Survey. Paris: IAU.

Kutinlahti, P. (2005) *Universities Approaching Market: Intertwining Scientific and Entrepreneurial Goals*, VTT Publication #589. Helsinki: VTT.

Kwiek, M. (2004) The emergent European educational policies under scrutiny: the Bologna Process from a Central European perspective, *European Educational Research Journal*, 3(4): 1–24.

Kwiek, M. (2005a) *Poland: a higher education policy*, Paper presented at the Turku Workshop, 11–12 February 2005.

Kwiek, M. (2005b) The university and the state in a global age: Renegotiating the traditional social contract?, *European Educational Research Journal*, 4(4): 324–41.

Kwiek, M. (2006) *The University and the State: A Study into Global Transformations.* Frankfurt am Main and New York: Peter Lang.

Lafer, G. (2003) Graduate student unions: organizing in a changed academic economy, *Labor Studies Journal*, 28(2): 25–43.

Lambert, B.H., Sandgren, A., and Strömqvist, G. (2006) *Swedish higher education, research and innovation policies: universities as engines of economic growth* (2006-11-15; European Commission project reference CIT2-CT-2004-506051). European Universities for Entrepreneurship: their role in the Europe of Knowledge; EUEREK database (http://www.euerek.info/Public_Documents/Documents/Sweden-HigherEdPoliciesData.pdf).

Levy, D.C. (2002) *Unanticipated development: perspectives on private higher education's emerging roles*, PROPHE Working Paper #1 (http://www.albany.edu/dept/eaps/prophe/publication/paper.html#WP1).

Levy, D.C. (2006) *An introductory global overview: the private fit to salient higher education tendencies*, PROPHE Working Paper #7 (http://www.albany.edu/dept/eaps/prophe/publication/paper.html#WP7).

Lundvall, B.A. and Johnson, B. (1994) The learning economy, *Journal of Industry Studies*, 1(2): 23–42.

Maassen, P.A.M. and Stensaker, B. (2003) Interpretations of self-regulation: the changing state–higher education relationship in Europe, in R. Begg (ed.) *The Dialogue between Higher Education Research and Practice*. Dordrecht: Kluwer Academic.

Marginson, S. and Considine, M. (2000) *The Enterprise University: Power, Governance and Reinvention in Australia*. Cambridge: Cambridge University Press.

Neave, G. (1985) The university and state in Western Europe, in D. Jaques and J. Richardson (eds.) *The Future for Higher Education*. Milton Keynes: Open University Press.

Neave, G. (2000) Introduction. Universities' responsibilities to society: an historical exploration of an enduring issue, in G. Neave (ed.) *The Universities' Responsibilities to Society: International Perspectives*. Issues in Higher Education. Oxford: Pergamon Press for International Association of Universities.

Neave, G. and van Vught, F.A. (1991) *Prometheus Bound. The Changing Relationship between Government and Higher Education in Western Europe*. Oxford: Pergamon Press.

Nowotny, H., Scott, P., and Gibbons, M. (2001) *Re-Thinking Science: Knowledge and the Public in an Age of Uncertainty*. Cambridge: Polity Press.

Organization for Economic Cooperation and Development (OECD) (2004) *Education at a Glance: OECD Indicators 2004*. Paris: OECD.

Organization for Economic Cooperation and Development (OECD) (2005) Entrepreneurship, *Journal of Higher Education Management and Policy*, 17(3) (Special Issue).

Ortega y Gasset, J. (1946) *Mission of the University* [translation of *Misión de la Universidad*, 1930 (in Spanish); 1998 reprint]. London: Routledge.

Page, N. (2003) Demolishing the ivory towers (university tech-transfer), *Intellectual Asset Management*, 1: 19–26 (http://entrepreneurship.mit.edu/Downloads/NigelPageArticle.pdf).

Perlman, B., Gueths, J., and Weber, D.A. (1988) *The Academic Intrapreneur: Strategy, Innovation and Management in Higher Education*. Westport, CT: Praeger.

Pinchot, G. (1985) *Intrapreneuring*. New York: Harper & Row.

Rinne, R. (2004) Searching for the rainbow: changing the course of Finnish higher education, in I. Fägerlind and G. Strömqvist (eds.) *Reforming Higher Education in the Nordic Countries: Studies of Change in Denmark, Finland, Iceland, Norway and Sweden*. New Trends in Higher Education. Paris: International Institute for Educational Planning.

Rinne, R. and Koivula, J. (2005) The changing place of the university and a clash of values: the entrepreneurial university in the European knowledge society, *Higher Education Management and Policy*, 17(3): 91–123.

Roberts, D. with Thompson, L. (2007) *University league tables and the impact on student recruitment*. Reputation Management for Universities, Working Paper Series #2. Leeds: The Knowledge Partnership.

Ross, J.E. and Unwalla, D. (1986) Who is an intrapreneur?, *Personnel*, 63(12): 45–9.

Schimank, U. (2005) *A comparative perspective on changes in university governance in Europe*, Public Lecture in the Australian National University.

Schimank, U., Kehm, B., and Enders, J. (1999) Institutional mechanisms of problem processing of the German university system: status quo and new developments, in D. Braun and F.-X. Merrien (eds.) *Towards a New Model of Governance for Universities? A Comparative View*. London: Jessica Kingsley.

Sharma, R. (2004) Performance-based funding in the entrepreneurial North American and Australian universities, *Journal of Higher Education Policy and Management*, 26(1): 109–18.

Shattock, M. (1988) Financial management in universities: the lessons from University College, Cardiff, *Financial Accountability and Management*, 4(2): 99–112.

Shattock, M. (2000) Strategic management in European universities in an age of increasing institutional self-reliance, *Tertiary Education and Management*, 6(2): 93–104.

Shattock, M. (2002) Re-balancing modern concepts of university governance, *Higher Education Quarterly*, 56(3): 235–44.

Shattock, M. (2003) *Managing Successful Universities*. Maidenhead: Open University Press.

Shattock, M. (ed.) (2004a) *Entrepreneurialism and the Transformation of Russian Universities*. Paris: UNESCO, International Institute for Educational Planning.

Shattock, M. (2004b) Generating non-state income in European universities, in M. Shattock (ed.) *Entrepreneurialism and the Transformation of Russian Universities*. Paris: UNESCO, International Institute for Educational Planning.

Shattock, M. (2005) European universities for entrepreneurship: their role in the Europe of knowledge. The theoretical context, *Higher Education Management and Policy*, 17(3): 13–26.

Shattock, M. (2006) *Managing Good Governance in Higher Education*. Maidenhead: Open University Press.

Siegel, D.S., Waldman, D.A., Atwater, L.E., and Link, A.N. (2003) Commercial knowledge transfers from universities to firms: improving the effectiveness of university–industry collaboration, *Journal of High Technology Management Research*, 14: 111–33.

Sinclair, U. (1923) *The Goose-Step: A Study of American Education*. Pasadena, CA: Upton Sinclair.

Sinetar, M. (1985) Entrepreneurs, chaos, and creativity – can creative people really survive large company structure, *Sloan Management Review*, 26(2): 57–63.

Skocpol, T. (2006) *Who 'we' are*, Dean's Speech at morning prayers, Graduate School of Arts and Sciences, Harvard University, 3 April 2006 (http://www.gsas.harvard.edu/dean_and_administration/morning_prayers_4_13_06_2.php).

Slantcheva, S. and Levy D.C. (eds.) (2007) *Private Higher Education in Post-Communist Europe: In Search of Legitimacy*. New York: Palgrave.

Slaughter, S. and Leslie, L.L. (1997) *Academic Capitalism: Politics, Policies and the Entrepreneurial University*. Baltimore, MD: Johns Hopkins University Press.

Sporn, B. (1999a) Towards more adaptive universities: trends of institutional reform in Europe, *Higher Education in Europe*, 24(1): 23–33.

Sporn, B. (1999b) *Adaptive University Structures: An Analysis of Adaptations to Socioeconomic Environments of US and European Universities*. London: Jessica Kingsley.

Sporn, B. (2001) Building adaptive universities: emerging organisational forms based on experiences of European and US universities, *Tertiary Education and Management*, 7(2): 121–34.

Stringfellow, W. (1975) *The absurdity of ARIL*, Paper presented at the 40th Anniversary of the Church Society for College Work, CSCW (http://www.crosscurrents.org/stringfellow.htm) (online version edited and updated by successor organization ARIL, the Association for Religion and Intellectual Life).

Sykes, C.J. (1988) *ProfScam: Professors and the Demise of Higher Education*. New York: St. Martin's Press.

Temple, P. (2006) Intervention in a higher education market: a case study, *Higher Education Quarterly*, 60(3): 257–69.

Tirronen, J. (2005) *Modernin yliopistokoulutuksen lähtökohdat ja sivistyskäsitys* [*Modern University Education: The Foundations and Concept of Education*], Kuopio University Publications E, Social Sciences #122. Kuopio: University of Kuopio.

Trow, M. (1974) *Problems in the Transition from Elite to Mass Higher Education: Policies for Higher Education.* Paris: OECD.

Trow, M. (1996) Trust, markets and accountability in higher education: a comparative perspective, *Higher Education Policy,* 9(4): 309–24.

UNESCO-CEPES (2004) *Higher Education in Europe,* XXIX(2) (whole issue).

van der Ploeg, R. (2006) *European universities must get their act together,* The Transformation of Public Universities (SSRC project) (12 September 2006). New York: Social Science Research Council (http://publicuniversities.ssrc.org/commentaries/european_universities/).

van Vught, F. (1990) *Recent developments in higher education governance,* Paper presented at the Conference on Policy Change in Higher Education, 4 June, Turku.

Veblen, T. (1918) *The Higher Learning in America: A Memorandum on the Conduct of Universities by Business Men* (http://socserv2.mcmaster.ca/%7Eecon/ugcm/3ll3/veblen/higher).

Vidich, A.J. (1994) The higher learning in America in Veblen's time and our own, *International Journal of Politics, Culture and Society,* 7(4): 639–68.

Walshok, M.L. (1995) *Knowledge without Boundaries: What America's Research Universities can do for the Economy, the Workplace, and the Community.* San Francisco, CA: Jossey-Bass.

Weber, L. (2004) *Governance and Capacity for Change.* Brussels: European University Association.

Wells P.J., Sadlak J., and Vlasceanu, L. (eds.) (2007) *The Rising Role and Relevance of Private Higher Education in Europe.* Bucharest: UNESCO-CEPES.

Williams, G. (ed.) (2004a) *The Enterprising University: Reform, Excellence and Equity.* Maidenhead: Society for Research into Higher Education and Open University Press.

Williams, G. (2004b) The changing political economy of higher education, in M. Shattock (ed.) *Entrepreneurialism and the Transformation of Russian Universities.* Paris: UNESCO, International Institute for Educational Planning.

Williams, G. (2004c) The higher education market in the United Kingdom, in P. Teixeira, B. Jongbloed, D.D. Dill, and A. Amaral (eds.), *Markets in Higher Education: Rhetoric or Reality?* Dordrecht: Kluwer Academic.

Williams, G. and Kitaev, I. (2005) Overview of national policy contexts for entrepreneurialism in higher education institutions, *Higher Education Management and Policy,* 17(3): 125–41.

Winston, G. (1999) Subsidies, hierarchy and peers: the awkward economics of higher education, *Journal of Economic Perspectives,* 13(1): 13–36.

Wolf, C. (1993) *Markets or Governments: Choosing Between Imperfect Alternatives.* Cambridge, MA: MIT Press.

Index

SUSTAINING CHANGE IN UNIVERSITIES
CONTINUITIES IN CASE STUDIES AND CONCEPTS

Burton R. Clark
University of California, Los Angeles, USA

● What can be done to ensure universities are well positioned to meet the challenges of the fast moving world of the 21st century?

This is the central question addressed by Burton R. Clark in this significant new volume which greatly extends the case studies and concepts presented in his 1998 book, *Creating Entrepreneurial Universities*. The new volume draws on case studies of fourteen proactive institutions in the UK, Europe, Australia, Latin America, Africa, and the United States that extend analysis into the early years of the twenty-first century. The cumulative international coverage underpins a more fully developed conceptual framework offering insight into ways of initiating and sustaining change in universities.

This new conceptual framework shifts attention from transformation to sustainability rooted in a constructed steady state of change and a collegial approach to entrepreneurialism. It contains key elements necessary for universities to adapt successfully to the modern world.

Lessons for reform can be drawn directly from both the individual case studies and the general framework. Overall the book offers a new form of university organization that is more self-reliant and manages to combine change with continuity, traditional academic values with new managerial values.

Essential reading for university administrators, faculty members, students and researchers analysing higher education, and educational policymakers worldwide, this book advocates a highly proactive approach to university change and specifies a new basis for university self reliance.

Contents
Part 1: Sustaining Entrepreneurialism in European Universities – *Introduction* – *Sustainability at Warwick: A paradigmatic case* –*Strathclyde: Sustaining change in a place of useful learning* – *University of Twente: Balancing on entrepreneurial seesaws in a Dutch university* – *University of Joensuu: Balancing sustainability in a regional Finnish university* – *Chalmers University of Technology: Entrepreneurialism redeemed* – *From transformation to sustainability* – *Part 2: Amplifying Variations in University Entrepreneurialism: Africa, Latin America, Asia, North America* – *Introduction* – *Makerere University: Entrepreneurial rebound from academic pits in Uganda* – *The Catholic University of Chile: Lessons from South America* – *Monash University: Seizing the revolutionary moment in Australia* – *Genetic entrepreneurialism among American universities Stanford; Massachusetts Institute of Technology; University of Michigan; University of California, Los Angeles; North Carolina State University; Georgia Institute of Technology; conclusion* – *Part 3: The Self-Reliant University* – *The entrepreneurial road to university self-reliance:* – *Why many universities will not become entrepreneurial; Key features of entrepreneurial organization in universities; The modern pathway to university autonomy and self-reliance* – *Notes and References* – *Index.*

September 2004   232pp
978–0–335–21590–4 Paperback   978–0–335–21591–1 Hardback

MANAGING GOOD GOVERNANCE IN HIGHER EDUCATION

Michael Shattock

"Michael Shattock, former registrar of Warwick, can lay claim to having invented the serious study of university governance in Britain."

Public

- How has university governance changed and developed over the last quarter of a century?
- How can people actively engaged in university governance manage the increasingly complex issues that confront them?

This book addresses university governance as extending throughout an institution from the governing body to senates/academic boards and the organs of governance at faculty and departmental levels. It considers the legal structure of higher education institutions; the impact of developments in corporate governance in the private sector; the reforms in modern university governance, including in academic governance; the practicalities of managing governance, drawing on selected case studies; and the role of governance in relation to institutional performance.

Whilst the primary market for the book is the United Kingdom, many of the themes addressed are of international applicability. The book provides both a practical guide for those actively involved in governing universities – lay governors, senior managers and academics – and a key scholarly text for students of higher education, managers in universities and colleges, and policy makers.

Contents

2006   192pp

978–0–335–21666–6 (Paperback)   978–0–335–21667–3 (Hardback)